WHITE SHELL WATER PLACE

WHITE SHELL WATER PLACE

An Anthology of Native American Reflections
on the
400th Anniversary of the Founding of Santa Fe, New Mexico
with a
Traditional Native Blessing by N. Scott Momaday

Edited by
F. Richard Sanchez
with
Stephen Wall and Ann Filemyr

The Official Commemorative Publication

SANTA FE

Note to Readers

Kindly report any errors in this book to:
Sunstone Press
Box 2321
Santa Fe, NM 87504-2321

© 2010 by Institute of American Indian Arts.
All Rights Reserved.

No part of this book may be reproduced in any form or by any electronic or mechanical means including information storage and retrieval systems without permission in writing from the publisher, except by a reviewer who may quote brief passages in a review.

Sunstone books may be purchased for educational, business, or sales promotional use. For information please write: Special Markets Department, Sunstone Press, P.O. Box 2321, Santa Fe, New Mexico 87504-2321.

Book and Cover design ❦ Vicki Ahl
Body typeface ❦ Adobe Garamond Pro
Printed on acid free paper

Library of Congress Cataloging-in-Publication Data

White shell water place : Native American reflections on the Santa Fe 400th commemoration / edited by F. Richard Sanchez ; with Stephen Wall and Ann Filemyr.
   p. cm.
 Includes bibliographical references and index.
  ISBN 978-0-86534-786-1 (hardcover : alk. paper) --
 ISBN 978-0-86534-787-8 (softcover : alk. paper)
  1. Pueblo Indians--New Mexico--Santa Fe--History. 2. Santa Fe (N.M.)--History. 3. Santa Fe (N.M.)--Historiography. 4. Indians of North America--Historiography. I. Sanchez, F. Richard, 1954-

E99.P9W47 2010
978.9004'974--dc22
                                    2010036093

Published in

WWW.SUNSTONEPRESS.COM
SUNSTONE PRESS / POST OFFICE BOX 2321 / SANTA FE, NM 87504-2321 /USA
(505) 988-4418 / ORDERS ONLY (800) 243-5644 / FAX (505) 988-1025

The Publication of This Book
is Generously Supported by

The only Santa Fe Hotel that welcomes you
in the Ancient Spirit of the Picuris Pueblo.

CONTENTS

Blessing / N. Scott Momaday__9
Acknowledgements__11
Map of the Pueblos Circa 1600s__12
Map of the Pueblos 2010__13
Introduction / F. Richard Sanchez__15

1
A Pueblo Perspective of the History of Santa Fe / Gregory A. Cajete__19

2
Indian Slavery and the Birth of Genízaros / Ramón A. Gutiérrez__39

3
Ohkay Owingeh: New Mexico's First Capital, This is Much of What I Believe,
Know and Have Learned / *Kaafedeh,* Herman Agoyo__57

4
Historia De Mañana / Storyteller Evelina Zuni Lucero__71

5
Indians, Colonialism, and the Santa Fe Trail of Tears and Conquest,
Challenging the Master Narrative / James Riding In__81

6
"The Porch" / Kim Suina__101

7
"A Living Exhibition," Labor, Desire, and the Marketing of American Indian Arts and
Crafts in Santa Fe / Matthew J. Martinez__108

8
Regarding Ethnicities and Cultures, / Diane Reyna__126

9
Grounded in Faith / Carol Harvey__132

10
Sustaining the Revolution, Adaptations and Transformations
In New Mexico State-Tribal Relations / Alvin H. Warren__155

Notes__167
Contributors__173
Study Guide__177
Index__181

Blessing

On this place
May blessings abound
Among these valleys and mountains
Along ancient trails of trade and pilgrimage
Where the waters of the sky fall
In fringes of rain and grain rises from the fields
Where animals graze in the meadows
And run wild in the forests
Where ravens and hawks have dominion
Over the blue and purple summits

On this place
May blessings abound
Bless our ancestors, may we honor them
Bless our children, may we be ever thankful for them
Bless the unborn, may they inherit the good in us
Bless us who make this prayer, may we be worthy

On this place
May blessings abound
Here in this house of art and learning
May our bodies be strong
Here in this house of art and learning
May our minds be open and clear
Here in this house of art and learning
May our spirits be one with Creation

On this place
May blessings abound
All our lives may we know truth
All our lives may we know the beautiful
All our lives may we know inspiration
All our lives may we know the sacred within us

On this place
May blessings abound
Let us live happily inside these words
Let us live peacefully inside these words
Let us live thankfully inside these words
Let us be wholly alive inside these words
In holiness do we make our prayer
In holiness do we make our prayer

—N. Scott Momaday

Acknowledgements

I would like to extend my gratitude to all who made this anthology possible: The All Indian Pueblo Council (AIPC); Maurice Bonal, Sandra Brintnall and The Santa Fe 400th Commemoration Board and Committee, for their collective and collaborative efforts and unflagging support; the authors, for their patience and efficiency; The Institute of American Indian Arts, most notably Ann Filemyr and Steve Wall, for their diligence, input and contributions; James Smith and the staff of Sunstone Press for their professionalism, support and continuous optimism throughout this undertaking; Laura Holt for preparing the index; Jason Garcia, for donating the art work for the book cover and cartouche; Mayor David Coss, the Santa Fe City Council, and private contributors for their financial support; and most important, the Native American tribal communities, both past and present, who throughout the centuries have endured and maintained the sacred history and memory of *O'gha Po'oge*.

—F. Richard Sanchez

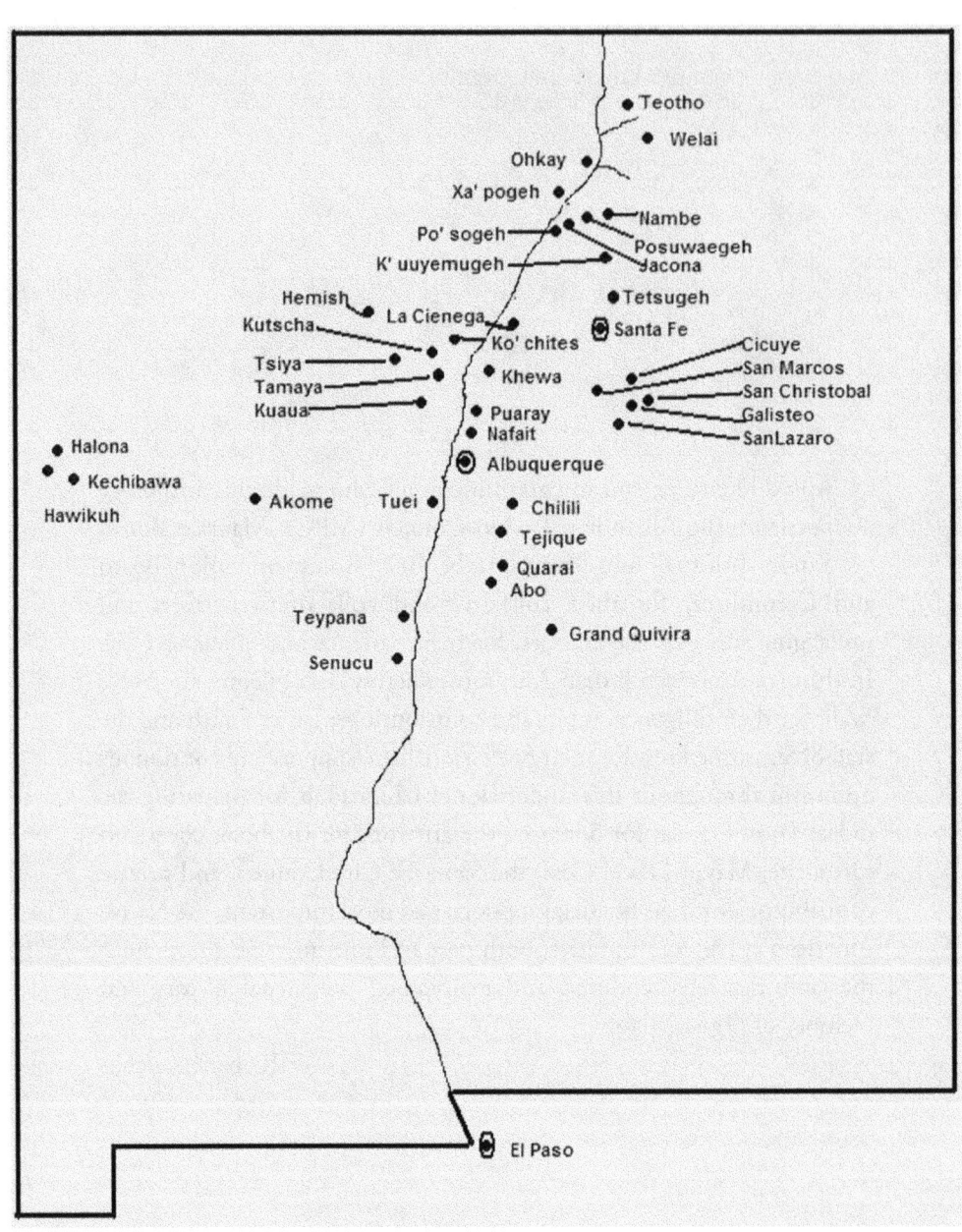

The Pueblos Circa 1600s

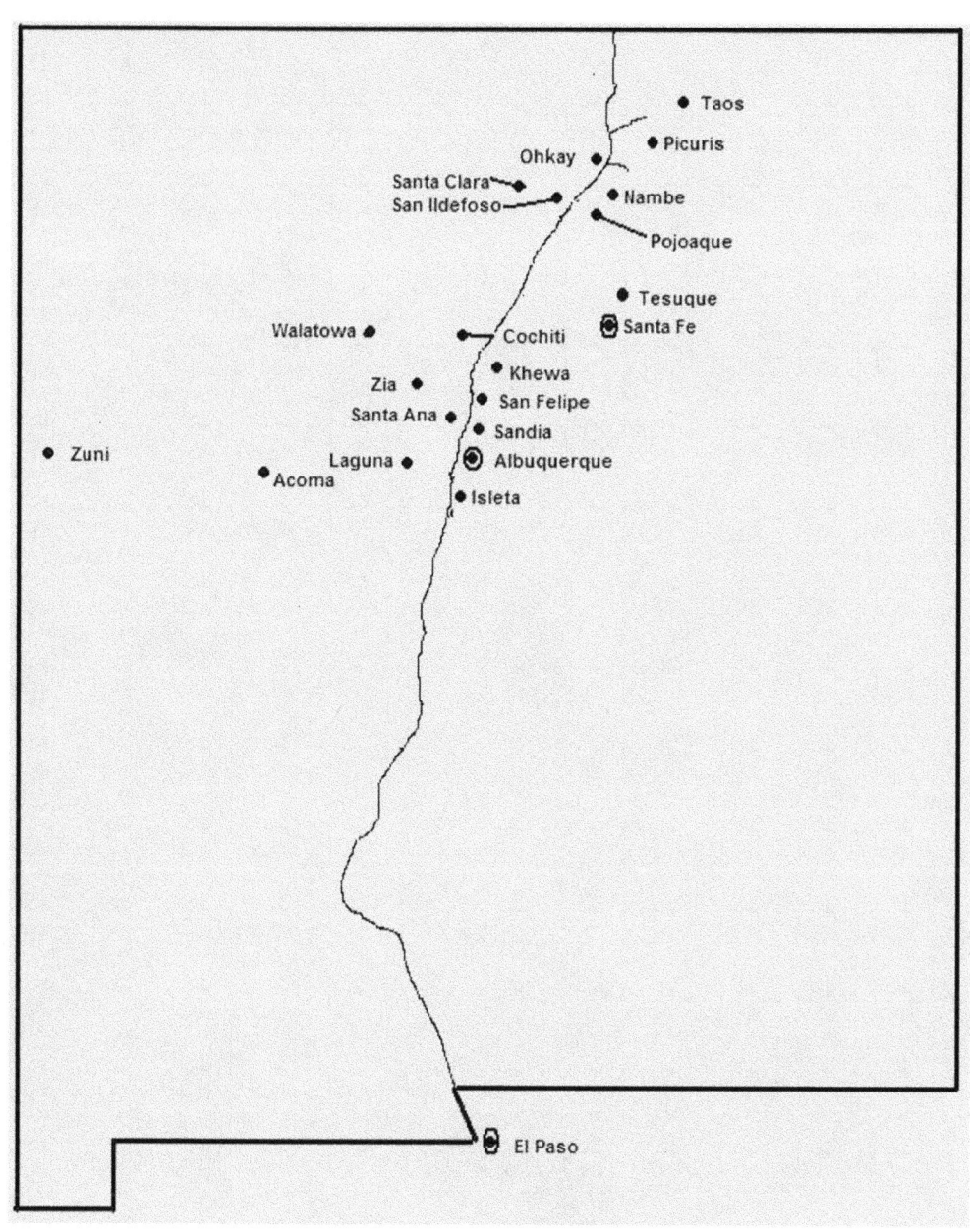

The Pueblos 2010

Introduction
by
F. Richard Sanchez
Isleta Ancestry

This anthology, a companion to the Santa Fe 400th Anniversary Commemorative publication, *All Trails Lead to Santa Fe*, affords Native American authors the opportunity to unreservedly express their ideas, opinions and perspectives on the historical and cultural aspects of Santa Fe using their own voice and preferred writing styles that are not necessarily in accord with western academic and writing conventions.

One cannot truly contemplate the history and culture of Santa Fe without the voices of the Native Americans—the original inhabitants of *O'gha Po'oge*, "*White Shell Water Place*." To be sure, much of Santa Fe's story is conveyed from a western colonial perspective, which, until fairly recently, has predominantly relegated Native Americans to the fringes. However, over the last thirty years colonial narratives regarding Native American history and culture have been, and continue to be, disputed and amended as the pursuit of academic, intellectual and cultural self determination gains momentum in respective Native American tribal and academic communities. Thus, the Santa Fe 400th Commemoration committee and Maurice Bonal, Chairman and President of the Board of the Santa Fe 400th Anniversary, Inc., cooperated to create an opportunity for the Native American voice to be heard in this unique publication.

Indeed, this anthology is a ceremony of Native voices, a gathering of Native people offering scholarly dialogue, personal points of view, opinions, and stories regarding the pre-and post-historical and cultural foundations of Santa Fe.

Like most Native American ceremonies, this ceremony commences with a blessing, eloquently composed by N. Scott Momaday. And, rather than providing a synopsis of each chapter, I invite you to the ceremony, to listen, learn and hear the voices of the authors—some familiar and others not—and to form your own opinions and draw your own conclusions. To be sure, this anthology imparts engaging accounts of the struggles, strife and challenges created, both past and present, by imperialistic colonial influences and, of course, the Native Americans themselves, as well as thought provoking commentaries and personal pieces, some told in the tradition of Native storytellers.

The voices that comprise this anthology include: Herman Agoyo–Ohkay Owingeh, Gregory Cajete–Pueblo of Santa Clara, Ramón Gutiérrez–Genízaro of Laguna–Zuni ancestry, Carol Harvey–Diné, Evelina Zuni Lucero–Pueblo of Isleta/Ohkay Owingeh, Matthew J. Martinez–Ohkay Owingeh, N. Scott Momaday–Kiowa, Diane Reyna–Pueblo of Taos/Ohkay Owingeh, James Riding In–Pawnee, Kim Suina–Pueblo of Cochiti, and Alvin H. Warren–Pueblo of Santa Clara. Nine of the authors are enrolled tribal members and the tenth, Ramon Gutiérrez, is a Genízaro, a person of majority-detribalized ancestry, or mixed-blood if you prefer, but does not meet the membership criteria established by his relevant ancestral tribes.

Regarding Genízaros, as a child growing up in Santa Fe I was taught, as were the children of Santa Fe's "Spanish families"(never mind the occasional trips to Isleta Pueblo to visit relatives on my father's side), that we were Spanish, direct descendants of the Conquistadores and Spanish colonials that established and colonized Santa Fe in 1604–1610. This was and continues to be the prevailing belief of many Native New Mexicans. As I grew older I became very aware of the inconsistencies in the above declaration. The idea of being a direct descendent of white European Spaniards—while possessing a brown skin tone—became problematic. Numerous volumes of anthropological and historical research have borne out the fact that New Mexico's isolation on Spain's furthest frontier created through the centuries an exceptional non-tribal Native population in New Mexico of *Mestizos*, people of mixed Indian and Spanish blood. The detribalized Genízaros are unique among this group. Their blood lines, usually established through genealogical research, readily identify their mixed-blood Native American ancestry, but they do not meet the minimum blood-quantum requirements for any single tribal membership. Ramon Gutiérrez is a Genízaro and was chosen for this project for his unique historical perspective of Genízaro history.

In her book, *Caballeros,* Ruth Laughlin writes, "Like the roads to Rome, all trails led to Santa Fe." The delight of this anthology is in the reading of those whose ancestors blazed these trails and, for a brief time, regained and recovered their ancient ancestral homes and traditions, only to be, once again, usurped by imperialistic colonialism. However, the notion of trailblazing continues today as Native Americans progress concomitantly with the creative aspects of their lives as modern-day warriors, both male and female, who continue to perpetuate the Native American ideals of sovereignty and self determination through political, cultural, economic and academic venues.

A Pueblo Perspective of the History of Santa Fe

by
Gregory A. Cajete
Santa Clara Pueblo, New Mexico

Introduction

The Tewa have a long and historically dynamic history with Santa Fe (*O'gha Po'oge*). Before the founding of Santa Fe by the Spanish, ancestors of the Northern and now extinct Southern Tewa (*Tanos*) settled in villages in and around the area dating back thousands of years. The Tewas and Tanos were certainly conscripted to build Spanish Santa Fe and would later lead the Pueblo Revolt and the siege of Santa Fe in 1680; thus, re-occupying Santa Fe for a period of thirteen years. Many Tewa and Tanos remained inhabitants of Santa Fe even after the reconquest by Don Diego de Vargas. Indeed, many Tewa and Tanos remained in Santa Fe after the reconquest as laborers, servants and farmers; to be eventually integrated into the population of Santa Fe.

Throughout the Spanish and Mexican periods, Santa Fe was a place where cultures, traders, settlers and Indians alike interacted, traded, and intermarried to form the tapestry of people and ways of life unique to this region of the Southwest. Pueblo people from the surrounding villages interacted with Santa Fe in multiple ways ranging from providing labor and selling wares to serving in the militia and interacting with government officials.

Today, Santa Fe is the seat of state government as well as the regional center for Northern New Mexico. Santa Fe has always been, and continues to be, the "big town" to which all people of Northern New Mexico traveled to do business. As the State Capitol, Pueblo people come to do political business. As the Archdiocese, Pueblo people come to attend mass at the Cathedral. As the location of the Santa Fe Indian School and St. Catherine's Indian School, Pueblo people come to attend school. As a center for Southwest Indian Art, Pueblo people come to Santa Fe to sell their arts and crafts usually in and around the portal of the Palace of the Governors.

Growing up at a time when Pueblo history was, for the most part, relegated to cultural traits more so than events, it is interesting that these many years later I find myself writing and offering a personal and Pueblo historical perspective of Santa Fe and the 400th commemoration of its founding.

Personal Perspective

Like many Pueblo children, I was born in Santa Fe at the Santa Fe Indian Hospital. My first actual memory of visiting Santa Fe is riding the Greyhound bus with my mother and grandmother. It was one of many bus trips to Santa Fe from Española that I would make during my childhood. Although I certainly went to Santa Fe many times as an infant, this was the first time I actually remembered the trip. I must have been about four years old. Many people from Española and Santa Clara Pueblo would catch the bus at the Española Drug Store and travel the twenty five miles to Santa Fe. At that time the Santa Fe bus depot was located one block south of the plaza so it was any easy walk from the depot to any part of downtown Santa Fe. I remember that this visit was an adventure. Many stores were located in and around the Plaza. I remember having a hot dog, coke and banana split at the Woolworth's Soda Fountain. I also remember my mother buying me toy soldiers, marbles, crayons and coloring books at Woolworths. I remember walking in and out of many stores with my mother and grandmother. It seemed to be taking a long time so my grandmother and I sat in the plaza waiting for my mother some of the time. I had plenty to keep me occupied playing with my toy soldiers and coloring. I especially remember my grandmother visiting with people, many of them Tewa, as we sat there and waited. It seemed as if she knew everyone who passed by, Indian and Spanish, and they knew her. I remember going with my grandmother to the Plaza Café to visit with the "grandma" of that place. Apparently my grandmother was friends with the people who owned the restaurant. I remember eating a huge hamburger at the Plaza Restaurant that day. Late in the evening I remember buying tickets to go home—I would always fall asleep on the bus ride home, anticipating the next bus trip to Santa Fe. This remembered trip was one of many trips to Santa Fe: to visit the Santa Fe Indian Hospital, to shop at Woolworths, Penneys, Sears and many other stores in and around the Plaza. Then there was the Santa Fe Fiesta whose history has always been clouded in the mists of history, myth and the "marketing" of the Santa Fe mystique. Yet, as was true of many Pueblo people and Hispanic New Mexicans of my generation, I would not be exposed to a comprehensive history of New Mexico that included the role of Pueblo Indians until I entered college.

Santa Fe, (*O'gha Po'oge*) "The Place Of White Shells By the Water," has always been a gathering place. It has also been a place of contradiction and conflict while at the same time being a place of great significance for Pueblo people in particular and at one time for other Indians like the Apache, the Navajo, the Ute and even the Comanche. This "Indian" history of Santa Fe has largely been hidden from view; usually left to the providence of historians, archeologists or anthropologists who have researched this history of "Indian" Santa Fe. Little of the true history of Santa Fe is known among even the native New Mexico inhabitants. For the most part this history has been shrouded in the mist of forgotten memories. Yet, the history of Santa Fe is tied to a larger history that is complex and conflicting but, at times, also a history of cooperative relationships between Pueblo peoples, Hispanos, and Genízaros spanning four centuries. The resettlement of Santa Fe cannot really be understood as a stand alone event but rather as an event that resulted from prior events. This comprehensive telling of history is still largely absent from New Mexico school curricula and is equally absent from the "marketed" image of Santa Fe as a tri-cultural ideal.

This following narrative presents an overview of various published perspectives of the history of Santa Fe relative to the Pueblo people of New Mexico. It reflects on an Indigenous history of this place which in two dialects of Tewa, from Ohkay Owingeh and Santa Clara Pueblo, is respectively called, *Kua' p'o – oge* or *O'gha O'gha Po'oge,* "The Place of Shell-Beads Near the Water," or "Bead Water Place."

Ancient History

The area around Santa Fe has likely been periodically inhabited by Pueblo peoples and their ancestors for at least 3,000 years. Even earlier, at the end of the last ice age, Paleo-Indian hunters likely followed herds of deer, elk and even mastodons along the foothills of the Rocky Mountains as far south as the Santa Fe basin. This is evidenced by various Paleo-Indian hunter campsites found along the foothills of the western side of the Rockies. Sandia Cave is a well known archeological site that exemplifies this semi-nomadic habitation pattern of Paleo-Indian hunters along the western slope of the Sangre de Cristo Mountains of New Mexico.

This long history of visitation and periodic habitation of the Santa Fe area is likely due to its unique geographical positioning at the southern most tail of the Rocky Mountains, which also form a natural causeway from their western side to the southern plains. No doubt this natural corridor combined with the natural gateway to the southern Rockies marked Santa Fe as a place where Indian people traveled through and stopped as they moved about Northern New Mexico, first, as hunter and gatherers, then as agriculturalists and traders.

In her chapter, "Down Under An Ancient City" in *Santa Fe: History of An Ancient City*, Frances Levine states, based on the remains of village and garden sites, that "between about A.D. 600 and 1425, ancestors of the modern Pueblos lived along the Santa Fe River." These sites are pre-dated by even older Archaic Pueblo sites dating to around 3000 B.C. During this long history of activity in the Santa Fe area, Puebloan people and their ancestors experienced extensive changes in the climate and ecological community in the area, which in turn affected settlement and habitation patterns. This movement of Pre-Colombian Pueblo peoples culminated in the abandonment of most of village sites during the early to late 1400s. Likely, this abandonment was due to drought and other climatic changes which led to the abandonment of many Pueblo villages along the foothills for sites nearer to the more constant source of water along the Rio Grande. Levine goes on to state that:

> "Archeological remains of the Coalition period, which began A.D. 1150 and ended about 1325, are found widely throughout the northern Rio Grande. Coalition period sites underlie parts of downtown Santa Fe and are found in the nearby settlements of Agua Fria and Arroyo Hondo… The archeological Pueblo sites dating from the late Developmental Period through the Coalition period include *Pindi* Pueblo on the west side of the Santa Fe River in Agua Fria; the Arroyo Negro site in South Santa Fe: and a number of sites in the vicinity of Fort Marcy and the Hillside neighborhood. The Early Classic period seems to mark the end of Pueblo occupation in Santa Fe, Agua Fria, and Arroyo Hondo, although there was a brief interval of Pueblo re-occupation of Santa Fe following the Pueblo Revolt of 1680. Toward the end of the Classic period and continuing into the seventeenth century, the population of the northern Rio Grande pueblos declined dramatically. Diseases introduced by the Spaniards decimated the Pueblo. A collapse of the aboriginal social and economic networks accompanied this decline, leading to the abandonment of some villages and the concentration of population into others. Santa Fe was not one of the areas in which the Pueblo concentrated. It would be more than two and half centuries before Pueblo people again occupied Santa Fe, and then their brief occupation was abruptly terminated when they were removed by Spanish troops." (Levine in Noble, ed., pp.9-11).

Based on the most recent scholarship, the founding of the Spanish settlement of Santa Fe is now credited to Juan Martinez de Montoya who reported to the

Viceroy in Mexico that he had made a settlement in Santa Fe. Montoya was apparently one of the settlers who had brought charges against Juan de Oñate for gross mistreatment of the Pueblos as a result of the slaughter of the people of Acoma and overall mishandling of the colony. These charges led to the resignation of Oñate as governor of New Mexico in 1607 and the appointment Pedro de Peralta in 1608. Peralta had instructions from the Viceroy to move the capital from Oñate's seat of administration at San Gabriel (present day Ohkay Owingeh) to Santa Fe. (Ivey, p.6).

Pueblo People and Spanish Colonization

Colonization of the Pueblo communities under the Spanish was every bit as brutal and disastrous as it had been for other Indigenous peoples in the Americas and in other parts of the world where European colonization occurred.

The story of the colonization of New Mexico begins with Alvar Núñez Cabeza de Vaca who, after the failed Narváez expedition of 1528, survived a shipwreck not far off-shore from present-day Galveston Island, Texas. Enduring a long trek through the American Southwest, Vaca, along with three other survivors, eventually carried back to the Spanish government in Mexico City stories of the "lands to the north where emeralds could be found and where there were towns of great population and houses." (Weber, pp.45). These were stories he had been told by Indians during his journey through the American Southwest. The stories of great wealth intrigued Antonio de Mendoza, the Viceroy of New Spain and thus commissioned Fray Marcos de Niza to lead an expedition north to substantiate Vaca's claims. Niza reached *Hawikuh* (Zuni Pueblo) in May of 1539. He sent *Estevanico* (Esteban), a black Moorish slave from Morocco, who also survived the shipwreck and returned to Mexico with Cabeza de Vaca, as a representative of the expedition into Zuni. The fact that Estevanico arrived at one of the most sacred times in the Zuni ceremonial cycle, coupled with his demands and demeanor, led to his capture and subsequent death at the hands of Zuni warriors. Upon hearing of Estevanico's death, Niza fled back to Mexico. Although Niza actually only saw Zuni from a distance he none-the-less managed to fabricate a fantastic tale of Zuni as being one of the fabled 'Seven Cities of Gold'. Niza's story created a frenzy of Spanish imagination about the actual existence of such cities. The Viceroy commissioned a second and much larger expedition into New Mexico led by Francisco Vasquez de Coronado in 1540.

Tewa scholar Alfonso Ortiz describes the Coronado Expedition as "a rampage of death, deceit and destruction through Pueblo country." And while the "sanitized" historical version of the Coronado Expedition presents him as the first European explorer of the Southwest, the actual record of Coronado's acts among the Pueblos supports Ortiz's assertion. The real purpose of the Coronado Expedition was not exploration after all, but a search for riches. *(Surviving Columbus: The Story of the Pueblo People, 1992)*. The most egregious of the many acts of death and destruction committed by the Coronado Expedition occurred in and among the several villages located in what the Spanish chroniclers called the *Tiguex* province.

Somewhere near present-day Zia and Sandia Pueblos the Coronado expedition set winter camp in 1541. Lacking adequate supplies, Coronado and his men demanded provisions from the now extinct Pueblo the Spanish called "*Alcanfor*." Needing food themselves the inhabitants of Alcanfor were reluctant to comply. However, the rape of a Pueblo woman by Coronado's men sparked a confrontation between the Pueblo men and the Spanish soldiers. The soldiers confined many of the Pueblo inhabitants in tents and then attacked, setting the tents on fire with the people still in them while others were slashed to pieces trying to escape. Those who were captured were burned at the stake to set an example of the retribution that would happen to any Pueblos who opposed Coronado's demands. Over 300 people were slaughtered. During that winter all of the other Pueblos in the Tiguex Province were attacked. Many villages were burned to the ground. Then, in April 1541, Coronado left the Tiguex Province with part of his forces heading east toward present day Kansas in search of a place called "*Quivira*" led by a guide whom the Spanish named the Turk for his prominent nose. The Turk described Quivira as the land of riches Coronado sought. Coronado never found Quivira and set his war dogs on the Turk for his trouble. Coronado returned to the Tiguex province and, in April of 1542, led his expedition back to Mexico City. Having experienced their first taste of Spanish greed and violence the Pueblos were certainly happy to see the Spanish leave Pueblo country. The Coronado Expedition was only the first storm cloud of many more to follow. For 39 years no Spanish were seen in New Mexico. It was a proverbial calm before the storm.

The Spanish chronicles tell of five ill-fated attempts to colonize New Mexico between 1582 and 1593 per the decree of the King of Spain. The most notorious of these expeditions was led by Antonio de Espejo who attacked the pueblo of *Puaray* and placed an unspecified number of captives in a kiva and set it on fire thus resuming the death and destruction introduced by Coronado.

It was not until the expedition of Juan de Oñate that the Spanish made it clear that they were in New Mexico to stay. Leading a caravan of eighty ox-drawn wagons and carts, 560 colonists, 129 soldiers, over a thousand Mexican Indians, a large unspecified number of women and children, and 7,000 cattle, sheep, goats, oxen, donkeys, mules and horses, Oñate crossed the Rio Grande near present day El Paso on April 30, 1598, claiming New Mexico for King Philip II and Spain. It took until July 11, 1598 for Oñate to lead this huge entourage through Pueblo country and arrive at *Yungeh,* near present day Ohkay Owingeh, where he established the first capital of New Mexico.

The Pueblo Revolt

John Kessell, in his book *Pueblos, Spaniards and the Kingdom of New Mexico*, 2008, presents an interesting narrative history of the social, political, cultural dynamics along with the personalities that played an important role in the history of Santa Fe.

According to Kessell, the relationship of Pueblos and Spaniards began primarily as a one-sided cycle of conquest and atrocities inflicted on Pueblo peoples by the Spaniards interested only in creating personal fortunes and glory for themselves. This was followed by continued conflict at levels interspersed with cooperation and co-existence when times were hard and situations presented this course as the best resort. In the final analysis, this period was disastrous for the Pueblos. The Pueblo population was reduced by 90%, from a conservative estimate of 80,000 to a mere 8,000, from the time of the Coronado Expedition to the American Annexation of New Mexico in 1848. At the time of the Coronado Expedition over 100 Pueblos, stretching south to north from El Paso to Taos and east to west from Pecos to Hopi, were in existence, however, only 19 Pueblos survived into the American period. In fact, some Pueblos had less than 200 members at the time of American annexation.

To understand the establishment of Santa Fe in the middle of Pueblo territory, it is important to know something of the colonial history of New Mexico before and after the Pueblo Revolt of 1680. The Revolt was in reality an act of desperation; the result of almost three generations of Spanish colonial rule and oppression, whose systematic application began with the arrival of Oñate.

During the 82 years leading up to the Pueblo Revolt, Pueblo people endured the *encomienda system,* which, at times, taxed each Pueblo household more than half of their harvest, textiles, pottery and hides to maintain the Spanish colonial government and missions. Added to this was the *repartimiento system,* which exacted labor from the Pueblos to build and maintain the missions and colonial government buildings in addition to a period of servitude in Spanish households. (Tanoan and Tewa laborers along with laborers from Pecos, San Marcos, Galisteo, San Lasaro, La Cieneguilla, Cochiti, and Santo Domingo were largely responsible for building Santa Fe under the governorship of Pedro de Peralta). Indeed, the pressure on the social and economic infrastructure of Pueblo communities combined with continual religious persecution were certainly key factors in precipitating the revolt.

Added to the oppression of the *encomienda* and *repartimiento* systems, by the early 1600s Pueblos were dealing with region-wide epidemics of smallpox, drought, famine and raids of Apache, Navajo, Ute, and Comanche, all of whom now possessed Spanish horses. It is important to note that Pueblos were not allowed to own or ride horses, possess firearms or metal weapons of any kind under Spanish colonial law. To the chagrin of the Pueblos, the raiders on the other hand, possessed all of these by the mid 1600s.

For example, an epidemic of smallpox took the lives of almost 3,000 Pueblo lives in 1640 with smaller epidemics taking their toll well into the 1660s. A severe drought plagued New Mexico between 1665–1668 decimating crops of many Pueblos and leading to starvation in some. With Spanish horses, the Apaches, Navajo, Utes and Comanches were able to raid both Pueblo and Hispanic communities with disastrous regularity. Unable to defend themselves, the *Piro, Tompiro* and *Tiwa* Pueblos of *Abo, Gran Quivira, Manzano, Tajique* and *Chilili* were largely abandoned as a result of these stresses.

Furthermore:

> "The Pueblo people had observed government officials struggling with Franciscan padres over who had ultimate authority over the Indians and who should collect tribute and labor from them. There were charges and countercharges that each side was profiting unfairly from Indians' labor and subverting the legitimate authority of the other faction." (Sando in Sando and Agoyo, ed., p.20).

In the eyes and hearts of Pueblo people the world was seriously out of balance and the Pueblos, seeing that the Spanish authorities and the Franciscans could do or would do little to protect them, began to revert to traditional Native religious practices, as they had done in the past, to address this imbalance and restore harmony to the Pueblo world.

Witnessing the rise of Native religious practice, the Franciscans felt increasingly threatened and pressed Juan de Trevino, Colonial Governor of New Mexico (1675–1677), to intercede and restore the authority of the Catholic Church and colonial government by banning Native religious practices and punishing those who led them. In 1677, Governor Trevino acted to do just this and exercised the power of his colonial authority. He commanded his soldiers to enter various nearby Pueblos and arrest those that were known leaders of Native religious practices. The soldiers arrested 47 alleged sorcerers (Pueblo Medicine Men) for practicing witchcraft. They were brought to Santa Fe, put on trial, and convicted. Three were hanged in their respective villages of San Felipe, Jemez and Nambe and a fourth hanged himself rather than submit to the Spanish sentence. The others were publically whipped and sentenced to slavery. On hearing of this, Pueblo leaders and warriors from surrounding Tewa Pueblos marched on Santa Fe to demand the release of the prisoners. The large group of Pueblos entered the Palace office of Governor Trevino; pressing the case for the release of the prisoners. Trevino, seeing the resolve of the Pueblo delegation and lacking the soldiers to defend his decision at that time, commuted the sentences of the remaining prisoners. Among those released was a leader little known to the Spanish named Po'Pay from Ohkay Owingeh. Upon his release Po'Pay traveled to Taos Pueblo, far from prying Spanish and Christianized Pueblo eyes, where he, along with other Pueblo leaders, began to plan a revolt against Spanish rule. Po'Pay became, in three short years, the central leader of the first successful revolt by an Indigenous group against a colonial power in the New World. Joe Sando writes:

> "The essence of the Pueblo Revolt was predicated on freeing Pueblo people from the colonial oppression of "an autocratic foreign government that ruled by decree, taxed them unjustly, gave them no voice in decision-making and denied them fundamental freedoms… Years of ongoing grievances and hostile, even cruel, treatment at the representative of the monarchy housed in luxurious palaces across the Atlantic Ocean had forced them to a point of no return. They had to drive the Europeans out of their country even though they lacked the empire's arms and military might." (Sando in Sando and Agoyo, ed., p.5).

The decision to go to war to the extent required by the Revolt was not taken lightly. It certainly required a coordination of effort which was unprecedented among the Pueblos. The level of secrecy required was equally daunting since Pueblo people sympathetic to the Franciscan Friars and the Spanish Colonial authority existed in every Pueblo. For almost three years careful plans were laid for the Revolt. There is no doubt that many secret meetings were held in various Pueblos; gauging the level of support for the idea and then actually preparing for the Revolt while continuing to appear outwardly as conforming to the mandates and rules of Christian and Colonial authority was a major feat. Much deliberation among numerous leaders had to have been conducted before a final consensus was reached regarding the date of the revolt and how it was to be conducted.

The northern leaders often mentioned along with Po'Pay were men such as Francisco El Ollito and Nicolas de la Cruz Jonva, both of *Po-sogeh* (San Ildefonso); Domingo Naranjo, a half black from *Ka-'p-geh* (Santa Clara); and Diego Xenome of *Nampe* (Nambe). Other leaders included Luis Conixu of *Walatowa* (Jemez); El Saca from *Teotho* (Taos); Luis Tapatu from *Welai* (Picuris); Alonzo Catiti, a mestizo from *Khe-wa* or *Kewa* (Santo Domingo). There were certainly others including representatives from the Hopi villages far to the West.

It was decided that a knotted cord would be used to count the days to the

Revolt. Before dawn on August 8, 1680, two young runners, Nicolas Catua and Pedro Omtua, were chosen from Tesuque Pueblo to carry these knotted cords from pueblo to pueblo to inform leaders when the Revolt would occur. They ran first to Pecos Pueblo where they were noticed by Pecos people sympathetic with the Franciscan, Fray Velasco. Fray Velasco sent word to Pecos Governor Juan de Ye who was also sympathetic with the Spanish. Juan de Ye dispatched a warning to Governor Otermín in Santa Fe that the runners had been sighted carrying knotted cords which almost certainly had to do with a communication regarding the impending revolt. When the runners entered Galisteo they were also seen and the padre of Galisteo, Juan Bernal, also sent word to Otermín. The next day, August 9, word was also sent from the village of Taos regarding these communications using the knotted cords. Otermín sent his men to hunt down these messengers and bring them to Santa Fe. The runners were found near the Tano villages and imprisoned in Santa Fe. Word spread among the Pueblos that the runners were captured. The next morning, August 10, Fray Pio escorted by a soldier named Pedro Hidalgo, rode to *Tesugeh* to say mass. Arriving to a deserted village, Fray Pio began to search the nearby hills for his congregation. He ran into a contingent of Tesugeh warriors gathered in a nearby arroyo with their faces painted red for war. Fray Pio approached them to try to convince them to lay down their arms. He was killed immediately. Almost being killed himself, the soldier Hidalgo fought his way out and rode away as fast as he could to Santa Fe to report to Otermín what had happened. The Revolt had begun.

Runners were sent to all the Pueblo villages to announce that the battle had begun. In each of the Pueblos the war cry was sounded by the War Chiefs and warriors gathered in their respective clan areas. In each Pueblo, warriors went to the convent homes of the Franciscan Friars while others went to haciendas and homes of the Spanish Alcaldes and other Spanish officials and ordered them to leave. Those that refused were killed. The mission churches were raided, burned, or other wise destroyed. During the next two days, August 11 and 12 over 1000 refugees from areas around Santa Fe gathered in the Capitol. (Sando in Sando and Agoyo, ed., pp.29-39).

> "On Tuesday, August 13, the tribes closest to Santa Fe invaded the Capital. These were the Pecos, Tanos from *Tonogeh* composed of Galisteo, San Cristobal, San Lazaro, plus the Keresan villages of San Marcos and La Cieneguilla de Cochiti…. The battle lasted for most of the day. When the Spanish, with their firearms and military training, thought they had overcome the rebels, Tewa warriors and the *Hemish* from Walatowa approached from the north to join the battle. As it grew dark, fighting diminished, and the Indians withdrew to the eastern hills for the night. The next morning, August 14, the warriors

returned to the villa but the day passed without further combat. (Little fighting occurred on August 15)". (Ibid, p.33, p.35).

The battle for Santa Fe continued again on August 16 and the Spanish continued to hold out. Reinforcements to the Pueblo ranks arrived from Picuris and Taos. Alonzo Catiti of *Kewa* (Santo Domingo) led a force of warriors from the Keresan Pueblos to join the siege. Soon, an estimated 2,500 warriors surrounded Santa Fe. Pueblo warriors occupied houses and blocked all streets leading outside the fortified walls. Pueblo warriors also blocked the Santa Fe River and the various acequias leading to the *casa reales* thereby cutting off the water supply to the town. This was a pivotal act in the siege because without water for themselves and their livestock, the Spanish could not hold out for much longer and their situation rapidly became hopeless.

At dawn on Saturday morning Pueblo warriors attacked once again. The Spanish, extremely thirsty, were becoming increasingly disheartened. Spanish horse and livestock were also dying from hunger and lack of water. In desperation, the Spaniards chose to make an all out counterattack. With every able bodied man armed with anything at his disposal, the Spanish attacked, catching the Pueblo warriors off guard. Otermín later reported that over three hundred warriors were killed with a minimum of losses to his forces. Forty seven Pueblo warriors were captured. Despite Otermín's perceived victory, the Pueblo siege had indeed effectively cut off food and water supplies. Santa Fe lay in ruins, the fields of crops had been burned, and there was little food or water left. Seeing that the situation was hopeless Otermín decided to abandon Santa Fe on Wednesday, August 21. Pueblo warriors watched as the Spanish caravan of wagons, settlers, soldiers and Mexican Indian allies left Santa Fe heading south and back to Mexico. It is likely that Pueblo warriors gathered in the plaza of the now reoccupied Pueblo of Santa Fe to offer prayers and thanks for their victory. Santa Fe would remain in Pueblo hands for twelve years. *(Surviving Columbus: The Story of the Pueblo People, 1992).*

Although western historians have provided many perspectives as to why the Pueblo Revolt took place, Tewa scholar Alfonso Ortiz perhaps best articulates the Pueblos' point of view, writing:

"The Pueblo Revolt of 1680 represents the story of Pueblo peoples' restoration of their commitment to their beginnings. It is, therefore, to be understood first and foremost as a religious restoration. All of the events of 1680 and in the subsequent relations in New Mexico are better understood in relationship to this fact. The Pueblo people suffered political and economic exploitation from the time the Spaniards settled among them in 1598, true, but these they had been able to endure. What they could not endure any longer were the unrelenting attempts on the part of the Spaniards in power, at times clergy and at other times civil authorities, to stamp out their ancient religious practices." (Ortiz in Sando and Agoyo, ed., p.4).

A Reprieve From Colonial Domination

For twelve years the Pueblos had a reprieve from colonial domination. During this time the pueblos would struggle to adjust to their hard won political independence. But the threat of reconquest remained ever present.

After the revolt and Otermín's retreat to El Paso, attempts were made by Otermín and subsequent others to retake Santa Fe and New Mexico from Pueblo control. Setting out from El Paso in November of 1681, Otermín attacked the Pueblo of Isleta. Isleta warriors offered only nominal resistance and quickly laid down their arms telling him that they thought the Spaniards were Apaches attacking from the south. Otermín made Isleta his headquarters. Encouraged that the reconquest might be equally easy as he had experienced at Isleta, Otermín sent out parties of soldiers to the Pueblos instructing them that they were to tell the governors of each of the Pueblos that they were to lay down their arms and surrender to the returning Spaniards.

As Otermín's various parties of soldiers approached they found the Pueblos of *Alameda, Purary, Sandia, San Felipe, Kewa* and *Cochiti* deserted. The inhabitants of each of these Pueblos had fled to the hills and mesa surrounding their villages. Otermín's soldiers burned each of these Pueblos as a warning to the Pueblo's inhabitants. Only in Cochiti did the Spaniards see large number of warriors gathering atop a mesa preparing for battle. Seeing that they were completely outnumbered by the gathering force of Pueblo warriors they returned to Isleta. A large number of Puebloan warriors mounted on horseback followed the retreating Spaniards and surrounded Isleta for a week. Not knowing the true size of the Puebloan force surrounding him as well as his soldiers and settlers losing heart for battle, Otermín decided to return to El Paso where he was relieved of the governorship of New Mexico in 1683.

The next attempt at the Spanish reoccupation of New Mexico was six years later in 1689 and conducted under the newly appointed governor in exile Governor Domingo Jironza Petriz de Cruzate. The Cruzate expedition fought a pitched battle with the warriors of *Zia* Pueblo in which fifty of his eighty men were wounded while over six-hundred people from Zia were killed and the Pueblo burned; again a reminder to the Pueblo people of the costs of attempting to remain independent nations.

The Reconquest of Santa Fe

The reconquest of Santa Fe, contrary to popularized accounts, was not "bloodless" and, in fact, the full reconquest of New Mexico actually stretches over a period of four years, 1692–1696.

Don Diego de Vargas was appointed governor of New Mexico in 1691. He arrived in El Paso and immediately set upon creating an expedition to re-conquer New Mexico once and for all. On August 10, 1692 Vargas led his expedition of reconquest into New Mexico. The Vargas expedition is documented in great detail in various writings and has been presented by a number of historians, most recently by John Kessell and Rick Hendricks eds. 1998, *By Force of Arms: The Journal of Don Diego de Vargas, New Mexico, 1691–1693*. I will present only a brief summary of the events of that period.

Initially, Vargas was surprised by the lack of resistance as he traveled through New Mexico from El Paso. Indeed, almost all the Pueblos he came upon were abandoned because the Pueblos had seen the slow moving caravan coming. The inhabitants of the Pueblos took refuge on the mesas and foothills as Vargas's caravan approached. Only in San Felipe Pueblo did he encounter a few inhabitants who told him that many Tewa and Tano Indians now occupied Santa Fe.

As Vargas approached Santa Fe on the evening of September 13, he found a well fortified Pueblo "city." Since it was evening, at first the Pueblo defenders did not believe that Vargas and his soldiers were actually Spanish and challenged them to show evidence. Realizing that they were indeed Spanish, the warriors defending Santa Fe vowed to fight to the death. The back and forth of shouting, threat and speechmaking continued through out the night. By morning Vargas had shown the defenders his standard of the Virgin Mary (*La Conquistadora*), blown bugles and beat his war drum to demonstrate his resolve. He promised clemency and good treatment to those who would surrender. By mid-morning Vargas decided to cut off the water supply as the Pueblos themselves had done to the Spanish twelve years before. He gave the Puebloans one hour to surrender. The hour came and went and negotiations continued as Vargas promised to pardon those who would come out and surrender.

Finally, two unarmed Puebloans came out and pledged peace on the part of all residents of the Santa Fe Pueblo. By late afternoon Vargas had erected a cross in the Santa Fe plaza. He entered Santa Fe without firing a shot but this was not to be the real end to the reconquest of Santa Fe. This first encounter with the Puebloans of Santa Fe was accomplished without bloodshed and what would later be celebrated at the Santa Fe Fiesta every September as the "bloodless" reconquest. Within a year, however, blood would indeed be flowing in the streets of Santa Fe.

During the days that followed, Vargas set off to almost all the Pueblos along the Rio Grande and by October, he and his soldiers, traveling west, reached the villages of Zuni and Hopi. He subdued Zuni quickly in that the Zuni people had already heard of his imminent arrival from the Apache who warned that Vargas meant to destroy all the Zunis if they did not submit to Spanish rule. In Hopi he subdued *Awatowi* with his promises of pardons and protection and a few days later he subdued *Mishongnovi* and *Jongopavi* in a similar fashion.

In each of the Pueblos he entered Vargas repeated his re-entry performance from Santa Fe of taking formal possession of the Pueblo in the name of the Spanish Majesty, the declaration of each Pueblo's inhabitants as his vassals, the baptism of as many Puebloans as possible and the erecting of a huge cross in the middle of each Pueblo's principal plaza. However, being forewarned that the reception at the last Hopi village of old *Oraibi* might end in violence, Vargas decided not to press his luck and returned to El Paso to begin enlisting colonists to settle in New Mexico. By his own count, as mentioned in his journal, he had gained the submission of twenty-three Pueblos and baptized 2,214 Indians.

Vargas spent eight months enlisting colonists and gathering supplies for his trek back into New Mexico. He again crossed the Rio Grande from El Paso on October 4, 1693 leading a huge caravan of about 800 people comprised of 70 families, 100 soldiers, 18 Franciscan friars and a large number of Pueblo and Mexican Indian allies. The caravan included eighteen large supply wagons and a huge number of animals, over two thousand horses, one thousand mules, nine hundred head of cattle, assorted pigs, goats and chickens. (Roberts, pp. 182-183).

When the caravan arrived on the outskirts of Isleta Pueblo on November 10, Vargas began to realize that the Pueblos would not be as docile as he had left them. He discovered from the still loyal governor of Pecos, who visited Vargas in Isleta, that in his absence from New Mexico only the Pueblos of San Felipe, Santa Ana and Zia remained fully loyal to the Spanish. The Northern Pueblos, particularly the Tanos, Tewa, Towa and Tiwa, had vowed to fight the Spanish. The reason for this turn of favor was apparently the result of the warning Pedro de Tapia from Cochiti, an interpreter for Vargas the year before, had given Pueblo leaders when Vargas left for El Paso. Tapia had since passed away; however, before he died he warned a gathering of Pueblo leaders at Ohkay Owingeh that although Vargas had pardoned them, when he returned with a larger force he would put all of them to death, leaving only those twelve to fourteen years of age alive to work as servants. Upon hearing this for the first time, Vargas was furious that all his work of the prior year was for not and hoped he would be able to repair the grievous damage of Tapia's warning and convince the Puebloans occupying Santa Fe that he had come in peace. Ironically, in less than two months, Vargas found himself uttering something similar to the words of Tapia's warning as he took control of the Pueblo of Santa Fe. (Roberts, p.184).

Vargas took a contingent of his men and went further north, establishing a temporary headquarters at Kewa (Santo Domingo Pueblo), and gathered the rest of the caravan in preparation for the final leg of the journey to Santa Fe. The Vargas caravan arrived at the outskirts of Santa Fe around December 10th. He approached the walled Pueblo of Santa Fe and, as he did the year before, attempted to assure the Puebloans inside that he would not harm them. David Roberts writes:

> "Through an interpreter, Vargas addressed the Puebloan leaders who had come to hear him out. Because he had pardoned these apostates the year before, he explained, the King of Spain was no longer angry at them. For Vargas's own part, 'I had begun to call them my children again,' the King 'was sending many priests so that the Indians might be Christians again. And the King had dispatched Vargas and his soldiers to protect them from the Apaches." (Ibid. p.186).

As part of his continuing reconquest ritual, Vargas had some of the Franciscan friars sing psalms and brandish the standard of the Virgin Mary. He then erected a cross and enacted a ceremonial repossession of Santa Fe for the King of Spain.

Despite Vargas's efforts there was an impasse lasting for thirteen days. The Vargas caravan camped outside the walls and waited. Food was running low, it was bitterly cold and the colonists were angry. Vargas demanded food as well as labor from the Puebloans to repair the old San Miguel church, which was situated within the ramparts of Santa Fe, so that the colonists could conduct mass. However, due to deep snows in the surrounding countryside, the beams needed for the repair could not be cut and transported. The Pueblo Governor, Jose, offered a kiva as an alternative solution. Vargas accepted and had a door cut into the kiva wall for an entrance. However, the Franciscans refused to serve mass in the kiva, further increasing the tension between the two groups. (Roberts, p.187).

Dissension grew in the caravan as the days wore on. Some of the colonists who had lived in Santa Fe before the Revolt petitioned Vargas to remove the Puebloans immediately and restore their homes. By December 23, many of the colonists were becoming ill and hungry and expressed fears that their children would die from the bitter cold. Vargas waited until December 29.

By mid-morning the battle began "as the warriors unleashed volleys of darts, arrows, and many rocks from slings. At last galvanized to action, Vargas cried out to his soldiers, Santiago, Santiago, kill those rebels!".(Ibid, p.189).

Vargas and his soldiers set fire to the main gate. By mid-afternoon the Spanish soldiers had broken through the gate and breached the ramparts. They cornered the Pueblo defenders in the inner part of the city and by nightfall the Spanish were in full control of the Pueblo. The Pueblo defenders hid out where they could but were rooted out one by one by the soldiers. The captured warriors were gathered together and Vargas ordered their execution.

> "The soldiers led the prisoners out of the plaza. The priests absolved them. Then Roque Madrid commanded the firing squad. In a matter of minutes, seventy Puebloan warriors lay dead in the dirt.... As the women and children huddled outside the ramparts, the governor announced that every one of them would be sentenced to ten years servitude. He would leave it up to the colonists to distribute the women and children among their new masters." (Ibid. p.191).

Vargas reported that although some Spaniards were wounded, not a single one was killed. The number of Puebloans killed is unknown. The number of women and children cast into slavery is also unknown. There were a large number of Puebloan people inhabiting Santa Fe at the time of the reconquest. It is uncertain what may have happened to them. Some may have escaped to other Tewa villages. Many others would have certainly perished. Indeed, the reconquest of Santa Fe was not bloodless.

By 1696 the submission of the Pueblos was complete. Vargas made war on the Tewa gathered atop of Black Mesa and on the Towa of Jemez. Many of the Tanos, who comprised a large portion of the people living in Santa Fe when Vargas arrived, fled to Hopi land where they established the Tewa Pueblo of Hano. The Picuris people, fearing the retaliation of Vargas, fled to Kansas only to be captured and held by the Plains Apache. Other Puebloans are believed to have fled to the *Dinetah* to live among the Navajo. People from a number of other Pueblos fled where they could to escape Vargas. This exodus of Pueblo peoples, along with the battles fought through 1696, determined where many Pueblo villages are situated today. It also precipitated the eventual extinction of several Pueblos near Santa Fe such *as Cuyumangue, Jacona, Galisteo, San Cristobal, San Marcos* and *La Cieneguilla*. Ironically, it would be the Tewa, Tiwa and Towa warriors who would comprise the bulk of the Spanish militia one generation later.

The warriors from these Pueblos were enlisted in Spanish campaigns against the Comanches, Utes, Navajo and Apache throughout the 1700s. The cooperation between Spanish and Pueblo people for mutual defense was essential to the survival of the colony during this time. Also, as a result of these alliances of necessity, New Mexico gradually developed its own unique sense of identity. Through the Mexican period and into the early years of American occupation this unique play of shared history, borne of conflict but evolving into collaboration and cooperation based on a shared sense of place, eventually forged a shared sense of identity as New Mexicans.

Final Thoughts

The reconquest of Santa Fe was neither bloodless or a simple matter of re-subjugating the Pueblos! In reality, Don Diego de Vargas was involved with the aftermath of the reconquest for the rest of his life. And, like Vargas, the people of New Mexico have been dealing with the reconquest every generation since. The complex tapestry of people, events and relationships set into play by the reconquest formed the New Mexico that we see and experience today. The Pueblos that survived the reconquest created unique strategies to accommodate the re-imposition of colonial rule while maintaining their cultures, languages and traditions. Variation of these strategies would subsequently be later applied in response to the impositions of the Mexican and American governments.

As I researched the various accounts of prehistory, the conquest, Pueblo Revolt and the reconquest of Santa Fe and New Mexico, I was touched by many emotions. One might say these emotions were the echoes of "historical trauma" or generationally remembered experience of tragedy, loss, dispossession and subjugation. In the midst of such replay of emotions I could not help but also feel a sense of pride for the tenacity of Pueblo community and culture as it was expressed then and as it continues to be expressed today.

As mentioned earlier, the Pueblo population was reduced by 90% and the number of Pueblos was reduced from an estimated one hundred at the time of the Coronado expedition to the nineteen Pueblos that exist today. The fact that Pueblo people continue to survive and even thrive as distinct cultural communities is a monumental achievement. Yet, there is an irony in the retelling of this story of the reconquest of Santa Fe in that so few Native New Mexicans have been exposed to any in-depth history of New Mexico. For example, I did not learn New Mexico history, particularly Pueblo history, until I entered college in 1970. This educational dilemma has improved only slightly since that time.

Today, general aspects of New Mexico history are presented to students in mid school and high schools. But even in these presentations the role of Pueblo people is minimized and generally restricted to cultural traits. If the Pueblo-Spanish conflicts are presented, they are usually "sanitized." Few students, particularly Pueblo students, have the opportunity to develop a deep or critical understanding of their own history. Hispanic students suffer a similar cultural/historical amnesia of this period of New Mexico history. Knowing the history of this time period, balance in both perspective and content is essential in understanding how the unique people and "ethos" of New Mexico came into being. With the reconquest of Santa Fe the *Genízaro* (de-tribalized) population of New Mexico largely came into being. The active slave trade in the 1700s brought yet another level of cultural and racial mixing. And through collaboration also comes intermarriage and cross-cultural trading at many levels.

In my work as a Native educator in the areas of culturally based science education and Native American studies, I rely heavily on critical historical accounts as a foundational context for my teaching and research. The truthful telling of history is difficult and often clouded with levels of political correctness, emotion and ethnocentricity. Western telling of histories still revolves largely around the themes of "winners and losers" or "great men and heroes of history" as they forge a foundation for modern civilization and Western society. This inherently biased approach to history certainly has an affect on those that hear it. The story and the history of the 'other' are only minimally represented. There is a deep historically affected psychology which forms the consciousness of every group of people. This group consciousness often forms the backdrop for how some people relate and/or interact with one another. If these very important forms of consciousness are positive, it often reflects as positive self-image and self-esteem. If the stories of history and the consciousness that it forms are negative, self-image and self-esteem suffer.

A critical and balanced representation of this period of New Mexico history is largely absent from most secondary school curricula. What is of greater concern to me is that there is not an interest on the part of many New Mexico youth in the "history" of New Mexico. Yet, it is this history that forms the identity of many New Mexicans. It is their history.

As for the Pueblo peoples, understanding their history and the role they play in New Mexico today, the Pueblo Tri-centennial commission presented the following focus for Pueblo participation in the commemoration:

> "First and foremost, the Tri-centennial would provide a focus for Pueblo people to examine themselves within their heritage and to affirm their values and ways as a people. Second, it would increase the understanding of Pueblo culture and historical development, using the commemoration of the Pueblo Revolt of 1680 as a presentation of cultural identity, human dignity and social viability. Third, it would facilitate the understanding of unique issues and concerns that characterize Pueblo communities today. Fourth, it would clarify issues that characterize Pueblo and non-Pueblo community relationships." (Sando and Agoyo, ed., p. 95).

This statement embodies the essence of the role that a firm grounding in one's own history can play in ensuring the continuity and sustainability of Pueblo communities in the Twenty-First Century.

Epilogue

Recently, as I watched the re-enactment of the Vargas Entrada during the Santa Fe Fiesta, I looked at the faces in the audience and tried to pick out the "locals". You can still see an aspect of the aftermath of the reconquest of Santa Fe and New Mexico in these faces even after many generations. I wondered to myself how many really know the deeper history of Santa Fe and New Mexico in all its complexity and tribulation. History is essentially a story and its telling is always relative to the memories and perspectives of the people who tell it. But, then again, the *truth* of a history is something that can really only be glimpsed though its reflection... even when its reality has faded from memory.

References:

Agoyo, Herman, editor. *When Cultures Meet: Remembering San Gabriel del Yungeh Owingeh.* Santa Fe: Sunstone Press, 1987.

Dozier, Edward P. *The Pueblo Indians of North America.* New York: Holt Press, 1970.

De Marco, Barbara. "Voices from the Archives, Part 1: Testimony of the Pueblo Indians in the 1680 Revolt." *Romance Philosophy,* vol.53, no.2, Spring 2000. pp. 375-448.

De Marco, Barbara. "Voices from the Archives, Part 2: Ayeta'1693 Letter to the Viceroy." *Romance Philosophy,* vol.53, no. 2, Spring 2000, pp.449-508.

Flint, Richard, and Shirley Cushing Flint, editors. *The Coronado Expedition to Tierra Nueva.* Boulder: University of Colorado Press,1997.

Hackett, Charles Wilson, and Charmion Clair Shelby, editors. *Revolt of the Pueblo Indians of New Mexico and Otermin's Attempted Reconquest, 1680-1682* Albuquerque: University Of New Mexico Press, 1942.

Hammond, George P., and Rey, Agapito, editors. *Don Juan de Oñate: Colonizer of New Mexico, 1595-1628* (two volumes). Albuquerque: University of New Mexico Press, 1953.

Ivey, James. *Santa Fe 400: An Uncertain Founding.* Green Fire Times. Vol.1. No.5. September 2009.

Kessell, John L., Rick Hendricks, editors. *By Force of Arms: The Journals of Don Diego De Vargas, New Mexico, 1691-93.* Albuquerque: University of New Mexico Press, 1995.

Kessell, John L., Rick Hendricks, and Meredith D. Dodge, editors. *Blood on the Boulders: The Journals of Don Diego De Vargas, 1694- 1697.* (two volumes). Albuquerque: University of New Mexico Press, 1998.

Kessell, John L. *Pueblos, Spaniards, and the Kingdom of New Mexico.* Norman: University of Oklahoma Press, 2008.

Ladd, Edmund J. "Zuni on the Day the Men in Metal Arrived," in Flint and Flint, *The Coronado Expedition to Tierra Nueva,* Boulder: University of Colorado Press,1997, pp.225-33.

Levine, Francis. "Down Under An Ancient City: An Archaeologist's View of Santa Fe" in Noble, editor. *Santa Fe: History of An Ancient City*, Santa Fe: School for Advance Research Press, 2008, pp. 8-25.

Noble, David editor. *Santa Fe: History of An Ancient City.* Santa Fe: School of American Research Press, 1989.

Naranjo, Tessie. "Thoughts on Two World Views." *Federal Archeology,* vol. 7, no.3, Fall/Winter 1995, pp.16-17.

Ortiz, Alfonso, editor. *New Perspectives on the Pueblos.* Albuquerque: University of New Mexico Press, 1972.

Ortiz, Alfonso. "Popay's Leadership: A Pueblo Perspective," in *El Palacio* 86, Winter 1980-81

Ortiz, Alfonso. "Some Concerns Central to the Writing of 'Indian History." *The Indian Historian,* vol. 10, no.1, Winter 1977, pp. 17-22.

Preucel, Robert W., editor. *Archaeologies of the Pueblo Revolt: Identity, Meaning, and Renewal in the Pueblo World.* Albuquerque: University of New Mexico Press, 2002.

Reyna, Diane, director. *Surviving Columbus: The Story of the Pueblo People"* Larry Walsh (Writer and Co-Producer), Edmund Ladd (Producer), Dale Kruzic, George Burdeau and KNME (Co- Executive Producers) *A KNME – PBS Production, The University of New Mexico, Albuquerque, NM.*

Roberts, David.(2005). *The Pueblo Revolt: The secret rebellion that drove the Spaniards out of the Southwest.* New York: Simon and Schuster.

Sando, Joe S. and Herman Agoyo, editors. *Po'Pay and the First American Revolution.* Santa Fe: Clear Light Publishers, 2006.

Sando, Joe S. *Pueblo Nations: Eight Centuries of Pueblo Indian History.* Santa Fe: Clear Light Publishers, 1992.

Suina, Joseph H. "The Persistence of the Corn Mothers," in Preucel, *Archaeologies of the Pueblo Revolt,* Albuquerque: University of New Mexico Press, 2002 pp. 212-16.

Weber, David J. *The Spanish Frontier in North America.* New Haven and London: Yale University Press, 1992.

Indian Slavery and the Birth of Genízaros
by
Ramón A. Gutiérrez
Genízaro of Laguna-Zuni Ancestry

Four hundred years have passed since Santa Fe, the City of the Holy Faith, was founded as a Spanish royal town. Established in 1610, it was to serve as the secular capital of the Kingdom of New Mexico, which then encompassed much of what are today the state of New Mexico, Colorado and Arizona. A commemoration marking the city's existence for four hundred years naturally prompts reflection, if not explanations, for a town's longevity and life. Commemorations of this sort ignite imagination, perhaps even fantastic speculation, about what could have been. What if? What if? What if?

What if Santa Fe had not been established? What if the stunning valley in which the town now sits had remained pristine, how might the lives of the native peoples of the Upper Rio Grande watershed been different? What other possibilities for the area's eventual development were forestalled when Governor Pedro de Peralta arrived in 1610 to establish order over a profoundly conflict-ridden colony, to establish Santa Fe, and to take command of the Kingdom of New Mexico?

Easy answers for such complex questions are hard to find. We know for a fact that Santa Fe's spires ultimately flew the colors of three successive nations: Spain, Mexico, and the United States. There can be little doubt that Santa Fe, as a well-watered spot surrounded by high desert land, with fertile, verdant and wildlife-stocked hills nearby, with diverse native peoples and prosperous, relatively dense towns, ultimately would have gained the attention of those who coveted their neighbors' goods. This was indeed the case since antique times, as one group of people after another has bitterly fought for the area's control. Spain became enamored of this desert oasis primarily as a mission field that would augment the number of its Christian souls, as a fortified colonial buffer zone that would help protect its profitable silver mines further south in Mexico, and as a beachhead to curtail its acquisitive European imperial rivals, England and France.

For the native peoples of New Mexico, for those who today call themselves Navajos, Apaches and Pueblo Indians, the Spanish conquest in 1598, and the establishment of the Kingdom of New Mexico and later a capital in Santa Fe in 1610, altered the area's cultural geography in profound ways. Here was a vast sea of peoples who were marked mainly by whether they lived as nomadic hunters and gatherers or as sedentary agriculturalists, and much less so by any distinctive set of cultural characteristics that sharply differentiated one lineage-based group from the next. It was from this mix of hunters and farmers, of nomads and settled agriculturalists, that a complex tapestry of ethnic/national identities eventually emerged, identities that later in the nineteenth century would be called tribal in form. We now think of these ethnic/national distinctions as demarcating people into autonomous and unique groups, with their own languages, customs and ceremonials. But that was not the case in 1400, or in 1492, much less in 1598. These distinctions were born of the fact that when the Spanish colonists entered the Upper Rio Grande drainage they fixed and froze what was a fluid native geography, tied indigenous peoples to the ownership of those particular parcels of land they then had, and claimed the rest as their own. In 1610 it would have been difficult to predict which of the roughly 134 Pueblo Indian villages reported in historical documents would survive, which would be amalgamated into larger settlements, and which would completely disappear. Much the same thing can be said of the complex assortment of Apachean nomadic bands that in the early 1600s roamed the land raiding in times of need the granaries and livestock of their settled neighbors, and in times of plenty, trading for goods and products more ritually and peacefully. It would have been hard to predict in 1610, which kin-based groups would survive and ultimately settle into agrarian life, whether voluntarily or by force. This essay explores the impact that the establishment of a Spanish colonial capital at Santa Fe in 1610 had on the indigenous peoples who resided in the Kingdom of New Mexico.

For the next three hundred years, starting from the Kingdom's foundation in 1598, to the placement of the Navajo and Apache on reservations established by the government of the United States of America in the 1870s, a fierce battle ensued for control of this vast kingdom, for its land, for its natural resources, and most importantly, for its human labor. At the center of this struggle was the institution of slavery, the ability to take an individual's personal liberty and to transform that person into human chattel whose work could be extracted without mercy or recourse for an entire life, and sometimes way beyond through the stigma the children and grandchildren of slaves inherited.

When we think of slavery in the United States today and examine its painful history and toxic legacies, we usually imagine the institution largely in terms of black and white. Images of slaves captured in African tribal wars being marched to the coasts in chains to be sold off to Portuguese and Spanish merchants for shipment to the Americas, is the story we all know pretty well. Between 1492 and 1807 approximately fourteen million African slaves were transported to the Americas. Some ten million of these went to Brazil, the rest to the English, French and Spanish colonies.[1] What is perhaps less clearly understood, and certainly rarely mentioned in American history books, is that slavery was a widespread institution among Native Americans both before and after the Columbian expeditions began in 1492.[2] Colonial settlement and expansion intensified the importance of slavery as an institution, but its presence was well established among every indigenous group that ultimately claimed the Kingdom of New Mexico as their home.[3]

Before the arrival of the Europeans in what is now the American Southwest, the institution of slavery among Native Americans was extensive and always associated with war. Feasting and hosting one's neighbors was common enough, but when contests over land, over well-watered spots, over control of particular hunting grounds provoked war, captives were one of the first and most important spoils that justified the taking up of arms. Throughout human history and across cultures around the globe, death has been the most common punishment used to humiliate one's vanquished enemies, usually parading as trophies their scalps, their dismembered bodies, and their heads, ears and genitals as well. When memory of a group's defeat has been important enough to remember or to be used to establish local relationships of domination and subordination among neighboring groups or longtime foes, customary death sentences on the battlefield were substituted by perpetual slavery, a status that was a living testament of one's humiliation. Because this type of slavery was small in scale (two or three persons per household), because such slaves were always deeply enmeshed in domestic "familial" relations through rituals of incorporation that were often euphemistically called adoption and marriage, and because the institution was largely confined to women and children, it was frequently opaque to officials in the European center of empire and to moderns dependent on historical documents to understand the institution. Warriors captured in battle, if spared and kept alive, were always deemed too troublesome and potentially rebellious. Occasionally, they were indeed allowed to live but were sold off quickly to other indigenous groups as slaves, with the full intention of seeing them exiled far away. Women and children captured and pressed into slavery, on the other hand, were highly coveted for their labor and for their ability to adapt to their servile status, generating the necessary labor and love to reproduce the household in which they were held.[4]

Among the indigenous peoples of the Americas, as was the case among Africans of the fifteenth century, and among the Spanish colonists of the Kingdom of New Mexico in the sixteenth century, warfare was often premeditated, provoked and then rationalized as "just" for the simple purpose of seizing slaves who could be commercially bought and sold, who could be pimped out to work as prostitutes, or who could provide additional labor for any chore. For many years historians of African slavery in the Americas wondered why most of the slaves that arrived in North and South America were largely men. We now know that when the American market for African slaves developed in the 1500s, men who would have been killed on the battlefields of Africa were increasingly spared, shackled, sold to European slave merchants, and shipped to the Americas for resale here. For African women and children captured in warfare their futures and fate in Africa remained the same. They were incorporated into the households of their captors to work in subordinate status, most of them, for the rest of their lives.[5] So too were the politics and economics of slavery among Native Americans in New Mexico in 1610, explaining the preference for women and child slaves, and the paucity of slave men.

One sees similar practices of enslavement, though enmeshed in very different webs of political signification and obfuscation, in the varied and voluminous historical literature on the plight of British and later American colonials captured and pressed into domestic servitude by Native Americans. These captivity narratives (note how we speak of them generically as captivity narratives rather than slave narratives) have fascinated lay readers and scholars for several centuries.[6] The travails these slaves endured as they adapted and assimilated into indigenous societies are gripping stories that were told and recorded usually only after their release, rescue or flight. Of those white slaves never freed or rescued we know very little. American captivity narratives as a literary genre became popular fodder for the reading masses in the seventeenth and eighteenth centuries precisely because they offered a fantastical escape to a land of "savages," putatively living lives of godlessness, abandon, and wanton debauchery, devoid of all the hierarchical structures normal of a well-ordered society. For others, the barbarism of the Indians depicted in white captivity narratives justified whatever military action was necessary to rescue the white slave and annihilate the foe.

Much less is known about the mirror image, the stories of the Indians who were detribalized, those who were torn from their natal worlds and incorporated into Spanish colonial society as slaves. Obviously, such an experience was not unique or unfamiliar in the indigenous world. The native peoples of the Americas had waged war against their enemies since time immemorial and expected from such vanquishment women and child slaves.

If one surveys the cultural geography of North America, one finds from time-to-time indigenous words that referred to such slaves. For many years, for example, anthropologists and ethnohistorians believed that the word *Nixoras* signified a tribal group in southern Arizona. On closer examination it became clear that Nixoras was not a tribal designation but a word of Maricopa origin that was used quite widely in the *Pimería Alta* (roughly the modern state of Arizona) to refer to individuals pressed into slavery through conquest or to Indian slaves purchased from other tribes. In colonial America it was not uncommon for Indian slaves to pass into European hands through purchase, as gifts, or as prisoners of war. Since these persons did not speak or write the languages of their European masters, and infrequently became literate, their experiences are very little known.

In most regions where the incorporation of such indigenous slaves into colonial society was recorded, the phenomenon was of limited numeric dimensions. African slavery in the Americas is usually thought of in massive numbers equated with their employment on plantations devoted to the production of sugar, cotton, and tobacco. Indian slaves were often few in number, were usually attached to households, and never formed a significant portion of an area's population. Colonial New Mexico stands out as an exception. As one of the oldest and most densely populated of Spain's northern outposts, the kingdom developed a heavy reliance on indigenous servitude offered in a host of ways. By 1800 perhaps as much as one third of the Kingdom of New Mexico's total population had entered the colony as slaves. By 1848, when the United States annexed New Mexico at the end of the war with Mexico, Indian slaves were still widely employed and still very much objects of commerce in the province's complex trade relations. It was not until the late 1870s that indigenous slavery, increasingly masked as debt peonage, was finally outlawed and its prohibition more actively enforced by local authorities and the courts.

Slavery was one of the foundational institutions Spain transported to its new world colonies in the years following 1492, having inherited it as a trans-Mediterranean form that had been born in the Greek and Roman worlds. From 711 to 1492, Spain waged a perpetual war against the Moors to regain control over the Iberian Peninsula. To enslave one's enemies, part of the strategy for holding territory during these years of intense war against Islam, was always justified. The enslavement of Indians who were bellicose and unwilling to submit to Spain's rule or to accept Christian conversion, was fully lawful and was standard practice in the Caribbean by 1500, based as it was on these older legal precedents codified during the reconquista of Spain between 711 and 1492. As the level of exploitation and decimation of the native peoples of the Caribbean accelerated during the early years of colonial rule, clerical critics of Spain's colonial project in the Americas voiced their opposition to the enslavement of Indians, to their hyper-exploitation through the *encomienda* (tribute payments), and to the harsh punishments that were meted out to subject Indians on a routine and often arbitrary basis. Fray Bartolomé de las Casas is probably the most famous of these critics. These defenders of the Indians appealed to the King's conscience, challenging the ideological foundations of Spain's new world conquests through debates with the king's theologians and jurists. The provocations and disquisitions over the welfare of the Indians proved successful when the Crown issued the New Laws in 1542, which were to blunt the most exploitative elements of colonial rule on its subjects.

The 1542 publication of the New Laws in Spain's colonial empire explicitly outlawed Indian slavery. The 1680 Recompilation of the Laws of the Indies reiterated the prohibition. But the institution nevertheless persisted as a minor exception on the remote margins of Spain's empire—in places like Chile, the Amazon, and New Mexico—where it was tolerated as a way of compensating those colonists who might invest their money and time in the settlement of such areas known to be devoid of any mineral wealth. Accordingly, Native Americans in the Kingdom of New Mexico who refused to submit to Spanish rule, who resisted the word of God, could be justly punished with enslavement. The theoretical justification was that they had been kindly and peacefully enjoined to submit to Christian rule and because they had refused, a "just war" could be waged against them. The laws of slavery in the remote margins of empire stipulated that such captives could only be kept in bondage for ten to twenty years, but in practice, most remained thralls for their entire lives.[7]

This was the explicit justification New Mexico's first governor, Don Juan de Oñate, invoked in 1599 when he punished the residents of Acoma Pueblo. On December 4, 1598, or so the Spaniards tell the story, Captain Don Juan de Zaldivar and 31 Spanish soldiers, having recently arrived in the province and en route to Zuni, stopped at Acoma for provisions. When the corn flour that they demanded was not quickly handed over, a battle followed, leaving Zaldivar and twelve of his men dead. Governor Oñate, on learning of the massacre, quickly retaliated. On January 21, 1599, Oñate took 80 men and 500 women and children as prisoners to stand trial for their insubordination, leaving behind some 800 dead men, women, and children. The Acomas were found guilty of murder and failing to pay the tribute that was demanded of them. For these crimes all the men and women over the age of twelve were condemned to slavery in Spanish households for twenty years. All children under the age of twelve were distributed to monasteries and households as domestic servants. And the two Hopi Indians captured as collaborators at Acoma were dispatched home, having each lost their right hand, to serve as testaments of Spanish wrath. Several years later Oñate razed the *Tompiro* Pueblos of southern New

Mexico for similar resistance to Spanish rule and condemned all of their inhabitants to slavery.[8]

Spanish raids into Indian Territory, ostensibly to punish putative "heathen" insubordination and arrogance, but in reality to capture slaves, became a constant fact throughout the colonial period. At the beginning of the seventeenth century, however, as the level of nomadic Indian depredation on New Mexico's settlements intensified, the number of "just wars" against the Apaches and other enemy tribes increased, and as a result, scores of men, women, and particularly children were brought into Spanish towns enslaved as prisoners of war. In New Mexico these slaves became known as *Genízaros* (from the Turkish *yeni*, "new," and *cheri* "troops"). Like the janissaries of the Ottoman Empire, where the term derives, Genízaros were slaves, primarily children, who had been seized for use as shock troops, as the first line of assault against enemy Indian tribes in war. As we will see shortly, in the eighteenth century, as the number of Genízaros in the Kingdom increased, many of them were pressed into military service against the Comanche, Apaches, and Utes and eventually rewarded with grants of land for meritoriously having done so. Being feared as too troublesome, and eventually as too arrogant, many Genízaros were also resettled into new buffer communities that were situated along well-traveled raiding routes to blunt the force of attacks on Spanish towns by nomadic Indians.

Throughout the colonial period, New Mexico's Spanish residents characterized the constant state of war they waged as simple retaliation and punishment of the *indios bárbaros* (barbarous Indians). But a simple tally of the booty colonists seized in these raids unmasks their true intent and result. In mineral-poor New Mexico, slaving was one of the few ways of obtaining additional domestic service for the production of household goods and human chattel that likewise could be exchanged for luxury items at local markets and further away at commercial centers. Slaves "are the kingdom's gold and silver and the richest treasure" that one could find in New Mexico, claimed Fray Pedro Serrano in 1761. Slaves were a medium of exchange and deemed pieces of moveable wealth easily convertible into other forms. "I owe Felipe Saíz, a resident of Parral, a few pesos, which I agreed to pay with a little Indian girl," stated a 1718 will. Don Joseph Reaño paid for his purchases in Chihuahua in 1761 with a few *inditos* (little Indians or children), as did many other New Mexican merchants between 1598 and 1870.[9]

One index of the extent of this warfare and its effects on New Mexican society can be gained easily through a comparison of Spanish burial records for those killed during Native American raids and the corresponding records noting the baptism of nomadic Indians. Since captives were always baptized before they were incorporated into a Christian home, such christenings are a reasonable index of the levels of Indian enslavement. Admittedly, baptismal records underestimate the true levels of slave hunting because baptism was only expected of Indians who would be incorporated into Spanish households. Slaves bound for labor elsewhere were rarely christened and thus quickly disappeared from Spanish records.

Between 1700 and 1820, 584 Spanish residents were killed by nomadic Indians and 2,708 nomadic Indians were baptized. An analysis of these numbers, which I conducted, indicates that there was a strong positive statistical association between the number of Spanish settlers killed by nomadic Indians and the number of nomadic Indian baptisms. The strength of this statistical relationship grew over time. As the number of Indian captives rose, so did the number of Spanish deaths.[10]

Throughout the eighteenth and early nineteenth centuries New Mexico's slave population was augmented by a second source, the purchase of Indian slaves from the Apache, Comanche and other groups who visited New Mexico's markets with their goods. These captives were individuals that these nomads had seized from each other, from their enemies, and from European settlements. Thus, for example, a slave so sold by the Apache to the Spanish could have first been captured by the Comanche, sold to the French, only to be captured by the Apaches for resale again. The Apache and Comanche had regularly entered Pecos, Taos, and Picuris pueblos to trade meat, hides and captives for Pueblo blankets, pottery, corn, and turquoise since precolonial times. The Spanish colonists encouraged this trade starting in the early 1700s, initially offering the Native Americans manufactured products, agricultural implements, horses, and later liquor and firearms in exchange for slaves.

The Spanish Christians of the Upper Rio Grande Valley justified the purchase of these *Indios de rescates* (bartered Indian captives) because they had already been enslaved through intertribal warfare. Governor Tomás Vélez Cachupín encouraged the trade in 1752, fearing that if it were curtailed, endless bloodshed would result. What was best, the governor asked, to allow the Indians to kill their prisoners of war or to permit the Spanish colonists to "ransom" them and allow their "redemption" through the sacrament of baptism?[11] The 1680 Recompilation of the Law of the Indies stated that such ransomed Indians incurred a debt that had to be repaid to their master through work for an unspecified period.[12] Masters were to treat their captives well, to Hispanicize, and to Christianize them. The Crown repeatedly ordered that these captives not be "marketed as slaves," but as Fray Pedro Serrano asserted in 1761, no one paid these decrees much heed.[13]

Between 1700 and 1849, 3,294 nomadic Indians were baptized and placed in New Mexican households. Approximately two out of every five of these were identified explicitly as slaves with the notation in the baptismal registers indicating that they were "in the power of," "in the dominion of," or "a captive of" a particular person. Ethnically the Navajo represented largest group of these captives, totaling

37.5 percent. The Apache followed with 24 percent of the total, Ute at 16 percent, and Comanche at 5 percent.[14]

One out of every eight of these newly baptized Indians was explicitly identified as an Indio de rescate, a person who was already a slave purchased at the various Native American trade fairs. Baptism made spiritual salvation possible for such slaves, and it was to this that friars alluded when they occasionally penned in the baptismal registers that an Indian had been "redeemed" from the gentiles (un-baptized Indians). Thirty-three percent of these were referred to as "adopted" by Spanish household heads. Again, the use of the word "adoption" masks the true nature of the labor these slaves would perform in Spanish households and was perhaps more an expression of the officiating friar's hope that the master/slave relation would be a quasi-filial one. One out of every five slaves was listed as a *criado* or servant (from the Spanish verb rier, which means "to rear"). Criados were usually Indian boys and girls captured and sold in infancy or childhood to be reared and to service their lords. New Mexicans skirted the laws against Indian slavery and often avoided using the term slave for an individual, employing instead the euphemism criado.[15] Fray Juan Agustín Morfi made this point quite explicit when he wrote in 1776 that these Indian slaves were "called Genízaros; they are Comanche and Apache captives obtained as children and reared [criados] among us."[16] Over time, the words genízaro and criado were used interchangeably to refer to all Indians residing in Spanish towns who had entered in a servile status. Indeed, the emancipated residents of Abiquiu, who had been resettled there to form a buffer town against Apache and Comanche raids, referred to themselves in 1820 as Genízaros Criados.[17]

During the course of the eighteenth century the Genízaro population of New Mexico was swelled by a third source, the expulsion of individuals from their own Pueblo Indian villages. Whereas slaves captured by the Spanish or purchased by them from enemy Indians, were symbolically represented as intruders in society, those who had been shunned or expelled were deemed extruders. This category of Pueblo Indian extruders was a complex one. Some of these individuals were simply marginalized Pueblo Indians who had been shunned by their kinsmen. Others were exiled from their towns because of some transgression. And still others may have simply thought that life in Spanish towns was more appealing and so migrated. In Spanish society such Pueblo Indians fared poorly and were deemed as "fallen". Displaced and caught between two cultures, they too tended to enter Spanish households as domestic slaves and were also generally referred to as Genízaros.

The expulsion of such Pueblo Indians from their own villages seems to have been largely the by-product of Spanish labor demands. Though tribute payment had ceased with the abolition of the encomienda after New Mexico's reconquest in 1693, the Spanish governors continued to demand labor and raw materials from the Pueblo Indians through the repartimiento, a rotational labor levy. The entry of Pueblo women into Spanish towns to perform such labor often became a perfect occasion for their sexual abuse. The governors of fourteen of New Mexico's pueblos complained in 1707 to the viceroy in Mexico City that many of their women had been raped while performing their weekly labor.[18] "When Indian women enter Santa Fe to mill wheat and spin wool they return to their pueblos deflowered and crying over their dishonor or pregnant," attested Fray Pedro Serrano in 1761.[19] When Pueblo elders discovered the defilement of their wives or daughters, they banished them from the pueblo, observed Fray Carlos Delgado in 1750.[20] These victims of Spanish sexual abuse were permanently stigmatized and became outcasts. The only options such marginalized women had was to become servants in Spanish households or to join a nomadic tribe.

If somehow a woman managed to conceal her disgrace but later gave birth to a fair-skinned child or one that displayed visible signs of mixed ancestry, the child was abandoned on the doorstep of the local mission. The baptismal registers of every parish record these babies as hijos de la iglesia, or as children of the church, with parents unknown. *Hijos de la iglesia* were baptized and placed in Christian homes, and subsequently were also referred to as criados or fosterlings. Approximately one out of every ten persons living in Spanish households during the eighteenth century entered the baptismal registers as "children of the church."[21]

The number of Genízaros one finds living in Spanish households in eighteenth-century New Mexico greatly depends on who is included in the category. If one counts only persons explicitly identified as Genízaros on census records, the number is a small fraction of the total population. The 1765 census of New Mexico lists only 677 Genízaros, for example.[22] If one takes as a whole the nomadic slaves who entered Spanish New Mexico as "intruders" and the Pueblo outcasts who became members of Spanish households as "extruders" from their indigenous villages, then the number of Genízaros is much more substantial, reaching perhaps as high as one-third of all persons residing in Spanish towns. Taking this proportion, by 1800, Genízaros may have numbered as many as 7,000 individuals out of a total Spanish population of 19,276.

The Treatment of Genízaros

In colonial New Mexico bondage was a household institution and its meaning, particularly to Genízaros, is to be found at the interpersonal level. Before slaves entered a Spanish household, they were stripped of their former name, baptized, and given Christian names. Manuel A. Chávez noted in the early 1800s that after one of his slaving expeditions, "on arriving home the first thing to do was to take the children to the priest to baptize them and give them a name. They would naturally take your name."[23]

Kinship was the dominant mode of affiliation in colonial New Mexico; everyone was enmeshed in its web. Lacking genealogical ties to the community, slaves entered their owner's household as part of his or her symbolic capital by which their eminence and status was known in the local community. The enmeshment of Indian servitude in the language of kinship has led some historians to conclude erroneously that the treatment of Indian slaves was "benevolent." This claim is based primarily on declarations before the courts in which slaves spoke of their masters and mistresses as "father" and "mother," and were referred to by their masters as "son" or "daughter."[24]

The use of filial and kinship terms to refer to detribalized Indians in legal documents tells us little about the nature of slavery or whether it was benevolent or not. Rather, they were statements concerning authority relationship within the household, particularly of a father's right to rule over wife, children, and thralls. The Crown tolerated slavery in New Mexico as a way of "civilizing" the Indians. When slave owners came before the courts to answer to charges of slave mistreatment, it was in their interest to portray slave relations as governed by the same rules that regulated family. Fathers ideally were loving, stern, and guiding. To have said otherwise would have been to expose oneself to the loss of mastership over another.

The language of ownership one finds used in court documents to refer to slaves is more frequent and much more revealing than the fictive kinship terminology. To Don Francisco Guerrero, Santa Fe's chief constable, the escapee from the town's guardhouse in 1757 was simply "the genízaro Indian servant of Doña Feliciana Coco." "Manuela, the servant of Isabel Chávez," complained of mistreatment in 1763. And the words with which "the boy servant of Francisco Apodaca" was returned to his owner after a flogging for petty larceny revealed his legal status. The youth was entrusted to Apodaca in 1765 "with total power over his person."[25] In each of these instances, and in many others like them, the Spanish preposition "de," denoting ownership and possession, was used to refer to the slaves. As persons who had no honor, slaves had social and legal personalities primarily through their masters.

Within New Mexican households the treatment of Genízaros ran the gamut from kindly neglect to utter sadism. To be a slave or a criado in a Spanish household was to be a marginal and stigmatized person. This was evident in the type of duties Genízaros often performed, such as emptying chamber pots in the morning and clipping the master's toenails. Both inside the household and outside of it, Genízaros were addressed as children, in the second-person Spanish informal and personal *tu* (you), but had to address their masters and local citizens with the formal *usted*. In Indigenous societies, from which these slaves hailed, growing age would have brought them increasing respect but not for New Mexico's slaves. Many of them were permanently infantilized, even by the master's own children. Take the example of an Indian slave named Bárbara, described in 1762 as old, sickly, and no longer capable of working. She expected that when her master died, that his son, Joseph Gallego, whom she had suckled with her own breast milk, would free her. Bárbara requested her freedom from him, which he refused, and constantly beat her every time she raised the issue. Bárbara's children, who were not allowed to see their mother, sought the governor's intercession. Arrogantly Joseph Gallego explained to Governor Vélez Cachupín that he had taken Bárbara to his house "not because of her service but because my deceased father bought her." His behavior could not be deemed cruel, explained Gallego, because he was simply preserving his father's patrimony. The governor sided with Gallego, explaining that Bárbara has "no basis" for demanding her freedom.[26]

That detribalized Genízaros lacked genealogical ties to the Spanish community and had been torn violently from their communities was humiliation enough in a society that prided itself on ancestry. Some masters compounded the hurt by refusing to allow their slaves to marry, to establish families, or to retain the progeny they bore. When slave women bore children while in captivity, the children were sometimes sold or given to others as gifts.

The only extant statement about the ideal treatment of Genízaros in New Mexico comes from a rather late source, the testimony offered by Pedro León, an Indian trader from Abiquiu, as he stood accused of illegal slave trafficking in 1852. Begging for clemency from the court, and thus coloring what he had to say about slavery, León stated:

> "[Slaves] are adopted into the family of those who get them, are baptized and remain [and are] trusted as one of the family – The head of the house standing as Godfather – The Prefect has the right to free them whenever maltreated – The Indian has the right to choose a guardian – Women are freed whenever married – say from 14 to 16 – Men ditto from 18 to 20 – At the death of Godfather never sold – always freed – The Godfathers provide husbands and wives for them the same as their children – When the godfather dies they are free – As soon as they are baptized they cannot be sold any more…. It would be contrary to the laws of the Church."[27]

In some households Genízaros undoubtedly were treated as warmly as León suggests. For when a slave was obtained in infancy, close emotional attachments developed with the master. Slaves, after all, resided in the same house with their owner; they served the master and his children; they ate the same food the female servants prepared for everyone else; and they slept in their master's house, sometimes in his bed for his pleasure and frequently at his feet. Some slave women even offered their breasts to the master's children, suckling them with their own milk.

The sheer proximity between slave and master, the slaves' outsider status and their lack of honor and genealogical ties to the community regularly made them scapegoats for abuse. Frustrations precipitated by a poor harvest, by the low price one's livestock brought at market, by a wife's infidelities, or by an affront to one's honor, could be, and often were, vented on slaves. Trivial insubordination or impertinences, whether real or imagined, were paid for by slaves with beatings that could at times end in death.

The enslavement of Native Americans was illegal but tolerated in New Mexico, wrote Governor Vélez Cachupín in 1752, "so that the [captives] can be instructed in Our Holy Catholic Faith and made cognizant of the Divine Precepts, so that they may win their own salvation in honor and glory of God, our Lord."[28] Slavery "civilized" Indians by giving them the requisites of culture: clothes, life in a European-styled home, and knowledge of the one true God. At the baptismal font every friar reminded slave masters that these were the three things they had to provide their slaves. Slaves silently endured assaults, humiliations, and cruelties but were quick to seek legal redress when deprived of these minimal needs. A good master was supposed to clothe them, house them, and teach them how to pray.

New Mexico's settlers valued female slaves more highly than males and paid twice as much to acquire them. At the 1776 Taos fair, Indian slave girls between the ages of twelve and twenty sold for two horses and some trifles—roughly 60 to 80 pesos—while young men in the same age group cost half as much.[29] A preference for female slaves is easy to understand. In a province where only one out of every three children born was likely to reach the age of twenty, female slaves were essential for their ability to bear children, to perform the basic household chores that guaranteed food and shelter, and to toil in the production of local trade products such as blankets, gloves and tanned hides.

Indian male slaves, particularly those between the ages of fifteen and thirty, were a troublesome lot and posed serious threats to the tranquility of the province. These men were repeatedly brought before the civil courts for apostasy, for not knowing or respecting their state in society, for failing to respect the property of others, and for their unbridled lust with the colony's women. Throughout the eighteenth century male slaves escaped as soon and as often as possible from the households into which they had been pressed. The authorities always were distressed when Indian slaves fled "from the kingdom or dismembered themselves from Christianity," because, as one apostate, Pedro de la Cruz, put it in 1747, "I will return within a short time with the Comanche and will expel the Spaniards by the hairs."[30] For this reason the number of male slaves in the province was kept low. That is why they fetched a lower price at market than females. Indian captives regularly were marched south to work in the Parral silver mines. Some went on to plantations in Veracruz, and after 1800 many were shipped to Havana and to the Yucatán.

Representation of the Genízaros

The presence in Spanish towns and villages of significant numbers of Genízaro slaves and criados who had no genealogical ties to the Spanish community, who were dishonored by their status as thralls, and were deemed socially dead amid men and women of honor, generated negative stereotypes of what it meant to be a Genízaro. Indeed, much of what was considered Spanish culture on the New Mexico frontier gained its meaning in opposition to and as an exaggeration of what it meant to be a Genízaro or detribalized slave. It was by contrasting themselves with Genízaros that Spaniards, aristocrats and landed peasants alike defined themselves, their honor, and their standing in life.

Genízaros were first and foremost prisoners of war captured by the Spanish, but they were also as Fray Atanasio Domínguez put it in 1776, individuals "ransomed from the pagans by our people. [They] are then emancipated to work out their account." Because Spaniards "only as a last resort…serve themselves," wrote Domínguez, Genízaros are servants among our people."[31] Commenting in 1778 on the state of affairs in New Mexico, Fray Juan Agustín de Morfi said that Genízaros were:

> "Captive Comanches, Apaches, etc., who were taken as youngsters and raised among us…. Since they are the offspring of enemy tribes, the natives of this province, who bear long grudges, never admit them to their pueblos. Thus [Genízaros] are forced to live among Spaniards, without lands, or other means to subsist…. [They] desire sites for villages but fail to obtain any, either because no one wants to provide them or because most of the lands have been occupied…on account of their poverty, which leaves them afoot and without arms…they bewail their neglect and they live like animals."[32]

Domínguez further observed that New Mexico's residents as a whole spoke Castilian of various sorts. The European-origin Spaniards spoke "with courtly polish." The landed peasants spoke "simply and naturally among themselves." But the Genízaros did "not wholly understand it [Spanish] or speak it without twisting it somewhat." Domínguez offered several assessments about Genízaro character as well. They were, he said, "weak, gamblers, liars, cheats, and petty thieves" and comprised "examples of what happens when idleness becomes the den of evils." Belén's Genízaros had no way of supporting themselves, he added, and lived by their luck: "Only they and God know whether they have managed to get their hands on what belongs to their neighbors."[33]

The caricatures that Domínguez and Morfi reported so freely, portrayed the Genízaros as individuals of indigenous origins, who were initially pagans, who owned no land, lacked the means to earn a subsistence, owned no horses, carried no firearms, lived like animals, spoke a twisted form of Spanish, and were characterized by their depraved habits. Salvador Martínez, a Spaniard from Albuquerque, summarized the popular stereotype of the Genízaros when he complained in the early 1800s that those living in the vicinity of Belén "were fugitives from their masters, odious people, vagabonds, gamblers, and thieves without the political or economic organization of a Republic."[34]

These stereotypes remained ingrained in the popular memory, for to this day mischievous and unruly children in New Mexico are taunted with the saying, *"Genízaro! Genízaro! Puro indo de rescate"* (Genízaro! Genízaro! Pure bartered Indian). When New Mexicans say today, *"No seas Genízaro"* (Don't be a Genízaro), they mean "Don't be a liar." Anthropologist Frances Swadesh discovered that in northern New Mexico, when someone was referred to as a Genízaro, it meant crude, low-class, or *"indiado"* (Indian-like).[35] In the 1950s anthropologist Florence Hawley Ellis was told similar things about Belén's Genízaros by the Spanish settlers who lived across the river in the village of Tomé. Belén's Genízaros were, according to Ellis' informants, "semi-slave, low class and without ability."[36]

If Indian-ness, slave and former slave pagan origin, dishonor, crude character, bad habits, and distorted language defined the Genízaros, a list of antonyms defined what it was to be a Spaniard. The differences between aristocrats and landed peasants were of degree rather than of kind. Spaniards, whatever their estate, were men of honor in comparison with the vanquished Indians. Even the lowliest Spaniard felt a sense of honor among slaves. Landed peasants shared fully in the benefits of a timocratic culture because, unlike Genízaro slaves, they were longtime members of the Christian community and as such had been given land by the king. Landowners were *vecinos* or citizens with full voting rights in town councils *(cabildos)*. By owning land, Spaniards could earn their own subsistence and were not dependent on others for their livelihoods, as were slaves. Spaniards owned horses and firearms. And finally, not only did Spaniards speak Castilian well, they were also men of their words.

When men of honor said that Genízaros "lived like animals," they meant that they dressed poorly or scantily and showed little modesty or restraint in their sexual comportment. Because slave women bore illegitimate children, failed to establish stable unions, were frequently sexually assaulted, and reputedly licentious, to be a Spanish woman, regardless of one's class, meant that one was concerned for one's sexual purity and reputation, guarded one's virginity, sought marriage, and monogamy in matrimony. Finally, men of honor were men of their word; their words carried force and were as binding as a modern contract. Genízaros and former slaves accordingly were considered liars and cheats.

By the 1770s the processes of stigmatization, devalorization, and segregation had transformed Genízaros into a distinct and dangerous ethnic group. Spanish society viewed them as marginalized and degraded because of their slave and former slave status. They spoke a distinct (broken) form of Spanish. Fray Carlos Delgado observed that Genízaros practiced marriage class endogamy, taking "women of their own status and nature." And most importantly, at least in the words of Fray Carlos Delgado, was that Genízaros "lived in great unity as if they were a nation (*Como si fueran una nación*)."[37]

Toward Cultural Autonomy

Over time, the number of manumitted slaves residing in Spanish towns increased, and as it did, various attempts to congregate these former slaves into their own villages were undertaken. Genízaros were resettled on the margins of the kingdom at Belén in 1740, at Abiquiu and Ojo Caliente in 1754, and at San Miguel del Vado in 1794. Aside from ridding Santa Fe, Albuquerque, and Santa Cruz de la Cañada of slaves and former slaves who were deemed unruly, the authorities hoped that by strategically locating Genízaro villages as buffers along nomadic Indian raiding routes, the impact of Indian depredations on Spanish towns would be softened. Thus Belén guarded the southern approach to the Rio Grande Valley; Analco, the Genízaro suburb of Santa Fe, protected the town's eastern approach; Abiquiu and Ojo Caliente guarded the northwest approach to Santa Cruz de la Cañada; and San Miguel del Vado slowed the northeastern access route to Santa Cruz de la Cañada and Santa Fe.

With the emancipation and movement of Genízaros out of Spanish towns and onto the hostile frontier between nomads and settled agriculturalists, they finally had an independent space in which to express their own identity, an identity that was quite hybrid, the result of mixing European ways with the cultures of the Pueblo, Navajo, Comanche and Utes. Some Genízaros abandoned their Christian baptismal names for what appear to be indigenous ones. Antonio Jiménez started calling himself *Cuasipe*. Miguel Reaño became *Tasago*. Juana, the Apache slave of Diego Velásquez, was now *Guisachi*. As New Mexico's governors established Genízaro villages, locating them strategically to help defend Spanish towns, these now former slaves also began to take active roles in repelling attacks by their former Apache, Comanche, and

Navajo kin.³⁸ Fray Carlos Delgado reported in 1744 that the Genízaros at Belén were obliged to "go out and explore the country in pursuit of the enemy, which they do with great bravery and zeal."³⁹ They were "great soldiers, very warlike and the ones most feared by our enemies," wrote Fray Agustín Morfi in 1782.⁴⁰ When Governor Pedro Fermín de Mendinueta gave chase to a band of Apaches in 1777, he dispatched fifty-five Genízaros in their pursuit.⁴¹

For their services as soldiers, scouts, and interpreters during the second half of the eighteenth century, Genízaros solicited and were given special governmental distinctions. Manuel Antonio, a Genízaro, received a presidio post in 1768. Others must have been honored similarly, for when authorities in Tomé had to use force to arrest Marcos Sánchez for maltreating his concubine in 1793, he vigorously protested saying: "I am a Genízaro unworthy of such base treatment."⁴²

Conclusion

In 1790 a general census of the kingdom of New Mexico was undertaken. Therein a sizeable number of Genízaros were listed as artisans: as blacksmiths, silversmiths, masons, carders, spinners, and weavers. One out of every five Genízaros is listed as having acquired land, with "farmer" noted as their occupation. The majority of Genízaros, however, were employed as day laborers, field hands, and domestic servants. As the development of export-oriented agriculture and livestock production progressed during the first half of the nineteenth century, many Genízaros were emancipated, only to have no other option than a debt peonage relationship with their former masters. Fray Juan Agustín Morfi summarized the predicament of such Genízaros well when he wrote in 1776 that "without land, without livestock, without any other manner of subsisting than with their bows and arrows…they [Genízaros] have surrendered themselves into wage labor and suffer all sorts of tyrannies."⁴³ By the time of Mexican independence in 1821, the plight of many of the emancipated Indian former slaves of New Mexico was very similar to that of poor landless peasants. They remained marginal to the affairs of the kingdom, but as their independent towns grew in size, they developed a distinct and prideful sense of identity as Genízaros.⁴⁴

From the foundation of Santa Fe in 1610 until this very day, there has been a popular fiction about Spanish presence in the Kingdom of New Mexico that has saturated the historiography and folklore of the area, seen particularly in civic self-representation when commemorations and yearly celebrations are staged. Clearly, there is some truth to the mythology. The Kingdom of New Mexico was indeed founded by Spanish soldiers and colonists who were granted rights to aristocracy, to land, and to the labor of the area's native peoples for their investments in conquest.

Over the years these settlers came to think of their honor, their status, and their dominance as having a metaphysical quality, as rooted in their pure blood, which they claimed was free of taint from mixing with Indians and other peoples they deemed inferior. But an equally important, if often ignored, truth about New Mexico's history is that its settlers became a hybrid people by the beginning of the eighteenth century. In precolonial times indigenous nomads and sedentary agriculturalists mixed and melded in complicated ways, just as was the case in colonial times. As I have tried to show here, the institution of slavery was a constant source of labor and of wealth. But slavery was also a considerable source of biological mixing as indigenous women and their children were raided and traded between nomads and town dwellers as circumstances required and to meet particular needs. What emerged from this extensive commerce in slaves was a new ethnic group—the Genízaros. Their difference—neither nomads nor agriculturalists, neither kin nor citizens—marked their marginality. But the very processes that led to the formation of this new ethnic group were a theme repeated over and over again in the Americas. The history of the Kingdom of New Mexico is thus not a story of Spanish purity and Indian danger, of Spanish civility and Indian barbarism. It is instead the more familiar story of *mestizaje*, of racial mixing, and the process whence the emergence of new peoples and new identities was made possible. Historians and folklorists of New Mexico like to think of the ancient kingdom and the modern state as an exceptional place, as a place set apart. The history of Indian slavery in New Mexico shows just the opposite, that new peoples were there forged that are profoundly mixed and hybrid.

3

Ohkay Owingeh: New Mexico's First Capital

This is Much of What I Believe, Know and Have Learned
by
Storyteller Kaafedeh – Blowing Leaf (Herman Agoyo)
Pueblo of Ohkay

To the *Kwiyo vi Eh* and *Sendo vi Eh* of Ohkay Owingeh

The 400th Anniversary of the oldest capital of the United States, Santa Fe, New Mexico, causes me to reflect and refresh my memory on this historic event as *Ohkay Owingeh* plans to construct a Heritage Center, which will include the story of the first capital of New Mexico at *Yungeh*—San Gabriel, settled by Don Juan de Oñate y Salazar around late 1598 or early 1599. Of the Pueblo and people of Yungeh, the eventual resettlement of the capital to Santa Fe and of our continuing challenges into the modern era—this is much of what I believe, know and have learned.

The *Peh Tsi* (Story) of Yungeh, New Mexico's First Capital

San Gabriel will always remain a mysterious place because Tewa oral history is scant. Who made the decision and how did they decide to evict our ancestors from Yungeh (Mockingbird Village)? Where were the citizen soldiers, Mexican Indians (most likely Tlaxcaltecans who were part of the established settlement in Santa Fe in the mid-1700s), and Spanish families located? In what part of the village did Juan de Oñate and his ten year old son Cristóbal reside? Huge corrals were needed to manage the entire livestock brought into the area. Where were they located? And also, to what extent was the village remodeled to accommodate the lifestyle of the new residents? On the Pueblo side there are also unanswered questions. Was Yungeh occupied by both the summer and winter *Towa* (people)? Was there an aboveground ceremonial house or underground kiva? What other ceremonial chambers and sacred sites existed? The cacique's homes.—where were they? What kind of emotions did the arrival and relocation arouse? Was it fear, amazement, anger, hate, sadness, bitterness, relief, and inconvenience? Did the relocation result in the construction of a new *wha' k'aygi* (dwelling), people moving into vacant homes, or did they join relatives at Ohkay? The village itself—was it two or three stories high? Were there eagles or hawks caged on the rooftops? Were domesticated turkeys caged in and around the village? Where were the *poe kwin* (springs) for drinking, ceremonial, and domestic use located? Where were the beans, squash, corn and other food staples grown? What was the approximate population?

By 1601 the Spanish colony consisted of more that five hundred men, women, children, Mexican Indians and at least eighteen friars. Most of the colonists were from Mexico and Spain, but some came from such countries as Greece, Portugal, and one, Rodrigo Velman, was from Flanders (Dutch). Led by Juan de Oñate, who proclaimed New Mexico and its people as vassals of Spain and under Spanish rule in 1598, they arrived in two main groups. The first group journeyed in extreme hardship conditions for seven to eight months before reaching Ohkay Owingeh. The second group arrived on December 24, 1600. At first, the Colonists occupied the east area of Ohkay Owingeh, which was fertile and close to the confluence of the Rio Grande and Chama Rivers, naming it San Juan de los Caballeros (after Oñate's patron saint, Saint John). For unknown reasons, perhaps they were not willing to spend the time to build permanent houses of their own, Oñate persuaded the people of Yungeh, who lived on the west side of the rivers, to relocate to San Juan. How he persuaded them to leave their dwellings I can only guess but I do know that they left their home of hundreds of years. Oñate and his colonists occupied Yungeh, declaring it a Spanish town and renaming it San Gabriel (perhaps another of his patron saints), remodeling the dwellings and building a Catholic Church.

With the arrival and settlement of San Gabriel by the Spanish, many Spanish cultural and political 'firsts' were experienced at Ohkay Owingeh. This includes Ohkay Owingeh as the first permanent Spanish settlement in New Mexico, the first establishment of a Catholic Church, the first hornos, the first implementation and adoption of Spanish agricultural innovations by a Pueblo in the American Southwest and the first Pueblo adaptation of the *Matasina* dance as introduced by the Aztecs. Also, Ohkay Owingeh was the original site in which the Spanish first planned to wage a 'just' war in North America against the Acoma Pueblo, and sadly, the people of Ohkay Owingeh were the first victims of organized 'Indian

Removal' that would haunt North American Indians for centuries to come.

During the Valverde Investigation in 1601, Captain Velasco testified that San Gabriel was suitable for a great city, having many rivers, springs and woods very close by. Velasco also related that fortifications were not necessary because the people of Yungeh were of a gentle, passive, and peaceful nature; hence, the title given to the Pueblo, San Juan de Los Caballeros, became permanent. Conversion to Catholicism began immediately.

After the conclusion of a celebration, most likely the *Moros y Cristianos*, held on September 8, 1598 several friars were assigned to various Pueblo regions to minister to the people and when asked how many Indians had been baptized, Captain Velasco could not answer because he was always on expeditions and not permanently camped at San Gabriel. He had heard, however, that one hundred children, more or less, had been baptized at San Gabriel and surrounding areas.

Already discord and disillusion among the settlers began to show. The Oñate expeditions were long trips; one trip, which lasted six months, gave most of the colonists the opportunity to pack up and escape to Mexico. Prior to this time the soldiers, friars, military officers and citizens, meeting after a high mass on September 7, 1601, highly recommended that it would be in everyone's best interest if all were to get ready and leave the province.

Already disillusioned at the hardships caused by the Spanish, the Pueblo people grew more alienated and angry by Oñate's exploits in 1598 at the Acoma Pueblo where his nephew, Juan de Zaldivar, and eleven soldiers were killed by the Acoma people after Spanish troops, using extreme violence, raided the Pueblo, stealing food and clothing. Oñate, after determining that the Acoma people had violated their oath of obedience, set Zaldivar's younger brother, Vicente, and seventy-two men against the Acoma people, killing eight hundred men, women, and children and taking six hundred more captive as a reminder to the other Pueblos of the costs of resistance. After being found guilty at a public trial at *Kewa* (Santo Domingo Pueblo), Oñate punished the captives by condemning all men, women and children between the ages of twelve and twenty-five to twenty years of personal servitude. He further ordered the severing of one foot of all men over twenty-five, all carried out in public. Children under the age of twelve were considered innocent and placed in the care of the Franciscan friars. Other skirmishes between Pueblos, including the fierce battle between colonists and the Jumano and Salinas Pueblos at the Battle of Agualagu in 1601, further justified the colonists' escape into Mexico.

The colony of San Gabriel, which consisted of over five hundred men, women and children, was now reduced to fifty-three. Governor Oñate, who spent much of his time neglecting the welfare of the colony in pursuit of wealth, declared the majority who left to be deserters and assigned one of his lieutenants to chase them. However, the deserters had already reached Mexico and were under official protection. They told the Mexican officials stories of the problems and hardship in the north and of the troubles at Acoma and Jumano. In their opinion the land had nothing to offer and that Oñate's judgment as a leader was very poor.

Although Oñate, soon after the Acoma and Jumano battles, sent glowing reports of his trip to the southwest and his discovery of the South Sea (Gulf of California), Spanish officials agreed with the deserters that New Mexico was not another Mexico and decided to stop all further exploration, maintaining only a small colony in New Mexico under the leadership of a new governor. Also, the capital was to be moved from San Gabriel to a place where food could be raised and the settlers could not abuse or exploit the Pueblo people. Although there were plenty of reasons to leave, the only real incentive to keep a colony in Northern New Mexico was the Catholic Church's continuing efforts to convert the Pueblo people to Christianity.

As for Oñate and the Spanish presence in New Mexico, the Council of the Indies and the King of Spain decided in 1606 to recall him from New Mexico and to investigate his alleged excesses. In January of 1609 the investigation was completed, but the judgments were not handed down until 1614. Oñate was fined and exiled permanently from New Mexico and banished for four years from Mexico. Furthermore, Oñate's family lost their privileges and titles to New Mexico, and the colony was re-categorized as a missionary field to be maintained by a royal colony. It was also judged that a new villa was to be founded that did not encroach on lands occupied by the Pueblos. Governor Pedro de Peralta assumed control of the colony in 1610 and may have established the new villa of Santa Fe soon after. Also, no primary documentation exists to support the account that San Gabriel was largely abandoned by the colonists. However, there seems to be some evidence, as noted by historian Marc Simmons, that some of the Spanish colonists remained at San Gabriel as Oñate pleaded his case and, by 1624, seemingly cleared his name before his death in 1630.

Although some of the Spanish colonists may have remained in San Gabriel, the Pueblo was partially reoccupied by the relocated Yungeh people. With the exception of a few Spanish and Indian dwellings built on top of old mounds, the Pueblo eventually fell into neglect and remained this way until the late 1930s and early 1940s when interest in excavating the old mounds surfaced.

In many ways my love of history and the search for Yungeh's past has greatly influenced my life. As a child "helping" my Grandpa plant his fields, an incident that I still vividly remember during one of the corn planting times was the revelation of the plow splitting a black pot in half. This occurred during my rest period, but Grandpa stopped the horse and waved me over to the spot where he stood. I was witness to see the broken pot, which also contained white corn meal. Although I was young, I realized that this was an important connection to our past. Later, as a young man, I also remember attending a Tribal Council meeting with my mother where the subject of excavating the site and building a museum was discussed. It was decided that the ancient Yungeh past was important not only for its archeological value but also as a reconnection to our ancestors. It was further decided, with the full cooperation of the residents that lived on the site, to have it excavated. It seemed that much of my life's path was determined.

Unfortunately, many of the old mounds at San Gabriel were leveled in order to increase the size of the planting fields. Although much of the east mound was excavated, a large section remains untouched. South of the east mound many of the foundations and lower walls, where the colonists lived, and the original church were excavated and stabilized in the 1950s thanks to the efforts of Dr. Florence Hawley Ellis and her field archeologists from the University of New Mexico. This section is an important finding to the people of Ohkay Owingeh and has yielded several artifacts such as bell fragments and helmets. Now part of section 48, the area is fenced in and not accessible to the general public; however, from time to time visitors are shown around the site. Originally, the Museum of New Mexico planned to lease the site and complete the excavation and stabilization of the Spanish area; however, this did not occur. Currently, I am hoping that the State of New Mexico, the Federal government, and the private sector, with the cooperation of the Pueblo, will assist in the development of a commercial district along Highway 68, which would include the Heritage Center to preserve Yungeh's unique history.

Prior to the 1950s there were little or no protective efforts of Yungeh on the part of the people of Ohkay Owingeh. This was due in part to the continual struggle to provide for one's family and livelihood, which may have created a low level of interest, knowledge, and realization of Yungeh's greater historical significance not only to the Pueblo of Ohkay Owingeh, but also to the larger local and world community impacted by Spain's incursions into New Mexico. A good portion of the site was destroyed, and at this point of my story, the role of the Anglo comes into the picture.

Much credit is heaped on this segment of the population for creating an awareness of the First Capital's historic importance through the Camino Real National Historic Trail Legislation, excavations, lectures, contemporary history textbooks, the funding sponsorship of the "Coloquio Internacional El Camino Real de Tierra Adentro" series by Mexico and New Mexico, the Northern Rio Grande National Heritage Area Legislation and Nomination and most notably, the designation of Yungeh in the National Register of Historic Places,

With the help of these groups and many from the private and academic sectors, the people of Ohkay Owingeh and the public at large are now more aware of the importance of San Gabriel de Yungeh not only as an archeological focal point, but also for its significance to the initial exploration and settlement of the Spanish in New Mexico. The excavation of Yungeh has yielded several layers of artifacts revealing many of the ways in which our people lived and developed from pre-Spanish contact to the present. However, the excavated site also has significance to the current Spanish population in New Mexico in that much of their history and culture can be linked back to Yungeh as the first Spanish settlement in New Mexico.

Before I continue my story I must say that although much information can be gathered from the excavation sites, there are many oral histories passed between our people that cannot be ignored or discounted simply because they do not meet the standards for documentation required by most western universities. For example, among our people there is the story of some of the earliest visitors from outside New Mexico to Yungeh who were the Aztec, and according to our grandpa Jose de La Luz Cata, this is what happened at Yungeh a "long, long time ago":

"It is my understanding that a long, long time ago, in the village of Yungeh, the People were gathered to participate in and witness a sacred dance. To avoid any outside interruptions, guards were posted around the village to the North, West, South and East. It so happened on that day visitors were spotted heading for the village from the East Side. One of the guards stationed on the east side ran into the village to inform the Pueblo officials that strangers were approaching the village; immediately, the dancing stopped and appropriate leaders and warriors were sent to meet the intruders. Shortly, there was a confrontation between the two parties and the visitors were denied entrance into the Pueblo.

This denial made the leader of the visiting group very angry, and there upon announced who he was. He said, "I am Montezuma, and because you have denied me and my people entrance, I am ordering you to perform a dance in my honor which I will teach you, and the dance you are doing will be performed the following day after my dance.

Ever since that day, the people of Ohkay Owingeh have been performing the Matasina dance on Christmas Day and their sacred dance, the Turtle Dance, on December 26."

Many of these oral histories continue to enrich our culture and serve as reminders of who we are as well as maintain the remembrance and respect of our ancestors. Grandpa's story serves to remind us that there were visitors, perhaps in the company of merchants on trading routes, to Yungeh from the south long before the

Spanish arrived. Since then, many have made their way through Yungeh on their way to fame and infamy including Francisco Vasquez de Coronado and his expeditionary army in 1541 and the ill-fated colonization expedition of Gaspar Castaño de Sosa in 1590.

Po'Pay and the Holy War Against the Spanish

After the Oñate period and the appointment of Governor Pedro de Peralta, a series of regimes of Spanish Governors in the new capital of Santa Fe governed the Pueblos. The most notable was the regime of Governor Antonio de Otermín that ended in 1680 when the Pueblos, led by *Po'Pay* (Ripe Pumpkin), expelled the Spaniards for a period of twelve years. Most western scholars call this the 'Great Pueblo Revolt of 1680', but I simply prefer to call it 'The Holy War'.

There was a time, long before the visit of King Montezuma to Ohkay Owingeh and his teachings of the laws of Jesus Christ, when the people of Yungeh did not know of the Christian god and our religion and ceremonies were developed over centuries of natural and spiritual traditions. When the Spaniards arrived and introduced Christianity to our people, our religious practices were viewed as sorcery, idolatry and witchcraft and many of our people, as well as other Pueblos, were persecuted and even killed if caught attending to our religious duties. Such was a time in 1675.

At that time a great drought had taken hold and many of the Pueblo people were dying from hunger and disease. Many crops and herds were lost due to the drought, but moreover, Spanish law prohibited us from trading with the Navajo and Apache and, being hungry themselves, they turned to raiding our village. In that there was no relief from the drought, we, like many of the other Pueblo people, lost faith in the Christian god and returned to our traditional religious practices and ceremonies. The Spanish responded by harshly suppressing this return by hangings and lashings. And like the Salem witch hunts in the American colonies, the Spanish accused many of us of sorcery and sedition. Such was the case of Po'Pay, from Ohkay Owingeh, and forty-six Pueblo men who were charged and indicted, under the governorship of Juan Francisco de Treviño in 1675, in Santa Fe for the crimes of "sorcery and sedition". As a result, all were publicly whipped and condemned to slavery, three of the four religious leaders were hanged, and the fourth hanged himself. However, this did not end the continuing persecution of the Pueblo people and their religious practices and by 1680, Po'Pay organized a 'Holy War' against the Spanish with support of most of the Pueblos.

Much like the war between England and the American Colonies in 1776, the Pueblo Holy War was fought to regain our independence from Spanish rule and to end religious oppression. I have no doubt that Po'Pay, or El Popé as the Spanish called him, was a religious leader. It makes sense to me that a holy war would be planned and executed by such a man and from my point of view, such a spiritual man would indeed draw on our ancient deities such as *Poseyemo, Caudi, Tilimi povi* and *Tleume* for guidance and instruction.

From a kiva located at the Taos Pueblo, Po'Pay, who may have very well received instruction from our ancient ancestors, formed an alliance of war chiefs and spiritual leaders, some of them half-breeds, to coordinate the Holy War against the Spanish. This group of men included: *Tagu* of Ohkay Owingeh, Luis Conixu of Jemez, Luis Tapatu of Picuris, El Saca of Taos, Nicolas de la Cruz Jonva of San Ildefonso, Juan El Tano of Galisteo, Domingo Romero of Tesuque, Antonio Malacate of Cochiti, Diego Xenome, Francisco El Ollito and Antonio Bolsas and Cristóbal Yope of San Lazaro, Alonzo Catiti of Kewa (Santo Domingo), and Domingo Naranjo of Santa Clara who was not a Pueblo Indian but a product of a black father and a Tlascaltec Indian mother.

Although the 7,000 or so Pueblo people were of different villages and spoke different languages and dialects, we were united, for the most part, in the effort to expel the Spanish from our lands. As you study the history of the Pueblo Holy War you will find varying accounts and different points of view on Po'Pay, how the war was fought and what happened afterwards. However, this is what I believe to be true.

I believe that Po'Pay was a man who was able to balance the spiritual, political and cultural aspects of his life in such a way that his efforts and intentions in conducting the Holy War were truly for the benefit of all Pueblo people and those of the Hopi and Apache tribes. Both our oral and written histories and western colonial history verify that, in 1680, the Spanish were expelled from New Mexico for a period of twelve years. They also verify that after Governor Otermín's refusal to leave Santa Fe and New Mexico peaceably, many were killed on both sides of the conflict and that the wrath of the Pueblos was harsh towards the Spanish people and their priests because of the years of humiliation, brutality and oppression heaped upon our people. Did the Spanish expect any less punishment for their inhuman crimes against our people? I believe that the Spanish would not have listened to our anger unless we responded with the same brutality they showed towards our people. We sent a message to the Spanish government saying that they were not welcomed in our lands and that we would no longer permit another to rule over us as if we were stray animals to be kicked aside. Yet, the Spanish eventually returned.

In the twelve years that the Pueblos maintained their independence, Po'Pay, like many future North American Indian leaders, attempted to return the people to their traditional way of life before the Spanish came. In order to do such a thing and bring the people back into harmony with their cultural and spiritual past, he ordered the destruction of all that represented Spain and the Catholic religion. He directed the people to no longer use the Spanish language, to forsake the Catholic rituals of baptism and marriage, as well as reinstate the practice of public religious ceremonies at the Pueblos. At this point in my story I must tell you, however, that not all that was brought to our people by the Spanish was destroyed. There was wisdom in keeping the things that improved our lives, especially items made of metal, new breeds of livestock, especially horses, as well as improved agricultural techniques. Why would we pluck out the corn stock to get rid of the weeds?

In those twelve years of freedom many of the Pueblos returned to isolation and much of the old conflicts and disagreements re-emerged among our peoples. And much like today's political practices, Po'Pay became a victim of political maneuvering by those who disagreed with his policies. Many Western historians write that Po'Pay's initial downfall came about as a result of being a tyrant and contradicting himself by re-adopting many Spanish ritual customs. I believe this to be unreliable information in that much concerning Po'Pay comes from Spanish documents, which have a tendency to portray him in the worst possible light. Po'Pay was removed as the leader of the Pueblo people, but if he was such a bad leader why was he re-appointed? If he was a tyrant why not kill all his enemies instead of submitting to democratic elections? These are questions I cannot answer, however, unless more definitive documentation on Po'Pay can be discovered. I will always believe that he was a man of honor and deep spiritual convictions who truly cared for the welfare of not only the Pueblo people but for all people. I have dedicated much of my life to the teaching and lecturing of the history of Ohkay Owingeh and the legacy of Po'Pay. His is a legacy of hope and determination for all people and I am proud to have been a part of the successful efforts by Ohkay Owingeh, our Tribal Councils, my family and friends and the State of New Mexico to have a statue of Po'Pay carved and placed into the United States National Statuary Hall in Washington DC in September of 2005.

Thoughts on the Reconquest

Why the Spanish returned to our lands is speculative. Many write that it was at the request of the displaced and impoverished colonists who had survived the war, while others write that Don Diego de Vargas was in debt, his tarnished reputation in need of repair. Another theory is that Spain needed to take back our lands in order to create a buffer between warring Apaches and French incursions. Who knows? Perhaps the Spanish returned simply because Spain had been humiliated in the eyes of England and France at the hands of mere savages. In any event, after twelve years of freedom the Spanish, in 1692, returned under the leadership of now Governor Vargas, a man of questionable character and military savvy who eventually reconquered New Mexico with the help of sympathetic Pueblo warriors.

Today, the people of Santa Fe celebrate Vargas's peaceful re-entry into Santa Fe but his re-entry was anything but peaceful or bloodless. What were our people to do when under threat of Vargas's armed men and cannons? I believe they did what seemed wise and allowed Vargas to re-enter the city, which was now an inhabited Pueblo of men, women, and children. However, once Vargas moved on to reconquer other Pueblos perhaps the inhabitants of the Santa Fe Pueblo committed to fighting Vargas upon his return. Although no documents exist concerning the mood and intentions of the people, I believe that plans were made in Vargas's absence to defend Santa Fe upon his return. This was to no avail as Vargas's return ended in bloodshed in which the city was taken by force wherein many people were killed, executed, and enslaved.

The reconquest of Santa Fe was not the end to Pueblo resistance, as many Pueblo peoples continued to resist the Spanish. In 1696 a second rebellion broke out. However, under Vargas's command the Spanish army, much like General Sherman's march to the sea during the American Civil War, conducted a total war in which food supplies were burned, fields laid waste, and pueblo communities destroyed. Many of our people fled to Hopi and Navajo land and even to the Great Plains to avoid Spanish rule. In the end Vargas, with the aid of his Pueblo allies, eventually won the day.

In the following one hundred and twenty-five years of Spanish rule most of the Pueblos were destroyed. A few remained in their original locations and some were eventually relocated or re-established. Today only nineteen of perhaps one hundred Pueblos prior to the Spanish conquest are still in existence. Although Pueblo land titles were established under Spanish law, political, economic and especially religious oppression continued throughout this period.

Having learned a harsh lesson from the Holy War, many people believe that the Spanish returned with a policy of tolerance concerning Pueblo ceremonial and religious practices. For the most part we were no longer being subjected to public humiliation, whippings and murder for exercising our traditional ceremonial and religious beliefs; however, religious oppression, which was severe at times, continued. If any form of religious, economic or political tolerance ever existed it was during the Mexican Period only because our people were ignored by the Mexican government, leaving us relatively undisturbed, which allowed us to strengthen and revitalize much of our traditional ways of life. Unfortunately, wholesale oppression of our people returned when the United States defeated Mexico in 1849 and the ownership and title to our lands once again came into question. Before I continue I would like to share some of my thoughts concerning the inevitable blending of cultures and people that most certainly occurred during the one hundred and twenty-five years of Spanish rule and into the modern period.

As for the culture of the people of New Mexico, there was indeed a mixing of blood and blending of cultures between many native and non-native peoples. This includes the emergence of the Genízaros, who are mixed-blood descendants of Indian slaves, tribal outcasts, detribalized Indians and Spanish colonial ancestors. I believe that the majority of Spanish Native New Mexicans and Genízaros, for the most part, are one in the same. With this in mind, the New Mexico legislature in 2007 officially recognized the Genízaros as indigenous people. I often wonder how this recognition is defined and how it impacts Genízaros both culturally and legally.

Many people in New Mexico celebrate their Spanish ancestry without giving any thought to their Native heritage. Perhaps the opposite is also true for many of our people as well. However, I hope that someday many of those who only claim their Spanish heritage will also consider their distant native ancestry and view their lives, culture and heritage as a gift from both their Pueblo and Spanish ancestors. The combination of both Native and Spanish ancestry is what makes the culture and racial makeup of the Native New Mexicans (or Genízaros, if you prefer) unique. In many ways our worlds are very different yet the Spanish and Pueblos share much in the history and culture of our peoples.

Into the Modern Era: Our Tribal Lands

Spain's foothold in Mexico and New Mexico ended in 1821 and from that year through the Mexican period ending in 1846, the Pueblos enjoyed equal citizenship as well as a great amount of autonomy. However, the people of Ohkay Owingeh, as well as all Pueblos, continued to struggle with the local Spanish people and Mexican government over land issues.

After the defeat of Mexico in America's war against Mexico, and, in spite of the pledge for the protection of Spanish land grants to the Pueblos under the Treaty of Guadalupe Hidalgo, the Pueblo of Ohkay Owingeh, like the all Pueblos, began to experience wholesale encroachments by both local Spanish people and Anglos, which led to the loss of huge tracts of land. This was due in part to our inability to fully understand the American legal and tax system as well as the rationale of the U.S. government's policies concerning individual land versus communal land ownership. We especially did not understand the American mind-set of Manifest Destiny, which introduced unscrupulous land speculators and squatters onto our lands. Our people, and later local Spanish land owners, became victims of legal wrangling in that Ohkay Owingeh was not recognized and legally protected until 1913, in the way that reservations were for other Indian tribes. Thus, we were at the mercy of land legislation such as the Homestead and Taylor Grazing Acts. Later, decisions by the Pueblo Lands Board in the late 1920s and mid-1930s proved that in reality, the "new deal" for mainstream America turned out to be a raw deal for Ohkay Owingeh as well as for all the Pueblos of New Mexico.

There is an element of distrust of the intentions of many outsiders who come to our pueblo to conduct research. However, when outside research by archeologists, historians, ethnohistorians and anthropologists is conducted for the benefit of our people it is most welcomed. Such research has been valuable in terms of identifying and recovering ownership of much of our lands.

For example, when the American war with Mexico ended in 1846, our lands became part of the territory conquered by the United States. The Treaty of Guadalupe Hidalgo negotiated between the United States and Mexico stipulated that all rights, including title to lands, given by Mexico and Spain to our people and the Spanish people as well, be honored. However, proving land title was difficult and ownership of much of our land was under question, which meant having to deal with the encroachment of squatters. Issues of Pueblo land ownership came to a head and, in 1854, the office of the Surveyor General of New Mexico was established in order to verify and confirm land grants from the Spanish government to the Pueblos.

According to the Surveyor General, Spanish documents dated September, 1689, indeed outlined the specific land grant to the Pueblo of Ohkay Owingeh. Congress confirmed the Surveyor General's report and by 1864, the people of Ohkay Owingeh were in sole possession of 17,000 plus acres of their homelands. On the surface this seems like a victory for our people. However, the date of the Spanish document, 1689, makes no sense in that Spanish authority over our people did not exist at that time and was not re-established until the reconquest of 1692–1696. The only conclusion that can be drawn is that the Spanish land grants, supposedly made by Governor Domingo Cruzate, were fictitious and the subsequent documents of proof provided by the Surveyor General were nothing more than forgeries, which subsequent research in the nineteenth century verified.

Much of the Spanish law and policies concerning land ownership by our people as well as other Native peoples developed over the centuries of occupation in the Americas. These laws and policies stated that all lands owned and occupied by Pueblo people at the time of the arrival of the Spanish were to legally remain in their possession. I believe that the Surveyor General must have had knowledge of this but accepted the forgeries in order to appease the Americans who were invading our lands and pressuring the American government to free up Indian land that was, in their eyes, being neglected. As a result of the land patents in 1864 the People of Ohkay Owingeh were allowed only a fraction of our homelands with the rest falling into the hands of various government agencies, unscrupulous land speculators and private individuals.

Although our lands are for the most part unrecoverable, there have been times in which the terms of The Treaty of Guadalupe Hidalgo has assisted us in regaining small parcels of land occupied by non-Pueblo peoples. For example, with the assistance of the Pueblo Lands Board, which was created in the 1920s, we were able to recover an additional 330 acres of lands in the late 1920s from those who did not have title. The Pueblo Lands Board, however, is seen in a less favorable light to our people because of decisions made by the board in favor of private individuals as well as villages such as Alcalde, Hernandez, Chamita, El Duende and Ranchitos. These actions decreased our land size by one third to approximately 12,000 acres. We have, however, continued throughout the years to purchase as well as rely on donations to increase our land base.

Final Thoughts

I have spoken of many historical and opinionated aspects of the history of Yungeh and our people. What I know and believe is not the final account of Ohkay Owingeh's long history, for our history continues to unfold. It is my wish to establish a heritage center in which all that has made us who we are today continues to inspire and encourage future generations to continue the quest for knowledge and wisdom in respect for our people and our ancestors. I am now a tribal elder who has gained much knowledge, experience and wisdom over the years. All that I have learned in my life I will continue to pass on—as my gift to you—my *Kwiyo vi Eh* and *Sendo vi Eh* of Ohkay Owingeh.

Acknowledgements

I cannot end my account without acknowledging those who have impacted my life either with love, encouragement, wisdom, knowledge or a combination of the four. Foremost I want to express my profound love and gratitude to the people of Ohkay Owingeh and our ancient ancestors, to my family, and especially to my wife Rachele, my children, and my grandchildren who have shared and made my life's path and journey one of wonder that words will never be able to express.

I also would like to acknowledge those such as Joe Sando, Alfonso Ortiz, Simon J. Ortiz, Vine Deloria, David Weber, J. Manuel Espinosa, Helen Hunt Jackson, Florence Hawley Ellis, Marc Simmons, Miguel Encinias, Marcia Keegan, Elinore Barrett, Franklin Folsom, and John L. Kessell, to name a very few, whose research, writings and support influenced the ways in which my ideas, research and writings have been shaped throughout my life. I would acknowledge every last one if I were able; however; the list would be half as long as the article itself. I would also like to express my great appreciation to Maurice Bonal, Sandra Brintnall and the Santa Fe 400th organization whose efforts made it possible not only for the production of this anthology, but also for the final production of the film documentary concerning Po'Pay.

So, I will humbly end my story expressing gratitude for all in search of truth and knowledge who have helped me along my life's endeavors in finding a prominent place for Ohkay Owingeh and our people in the writings of American and New Mexican history.

—*Kaafedeh*—April 2010

Historia De Mañana
by
Storyteller Evelina Zuni Lucero
Pueblo of Isleta and Ohkay Owingeh

The following excerpt from a novel-in-progress, *Silicon Coyote*, is a historical imagining of the Spanish expedition into New Mexico led by Francisco Vasquez de Coronado in 1541. The events depicted are of the Spaniards' search for the fabled Seven Cities of Cibola, from the Pueblo perspective. Following Coronado's ill-fated exploration which did not yield the wealth expected, the Spaniards returned on later expeditions to establish missions and a colony. A capital was established across the river from San Juan Pueblo (now Ohkay Owingeh Pueblo) in northern New Mexico and later moved to Santa Fe in 1610. Mistreatment of the Pueblo people in these initial expeditions and settlement laid the groundwork for later rebellion during the Pueblo Revolt of 1680, which expelled the Spaniards for twelve years until Diego de Vargas returned to reoccupy Santa Fe in 1692. More recent political battles, centralized in Santa Fe, over New Mexico Indian gaming have also been fictionalized and illustrate the continued efforts of New Mexico Indian governments to assert their political, cultural, and intellectual sovereignty.

In 1991, our tribe went Bingo and eventually the whole nine yards of Indian gambling: video machines, slots, cards, dice, roulette, keno, everything short of horse races and cock fights out back— all because my cousin Elsie needed a job. It was as simple as that. Our tribal gaming enterprise, one mired in a tangle of legalities, was established solely for one person. The official mandate was given voice: We *must provide employment opportunities for our people!* Tribal council members solemnly nodded at one another.

I so move!

I second!

As the secretary bent over her notebook to dutifully record the motion in the minutes, council members leaned in closer. *For Elsie*, they whispered.

Throughout the spring and summer of 1541, a Native of unknown tribal origins called the Turk had the Intruders from the south, from the waters beyond, chasing across the eastern plains of what is now called *New Mexico*. The land earlier has had names in Spanish and before that, more ancient names in Indian languages. Even the Turk had a name of his own, with which the Intruders couldn't be bothered. The Turk was so called because, to them, he resembled one. If they had asked, he would have told them he had many names and was known by many native peoples—known throughout time. In his current circumstances, the Turk had been taken captive at Pecos Pueblo from the people of the plains. He was a talker, relying on his wits to get him out of the trouble his mouth got him into in the first place.

At first the *capitán* of the soldiers on reconnaissance was only interested in talking to the aged cacique of Pecos Pueblo and his assistant, a commanding young man. The two leaders had extended hospitality to the Spaniards and brought them to their settlement on the east plains. The captain had no time for a pesky, lowly, captive *Indio*. That is, not until the Turk told him what he wanted to hear: There exists a land to the east, Quivira, a kingdom filled with treasures and wealth, he said. In the finest tradition of his trade, the Turk spread open both hands, showed a yellow stone in the palm of one, closed both hands again, put them behind his back, and again brought forth his closed fists. *El capitán* pointed at one and when the Turk opened the fist, a fine spun dream, reminiscent of the Aztec riches, appeared before the captain, captivating him with all he desired. The hot sands beneath his feet turned to gold.

To the average person, these two events are seemingly unrelated. But as Elsie tells it, the job made to order for her actually was part of a cycle set into motion long ago. Four hundred fifty years ago to be exact, practically yesterday in Pueblo time.

Our new tribal gaming enterprise named Quivira Palace was built to look like one with a front facade bedecked with glittering lights, sparkles of neon that simulated gold, rubies and diamonds, a bit of Las Vegas relocated to reservation hills, where previously, cattle had grazed. Almost overnight, construction of New Mexico's classiest Indian casino was completed just as Elsie's unemployment benefits came to an end. She stepped out of her Toyota Celica into her palace, her heels clicking smartly. The job was Elsie's dream come true: generous pay, minimal commute, flexible schedule. She started out as a bingo caller, often the star of television and print ads for the Palace. Her face became synonymous with Quivira and its promises. In a few short years as business boomed beyond all expectations, she worked her way up, becoming a cashier, then floor manager, and eventually, assistant manager. A people person, she handled trouble with the same finesse a blackjack dealer shuffled a deck of cards. She soothed irate customers with a honeyed tongue and a gift certificate; she placated disgruntled employees or quietly fired them, making them think they came out ahead.

Within her first month at Quivira, the dreams began. Elsie was just getting into the role of bingo caller, singing out her B-7's and I-25s. The security guard who liked to flirt with her told her he enjoyed her voice—that it was like the tinkle of bells in his ears, sweet and lovely. She announced calls with a certain measured flair that she felt gave her control over people's destinies. Whether they would bingo or not depended on her call. At certain moments when players were only a number away from a jackpot, Elsie relished the tension in the air. People hung on her call. Their success was hers. She willed it or withheld it.

Sporadic at first, then with regularity, Elsie dreamed of the Turk. At first she watched him from a distance talking avidly to strange, bearded men. The Turk gestured wildly, always pointing east. Then he slowly spread open his arms to indicate an incredible vastness. Excited, the bearded men started talking all at once in Spanish, shouting "Quivira!" The Turk watched them closely, his face impassive. When the men turned away, his eyes went hard, dark and sharp as obsidian.

Over and over, she dreamt the same scene so that she came to know and recognize the Turk though she didn't yet know his name. His hair was black as night, coarse and flowing down his back, his skin baked a deep brown, shiny from sweat. He had an inner strength she knew was long lost. She wanted to touch his face, thought she might, but he turned away, his back muscled and strong, his gestures and movement somehow like the river with the glint of moonlight on its surface. In one dream, she asked the Turk, "What is your name?" He didn't answer, but one of the soldiers called out, "Turk!" and he turned around. Before Elsie could speak his name, the soldier seized the Turk. He put up no resistance.

To the horror of the Pecos people, without any provocation, the captain also seized their cacique and his assistant, as well as the Turk's companion, another slave, all the while ranting about gold. Gold? As the people watched helplessly, the four were placed in iron collars and chains and taken west to where the Intruders were encamped in the southernmost Tiguex village of Alcanfor on the west bank of the mother river. The Alcanfor people had graciously vacated their homes at the request of the Spaniards in order that the strangers might have shelter for the coming winter. From vantage points atop their multi-storied homes, the people of the other Tiguex villages watched as the two leaders of the largest Pueblo were led in like the horses of the Intruders. They muttered in anger, especially those who had given up their homes. *Is this how they repay the hospitality of the Pecos cacique? How will they repay our generosity?*

The Turk kept up a running conversation with the captain. "You'll find no gold in this valley," he told him. "All that's here is P'osoge, the Big River. The much bigger river is to the east on the other side of this mountain you call Sandia." He lifted his chains and his chin to gesture at the rugged desert mountain, which lay parallel to the river. "On the other side is where you want to be. I shall take you mañana. Vamonos." The captain said something about the river to one of his men. "Why do you call it Rio de Nuestra Señora? I told you it is called P'osoge. There is a more magnificent river than P'osoge to the east. You want to see it?"

The captain rode off when he heard a shout of welcome from a soldier atop the fortressed wall of Alcanfor.

In yet another dream that unfolded a continuing series, Elsie witnessed the Turk taken before a commander, perhaps a general, though he was young for one, tall and handsome. This is what Elsie knew came to pass during the encounter, though she didn't know how she knew for the conversation was in Spanish:

"Tell me. What of this Quivira?"

The Turk said nothing. He sized up the commander who feigned disinterest in his own question. When the commander turned sharp eyes on him, the Turk responded, "Far to the east beyond the bison herds lies a great, great river, two leagues across." He slowly spread his arms wide. The gesture was grand, conveying magnificence. "At sunrise and sunset, its smooth surface is golden; by day, it shines like silver. Its waters are filled with fish large as—" The Turk paused thoughtfully. After a moment, his eyes brightened. "As large as the general's horses."

The commander leaned forward.

"The great canoes of the ruler of this kingdom glide down this majestic river. Their sails billow in the soft winds, mighty oarsmen, twenty or more, on each side. A large eagle of solid gold graces the prow of each canoe, and the royalty recline under a canopy at the stern." The Turk looked wistfully off in the distance as if picturing them.

The commander's blue eyes glistened. "Go on."

"The land is filled with gold and silver. Silk, too."

"Gold like this?" The commander offered a tin ornament.

The Turk sneered. "This is not gold." He tossed the object aside.

"I know silver. And I know gold well. Of the two, I much prefer gold. I tell you there's so much gold in Quivira, silver is seen as an ordinary metal, used only for common utensils, small or inferior things. Larger items are crafted of pure gold into precious works of beauty. Bowls. Pitchers. Platters and the like. Heavy, but—" The Turk shrugged.

The commander's gasp was audible. "What else?" he breathed.

The Turk was silent for a moment, thoughtful, as if deciding which of the many pleasures to tell. "Each afternoon, the ruler takes his leisure beneath the shady boughs of large trees hung throughout with tiny gold bells which tinkle pleasantly in the breeze." He laughed as if delighted by the ruler's self-indulgence. Looking out the corner of his eyes at the officers, he said, "The sound pleases the women."

The commander turned to his men, seeing his own excitement reflected in their faces.

"You must see it for yourself," the Turk insisted. "I can show you."

"We must be cautious," the commander told his men afterwards, told himself, but his words were perfunctory. They were already convinced by the details of the Turk's story, by his open sincerity. He must be telling the truth, the officers reasoned. How could a savage know gold, know of royal living, except that he had seen it with his own eyes?

"I will hear more of Quivira as the *Indio* tells it," the commander decided, despite the fact that the cacique and his assistant refused, even under coercion, to corroborate the Turk's story. The commander was amused by the Turk, taken in with his adroit mind, his ability to quickly pick up Spanish, his brashness in the face of superiors.

Each night, the commander summoned the Turk before him, and with each telling the Turk's story grew. He recounted the wealth of silver and gold to be found in Quivira, so immense a quantity that horses alone couldn't bear the burden; the gold would have to be brought out in wagons. He added fanciful elements: the oars of the royal canoes were secured with golden oarlocks. The ruler dwelt in a fine palace made of precious stones and gracefully draped throughout with delicate cloths of cotton. The women were gracious and kind with a beauty beyond comparison, the noblemen refined. The fruit of the land was fit for kings, enough to sustain the many cities of the kingdom. And there was more to be found beyond the boundaries of Quivira. Far richer kingdoms, *Harahey* and *Guaes*, lay further east. The Turk could name the king there—*Tattarax*.

His incredulous stories spread throughout the camp, firing the imaginations of the soldiers, young men with no wives, nothing to lose, all thirsting for adventure in the New World. They could hardly contain themselves. Quivira, the answer to their miserable trek north and what they had to endure in the river valley they occupied: the extreme cold of winter and the sudden uprising by the Tiguex pueblos. What a bother! These Indians were like a colony of red ants stirred up, fierce in the face of an invasion. But once the insurrection was suppressed, once spring returned, they would immediately set out for this Quivira—the real business of the expedition.

For now, the rebellious *Indios* must be made to submit, to understand they were now subjects of the King of Spain, subject to the requisitions of his representatives. The soldiers' use of an entire town as army quarters, their demands for the Indians to bring in food, clothes and woven goods, were all reasonable requirements to ask of the King's subjects. So what if some of the Indians had taken the clothes right off their backs to meet the army's levy? Had they not been compensated with beads and bells? And was not the imprisonment of the Pecos leaders and the Turk a necessity for the securing of wealth for the Crown, the anger of the Pueblos notwithstanding? Turning the dogs on the stubborn cacique and his assistant, both of whom continued to feign ignorance about gold to the east, was justifiable. Anyway, the two suffered only a few dog bites. As for the Indians' charge that a soldier raped one of their women—Puh! That was nothing that gold couldn't fix.

"How do you know all this?"

"I just do. Night after night, they're relentless." Elsie ran her fingers through her hair. "My dream last night… It was so real."

"Oh yeah?"

A soldier, Cervantes, stood guard over the Turk who had been placed in seclusion during the uprising.

"Five soldiers are dead at Moho, including a captain," the Turk told Cervantes in a flat tone. "It was the captain well favored by the men, wasn't it?"

At his words, Cervantes stiffened. He knew a second battle was underway at *Moho* where Captain Ovando had been seized by the Indians, dragged into a tower porthole, and most likely killed. Four others had been fatally wounded. But Cervantes fervently denied anyone had been killed. The Turk remarked he knew it was a fact and didn't need anyone's corroboration. Curious of how the Turk came by this information, Cervantes hid to spy on him. The Turk, his back hunched, intently gazed into a pottery bowl of water set before him on the dirt floor. Creeping closer, peering over the Turk's shoulder, Cervantes made out a blur of movement on the water's surface. Looking inside the bowl, the guard saw soldiers, *Indios*, and horses swirling in the water as if in an eddy. Cervantes gasped. Even as he stared in amazement, the water became cloudy, and the Turk covered the bowl with a piece of cloth.

As Cervantes backed off, startled, the Turk calmly said, "It's not yours to know."

Ever since Cervantes had been assigned to guard the Turk, he had entertained a nightly audience of men eager to hear what new detail of Quivira the Turk had told him. It hadn't been beyond him to make something up even if the Turk had said nothing the whole of his watch. But this was different! He couldn't wait to tell. The Turk was a wizard!

Surely it must be, the soldiers repeated to one another as they readied for another assault, that looking into his bowl of water not only revealed the deaths to him but also the great wealth beyond.

"Aaaii! Quivira is real! We will soon be there!"

But the garrison encamped at the spring outside the pueblo of Moho could make no headway in the battle. Battering rams couldn't bring down the fortified walls of this large, multi-storied town. Warriors from other pueblos had gathered at Moho and were positioned on the upper levels. They shot down soldiers who managed to scale the walls with arrows tipped in rattlesnake venom.

Squatting, staring at the spring before him, the general threw in a pebble. The water rippled in concentric circles. He stared at the ripples. Then he rose decisively. "We control their water source. They won't be able to hold out long. Lay siege," he curtly ordered.

It seemed to Elsie to be a turning point in the conflict, for the noise of fighting subsided, and she saw soldiers entering the nearly empty pueblo. In one of the rooms, the soldiers found the strangely preserved, ghostly white, naked body of the fair-haired Captain Ovando, whose death the Turk knew about. The soldiers' voices were a buzz of awe and anger. The Turk was dragged out to witness the torching of part of the town. "Let this be a lesson to you," Cervantes hissed in his ear. The Turk watched, emotionless. He had already seen what was coming. Looking into the bowl of water into the future, he had seen a strange sight: thousands of mysterious lights throughout a large settlement brightened the night with a glow that extended into the sky, obliterating the stars. This city of lights, as large as all the Pueblo nations combined, filled the Tiguex valley on both sides of *P'osoge* and spread up the east side of the mountain as well as across the foothills west of the river and further south. Stunned, he had covered the bowl and sat wondering at the power of the people who could pluck stars from the sky and turn night into day. He was still staring into space when the soldiers yanked him to his feet and forced him to watch Moho burn.

The soldiers later burned down a second Tiguex settlement as a warning to the pueblos against further rebellion. As smoke drifted down the valley, an eerie silence descended on the deserted settlements of the Tiguex Nation. Then the whole Spanish entourage, fifteen hundred people strong, crossed the frozen river in mid-spring, marching for the eastern plains. The Turk was at the general's side, describing the marvels that lay ahead.

The Turk moved them over the Great Plains like wind, first here, then there, all the while palming his yellow stone, assuring them of Quivira's imminent nearness. "You are nearing the kingdom where you will reap rewards for your travel!" he promised. They moved over an immense sea of grass, leaving no visible sign of their passing. On and on and on they journeyed into the summer, until finally the general ordered the army back to the Tiguex valley to prepare for winter. The soldiers begged to stay, but the general was adamant. He himself and a small party of chosen men, following the Turk's lead, would continue the search for Quivira. He would send word immediately when he reached Quivira.

When the encamped army, and the general and his chosen few again met, it was September, a full year since their *entrada* into pueblo territory. The captain left in command went out to meet the general.

"Was King Tattarax like Montezuma?" he asked, eager for news of Quivira.

The general snorted disdainfully. For all their trouble, all they had seen was a decrepit, old chief, he said. His only riches consisted of a copper medallion hanging around his stringy neck. Whether the old man was even King Tattarax, the general couldn't say for sure.

"What about—"

The general shook his head before the captain could finish his question. There were no eagles of gold. No stately boats. No golden bells in trees. No gold. *Nada.*

The captain's eyes searched among the general's weary men. "And where is the Turk?"

The general's eyes flashed in anger. "Dead! *¡Ese cabron!* A dog's death is what he got. He was killed one night in the tent of López and Zaldívar, then buried in a hole before the light of dawn. Killed for his black heart. His lying ways. He had wickedly conspired with the people of Pecos Pueblo to wipe us out! The entire King's army!" The general was choked with rage. His eyes bulged. "The Turk was to lead us aimlessly till we weakened, our supplies depleted, our horses dead! If any found their way back, the Pecos warriors would do them in at this very pass."

The captain was appropriately horrified at the connivery against the King of Spain and his representatives. He quickly crossed himself twice, saying, "*¡Gracias a Santiago! ¡Gracias a Dios para favor!*" Then before the opportunity passed, he asked, "So there was no Quivira? No wealth?"

The commander sighed heavily, shook his head, no. "But the Turk with his lying heart insisted to his dying day that we were near the Royal River, near to our treasures. Our dreams and desires were soon to be fulfilled. Liar! He had promised that with every stop."

"So what did you find?"

"Plains on end. People in grass-roofed huts. Big wolves, white-pied deer, rabbits, grapes, nuts, mulberries and plums. Buffalo droppings everywhere." He waved his hand dismissively, shook his head in disgust. "Wagon load upon wagon load of cow manure."

And so her dreaming life went over the past five years, rich and detailed. In some of Elsie's dreams, the Turk dreamed of his death at the hands of the angry soldiers. And he often dreamed of Quivira Palace. Not the one he made up, but the one of the reservation hills of the future.

He had frequently watched the soldiers gamble at card games. Tribal peoples often feasted and gambled freely, so he was intrigued by a new form of gambling. When the officers were present, the men quietly played games of first or triumph, which involved no wagers for horses and saddles; but in the officers' absence, the soldiers played betting games with great earnestness and intensity of emotion, the very games the officers played among themselves. Dice was another pleasurable, furtive diversion which the Turk watched with avid interest. While he didn't understand the reason for it, he deduced that some games were frowned upon though the men derived their greatest pleasure from them.

One morning in particular, Elsie emerged through layers of dreams; she struggled to rise to consciousness. The effort turned strenuous as if she was buried in sand; her limbs grew heavy, immovable, her tongue thick, mouth dry. Her lungs burned. Her very efforts to move seemed to draw her deeper and heightened her panic. Exhausted, she ceased struggling and immediately experienced a release, a warm, strangely pleasant sensation of being in a mucky, swirling substance like quicksand that pushed her up.

When she awoke from this last dream, she came to see me.

"The state's not going to win, Angel, my boy," Elsie told me, her voice full of confidence. She was referring to the current state of affairs in Indian gaming. In last winter's legislative session of '96, state legislators and the governor battled one another over the legality of the gaming compacts the governor had signed with the tribes. The power struggle had been taken to court where the ruling went against the tribes, who were now appealing the decision which declared the compacts invalid. The whole gaming issue was stalled as everyone awaited the appeals court to issue a decision. In this election year, everyone was striking a pose.

"Legislators and the attorney general are fighting this tooth and nail. What makes you so sure the state won't win? " I asked out of idle curiosity. I was a little envious of Elsie's dreams. The most I've ever experienced has been *deja vu*—that little isolated warp in time and space that leaves me wondering what's really going on, if things don't happen over and over with only the names and dates changed to protect the ignorant.

"It's not in the cards. Not in the stars," she responded, her voice matter of fact. "I used to just have a feeling, but now it's more like I know."

I heard the conviction in her voice. Who was I to question it? Strange, mysterious things do still happen, even in the face of Western empirical science which states that if something can't be proved using scientific methods then it's not so. But not everything in life is for us to know, which is why I can accept everything Elsie has told me. Life is a mystery, full of twists and turns. Most people in New Mexico understand this. Everyone in the state is looking for mystery and miracles: in tortillas, in dirt, in the dry air, in the night sky over Roswell. Even in the spin of the slots. Who knows why the long ago people suddenly up and left Chaco Canyon as if a nuclear attack had been signaled, and everyone dropped what they were doing to head for the bomb shelters—okay, maybe it was a meteorite. Usually, I'm a rational person. A journalist asking, *Who, What, When, Where, Why, How? Can I quote you on that?* Rarely do I accept people's stories at face value. Everyone has their own version of the truth.

But believing her story was not the point; with Elsie, it never was. She simply told it like it was, and with a shrug of her shoulders left it to you.

"We'll see," I said.

"Four hundred and fifty-plus years and we're still doing the same dance. Mark my words," she said.

Indians, Colonialism, and the Santa Fe Trail of Tears and Conquest
Challenging the Master Narrative
by
James Riding In
Pawnee

Celebrations of famous people and events frequently arouse the indignation of American Indian activists because these occurrences almost always romanticize the oppressive past, denigrate Natives, and gloss over, if not dismiss, the horrors of ethnic cleansing, conquest, colonization, and genocide. Quite expectedly, many socially-conscious Indians fear that the 400th year anniversary of the founding of Santa Fe may set into motion a propaganda machine capable of feeding lies and half-truths to the public about Indian-white relations. If this scenario unfolds it will mean that mistakes and protests that have confronted previous commemorative events, such as the Columbus quincentenary in 1992, will have gone unnoticed.

Being an Indigenous scholar who has a long record of challenging racism, scientific grave looting, and oppression, I feel honored to have been invited to take part in this important book. It represents a forum where Native writers can express their uncensored views about various elements of a potentially divisive celebration. In what follows I am sharing much of what I have learned about Indians and the Santa Fe Trail through a research project sponsored by the National Park Service. My relating of this history begins with the words of one of my Pawnee forefathers.

During an 1822 Washington, D.C. speech before the "Great Father," Saritaris, a Chaui Pawnee leader, carried out his duty as a Pawnee leader by speaking in defense of his people's independence, sovereignty, landholdings, and cultural integrity. After comparing his people with those of the United States, he expressed a growing sense of uneasiness and concern among Pawnees toward white American encroachments, stating:

> "You love your country; you love your people; you love the manner in which they live, and you think your people brave. I am like you, my Great Father, I love my country; I love my people; I love the manner in which we live, and think myself and warriors brave; spare me then, my Father, let me enjoy my country, and pursue the buffaloe, and the beaver, and the other wild animals of our wilderness, and I will trade skins with your people. I have grown up and lived thus long without work; I am in hopes you will suffer me to die without it. We have plenty of buffaloe, beaver, deer, and other wild animals; we have an abundance of horses. We have everything we want. We have plenty of land, *if you will keep your people off of it*." (Morse, 244)

In essence, his words, albeit filtered through a non-Pawnee cognitive process of translation, invoke the principles of the inherent rights of his people to live undisturbed on, and exert authority over, their homeland.

Although Saritaris probably died from the effects of cholera within several years of his return from Washington to his Pawnee homeland in what became called Nebraska and Kansas, his words, which also essentially summed up the positions of surrounding Indian nations, fell on deaf ears. At that time, to the east the United States was aggressively pursuing a policy of expansionism aimed at opening Indian lands for white American settlement. The founding of the Santa Fe Trail about the time of Saritaris's address represented an important element in this process of territorial aggrandizement. Calling for actions to drive Indigenous peoples out of the way, proponents of this course of action often justified their positions with racial stereotypes that simultaneously denigrated Indians as an inferior people while proclaiming the racial superiority of their race. They considered territorial growth as being not only ethical but also vital for securing a future that promoted the freedom, democracy, and economic prosperity of their young nation. This rhetoric, which would be encapsulated in the term manifest destiny during the mid-1840s, also called for the United States to establish its hegemony over lands reaching to the Pacific Ocean.

Linking the United States with Mexico as an overland trade route, the Santa Fe Trail was the type of unwelcome intrusion that Saritaris feared. This intrusive road traversed the southern part of the Pawnees' territory, passing through some of their most productive buffalo hunting lands. Impacting other Indians as well, it was an important element in this history of expansionism that had dire consequences for Indian peoples.

On the macro level, the trail's imposition on Indian life must be contextualized within the framework of a colonialist process that began with the arrival of the first European explorers in the Americas during the fifteenth century. The earliest European invaders, seekers of lands to occupy, resources to exploit, and trading relationships to tap, claimed Indigenous lands by virtue of the myth of discovery. When positioned to do so, these newcomers unleashed the fury of their power against uncooperative Natives. Deadly microbes of foreign origin not only took millions of Indigenous lives but also made the imperialistic objectives of the colonists much easier to carry out. Falling one nation after another under foreign domination, either by the force of military might or the effects of attrition, these peoples lost their freedom and independence, meaning the aggressive acts of others imposed a substantial burden on the free exercise of their customary values, beliefs, and traditions. Oppression, dependence, genocide, and coercive assimilation served as tactics of colonial conquest.

Those Indians who had intimate contact with the Santa Fe Trail lived in differing circumstances, vis-à-vis their previous experiences with colonization. Dividing these nations into three broad groups enables us to see how the condition of their preexisting political status affected their relations with the trail.

The first group consists of free Indigenous nations that had not fallen under the political or economic domination of a colonial power. Extending in an east to west direction along the route of the Santa Fe Trail, they were the Osages, Kaws (or Kansas), Pawnees, Comanches, Cheyennes, Kiowas, Arapahos, Plains Apaches (often called the Prairie or Kiowas Apaches), Utes, and Jicarilla Apaches. By the early 1700s all of them had integrated horses into their cultures, giving them greater mobility in matters of economic pursuits and warfare. At the trail's onset, each of them had already experienced varying degrees of contact with one or more colonizing power, mostly in the forms of trade, diplomacy, and warfare, without losing their independence. With the trail's rapid development into a major thoroughfare being an element of a broader process of expansionism, they increasingly found themselves engaged in losing struggles to maintain the integrity of their sovereignty, lands, and cultures. However, factors such as population size, location, and settlement patterns would influence the course of action that each of them took pursuant to their relations to the trail.

In their interaction with the trail's traffic, they insisted that travelers must act in conformity with Indian protocols, which called for the sharing of such items as tobacco, gunpowder, balls, sugar, coffee, and food as a condition or price for crossing through their lands. When travelers resisted, Indian men would often collect a toll by taking livestock and property either by force or by stealth.

A second group comprises Pueblo Indians of New Mexico who had previously lost their elements of independence before coming into contact with the trail. Except for a twelve-year period of freedom gained through revolution, these peoples had toiled under the heavy yoke of Spanish domination for more than two hundred years. Although having lost most of their lands, political rights, and subjected to the burden of involuntary labor and taxation, they had continued to live in communal lives. In their compact towns, they grew customary crops of corn, beans, and squash as well as incorporating new foods of foreign origins into their diets. The Pueblo Revolt of 1680 taught the Spaniards the hard lesson that these Indians would rise in rebellion to preserve their religion and ways of life. Spanish accommodation of these Indian concerns lessened the burdens of colonization on the Pueblos.

When Mexico freed itself from the reins of Spanish control in 1821, the Pueblos fell under the political authority of another governing power. Although theoretically possessing the rights of Mexican citizens, they continued to experience oppression. Mexican policy had the ill effect of opening significant portions of their lands for Mexican settlement. In 1846, with the U.S. invasion of Mexico, they became subjected to U.S. domination. As in the past, the Pueblos endeavored to carry their customary ways of life despite gradually intensifying efforts to compel them to adopt white American manner of living.

It should be noted that surrounding Navajos, Utes, and Jicarilla Apaches evaded the fate of the Pueblo life during the Spanish and Mexican eras. Not living year round in permanent dwellings, their mobile lifestyles and remote migratory settlements enabled them to avoid subjugation until the first few years of the U.S. era. Until then, these peoples engaged in relations with the colonizers that involved trading, warfare, and diplomacy.

The final set is made up of Indian nations who had been removed from their eastern lands to new lands on the eastern edge of the central plains after the trail had come into existence. Consisting of Shawnees, Delawares, and others, these displaced peoples had previously battled the forces of colonialism to maintain their sovereignty, lands, and cultures but ultimately lost their ability to offer militarily resistance to U.S. expansionism. On their reservations in Kansas, many of them nonetheless remained committed to living in accordance with the customs and beliefs of their ancestors. Others, however, had previously or would convert to Christianity and embarked on a path of acculturation without disavowing their Indian identities or tacitly forfeiting their inherent political rights. As with the Pueblos, they generally had little choice but to have cooperative relations with the Santa Fe Trail.

Santa Fe is inseparable from this story of colonialism. The trail linked this town, New Mexico, and areas beyond, to the United States. Before, during, and after the trail's existence, Santa Fe served as a provincial capital for a succession of three foreign governments: Spain, Mexico, and the United States. As such, government officials seated in Santa Fe implemented decisions that affected Indian life over a vast landscape. Indian delegates often visited those officials to discuss such matters as war, peace, trade, policy, and water rights. Thus, this town played a central role in the intertwined processes of colonial expansionism and the colonizers' efforts to subjugate and maintain control over Indians. This chapter examines elements of these Indians' relationship with the trail within the contexts of colonialism and the master narrative.

During the early days of the trail's existence, as Saritaris declared so vividly, Indians along the way watched with suspicion and apprehension as mounted U.S. citizens with pack animals trespassed on their lands. Yet they were willing to trade with white Americans on Indian terms. Rut-carving wagons soon became the primary mode of transporting people and goods over the trail. In 1846, the United States invaded Mexico. This war of aggression forced the Mexican government to cede the northern half of its land claims, bringing the entirety of the trail's route under U.S. control. By the 1870s, pressure from U.S. expansion had literally cleansed the area surrounding the trail of its previously large Indian population. From the perspective of the independent Indians, the trail was the tip of a spear that brought them harm, suffering, and destruction.

Although numerous incidents of cooperation and friendly contact transpired over the course of the trail's history, the exertion of violence was the factor that shaped the outcome of this historical process. From 1825 to the 1870s, the U.S. Congress appropriated millions of dollars to protect travelers and to quash Indian opposition to the trail. In addition to covering the costs of a survey and treaty negotiations with and obligations to different Indians, these allocations also funded an expensive array of U.S. army operations including the deployment of escorts, the construction of a series of military posts, the garrisoning and supplying of troops stationed at those posts, and the manning of aggressive campaigns against Indian resistance.

The Master Narrative

Mainstream scholarship often tells the story of the Santa Fe Trail through the prism of American nation building and heroism, but this history is significantly more complex and nuanced than brave Euro-American pioneers overcoming the hazards of wild Indians, geographical barriers, and unpredictable weather. Scholars, or the guardians of the master narrative, have mostly done a poor job of incorporating Indians into this history. Consequently, the body of literature they created, whether expressed vividly or subtly, rests on the racist notion of Euro-American superiority and Indian inferiority. This literature seems to indicate that Indians had nothing better to do than attack innocent pioneers. It contains misconstructions of Indian cultures, biased interpretations, methodological defects, and conceptual flaws.

There are crucial points that must be understood for comprehending this history. The first is that, despite an axiom central to the master narrative asserting that an inherent belligerence within savage Indians was the root cause of the violence, colonialist expansionism, whether perpetrated by white American or Mexican aggressors, was the primary cause of conflict. The second is that Indians usually went to war to protect their lands, cultures, and sovereignty as well as to offset the harm caused by encroachments into their lands, property, and life-sustaining resources. The third is that the trail is a sub-story of a larger historical process involving Indian nations interacting with an expansionistic people of European ancestry vying for control of the lands and resources within an overarching colonial orbit. A fourth is that virtually all Indian nations at some point in time lost their ability to resist expanding colonial nations, leaving them susceptible to foreign tyranny and exploitation. A final is that Indigenous nations had three options: flight, cooperation, or resistance. (Ferguson and Whitehead, 17) Indians having an association with the trail exercised each of these alternatives,

Colonialism is defined as the expansion of a colonizing nation into the lands of Indigenous nations for the purpose of acquiring lands, resources, and labor. It is behavior that includes calculated militant and diplomatic measures, often one and the same, devised and carried out by colonizers to politically subjugate, control, and dispossess the Indigenous landowners. This aggression was essentially an armed invasion that took years to complete. Members of the colonizing society typically developed propaganda expressed vividly if not accurately through the language of racism, aimed at giving a sense of destiny, propriety, and morality to their nation's assault on Indian sovereignty, lands, cultures, and human rights. In doing so, they constructed a narrative based on such factors as ideology, discourses on conquest, expressions of racism, and innuendo to rationalize the westward spread of their people into Indian lands. They integrated the Santa Fe Trail into the master narrative. This story echoes a refrain, commonly held and expressed within U.S. society, depicting Indians as predatory and savage peoples who stood in the way of progress.

The Independent Indians

The trail's founding was a criminal act in that it involved U.S. and Mexican encroachments into Indian lands. In September 1821, William Becknell and a small party of mounted U.S. citizens departed Missouri en route to Santa Fe with a quantity of manufactured goods in anticipation of reaping enormous profits from trade. Unlawfully passing through the lands of the Osages, Kaws, Pawnees, Comanches, Utes, Jicarilla Apaches, and others along the way, these well-armed trespassers reached their destination in mid-November and fulfilled their wildest expectations. Several months earlier, Mexico had gained its independence from Spain by means of a violent uprising. Reversing the Spanish policy of excluding U.S. traders, Mexican officials allowed the white Americans to conduct business and return home several months later.

In the United States, news of the party's success touched off a frenzy of travel, commerce, and conflict with Indians that steadily escalated over time. With vast sums of money to be made in Santa Fe and Chihuahua, traders and the U.S. government initially ignored the territorial rights of Indians. Traveling in wagons and turning the trail through Indian country into a major thoroughfare, traders antagonized and harmed Indians by engaging in recurring acts involving the slaughter of buffalo; destruction of timber, plants, and foliage; pollution of water; desecration of burials; and camping on customary Indian sites.

Along the eastern side of the trail during the first few years of its existence, Kaws, Osages, and others occasionally extracted compensation for damages from parties of traders by stealthily appropriating livestock and property or by demanding provisions in open confrontations. Further west, along the Arkansas River in the central portion of the trail's route, Pawnees and Comanches occasionally took similar actions for the same reasons. By the mid-1820s, however, relatively few incidents of violence had occurred. Nonetheless, following a tradition that had been in place since the early years of European colonialism in the Americas, traders, local and national politicians, newspaper journalists, and expansionists exaggerated the extent of the conflict and distorted the cause of the tensions and violence. Casting travelers as innocent victims of uncontrollable Indian savagery, they petitioned their national government to intervene on their behalf.

Responding to these calls for assistance in 1825 to support the traders' relentless drive for profits, the U.S. Congress allocated funds to survey the trail and obtain right-of-way treaties with Indian nations whose lands lay along the trail's route on the U.S. side of the international border, which at that time was the Arkansas River. Although U.S. officials realized that Osages, Kaws, Pawnees, and Comanches claimed lands along the trail's route, they merely sought out leaders of the first two nations for treaty considerations and compensation. On August 10 and 11, Osage and Kaw representatives respectively accepted $500 dollars in trade goods or cash and merchandise valued at $300 in return for safe-passage agreements. Both treaties stipulated that the Indian leaders agreed "to the marking of said road, and to the unmolested use therefore to the citizens of the United States and of the Mexican Republic" and that "they will, on all fit occasions, render such friendly aid and assistance as may be in their power, to any of the citizens of the United States and of the Mexican Republic, as they may at any time happen to meet or fall in with on the road aforesaid." They further consented that the road "shall be considered as extending to a reasonable distance on either side, so that travelers thereon may, at any time, leave the marked tract, for the purpose of finding subsistence and proper camping places." (Kappler, 246-50)

U.S. officials proved too parsimonious and shortsighted to offer other Indians monetary considerations or protection. Rather, they opted to handle the matter by including a safe-passage clause in treaties of peace, friendship, and trade with many of those who might come into contact with the trail, which included the Oglala, Cheyenne, Otoe and Missouria, Crow, Omaha, and Pawnee peoples. The September 30 treaty with the Pawnees is reflective of these boilerplate agreements. On that date Pawnee leaders purportedly recognized the political supremacy of the United States and agreed to live under its protection. They also consented not to "molest or interrupt any American citizen or citizens, who may be passing from the United States to New Mexico, or returning from thence to the United States." (Kappler, 258-60)

Although Osage and Kaw relations with the trail improved somewhat after August 1825, this spate of treaty making suffered from at least three critical weaknesses. U.S. representatives failed to discuss this matter of travel with Comanche, Kiowa, Arapaho, and Plains Apache leaders, meaning that people from affected nations did not have an opportunity to express their views regarding this important matter. The treaties with the Pawnees and Cheyennes did not protect the interests of these peoples or provide reparations for damages inflicted by the trail's traffic. Finally, U.S. officials did not attempt to regulate or control the behavior of its citizens.

To understand these shortcomings we must fully recognize the attitudes of nineteenth-century white Americans. They were a fiercely self-righteous and very race-conscious people who viewed others without a Western European pedigree as being inherently inferior in intelligence and culture to themselves. Their political leaders simply refused to take actions that would safeguard Indian rights and curb the incendiary acts of their citizens in matters involving others deemed as lacking human worth. Then too, their nation's ambitions to appropriate Indian lands and open foreign markets promoted an environment in which discussion of human rights for Indians had no meaningful place for consideration.

In spring of 1828, a year characterized by a spike in violence, unknown Indians killed two travelers with a caravan on the Mexican side of the border. As the funeral service for the fallen men was ending, a group of eight Indians, most likely innocent Comanches, appeared. Striking out in vengeance, caravan members opened fire, killing all but one of the approaching Indians. Retaliating Indians drove off nearly 1,500 head of horses from the offending caravan. By taking this action, they sent a clear message saying they would not tolerate criminal acts committed by travelers.

Tensions continued to mount that fall with the circulation of an unsubstantiated rumor. In October, a U.S. government agent reported that 1,500 Pawnees had gone to war against the trail and if that failed they would kill all of the whites they could find in U.S. settlements in Arkansas. This assertion lacked truth, but officials in Washington and Santa Fe responded to pleas for military protection from trail travelers.

Brash U.S. political and military leaders proved too impatient to allow Indians to stand in the way of the lucrative economic ambitions of their fellow citizens. In May 1829, four companies of slow moving U.S. infantrymen departed Fort Leavenworth, then called a cantonment that had been established two years earlier, to protect commerce on the trail and the fur trade. Probably under Indian surveillance during much of their deployment, the command soon linked up with the annual caravan, which consisted of seventy men and thirty-five wagons, and escorted it toward the Arkansas River. At the Arkansas, a stream that served as a line that divided the lands claimed by the United States and Mexico, skittish caravan members wanted the soldiers to escort them further into Mexican territory, but the troops refused to cross the river.

On June 11, about six miles west of the border, Indians identified as Comanches, Kiowas, and Arapahos launched a surprise attack on the caravan, killing a trader. Opting to avoid the firepower of well-armed enemy force, they broke off the fight before the U.S. troops reached the scene. They allowed the soldiers to re-cross the river and set up camp near Chouteau's island before carrying out a campaign of guerrilla warfare, a typical form of Indian fighting. That summer and fall, they mostly employed hit-and-run tactics against such vulnerable targets as soldiers hunting buffalo and traveling in small groups. On occasion they attempted to stampede the soldiers' cattle herds. The soldiers ended their largely futile campaign later that fall and returned to Fort Leavenworth. For their efforts they had managed to kill only about eight Indians while suffering a number of casualties, including four deaths. (Cooke, 46-60) That fall Santa Fe officials dispatched a force of Mexican soldiers, assisted by forty Taos Pueblo allies, to escort a caravan en route to Missouri. On October 6 near Cimarron springs in Mexican territory, over a hundred unidentified Indians attacked. Both sides suffered a few losses in the fighting. (Cooke, Scenes and Adventures, 86) What these facts say is that the use of military troops was not only ineffective but that it also failed to discourage Indian resistance toward the trail's traffic.

During the 1830s, violent encounters along the trail diminished, but the Pawnees, whom trail travelers considered a deadly threat, sustained dramatic population losses. During the spring of 1831, Pawnees reportedly killed two white Americans. In May of that year, Indians believed to be Comanches took the life of Jedidiah Smith, a famed trapper and explorer who had become engaged in the Santa Fe trade. U.S. officials did not retaliate for these deaths, but traders may have. That fall in October, a devastating epidemic struck the Pawnees, killing about half of them. They swore vengeance against the Santa Fe traders for giving some of their people "gifts" infected with the deadly smallpox virus. In 1832, a Pueblo Indian traveling with an eastbound U.S. caravan reportedly shot and killed a Pawnee leader without provocation. (Pike, 287-88) The following year, Pawnees laid siege to the New Mexico town of Mora, a small settlement situated north of Las Vegas near the mountain route of the trail, causing its abandonment for two years. In 1837, smallpox once again broke out among the Pawnee towns killing hundreds of young people who had been born after the previous epidemic. At various times and place, diseases struck other Indians along the trail with devastating consequences.

During the 1830s, in an apparent act to discourage Indian resistance, U.S. officials adopted a compensation policy that enabled travelers who lost property to obtain reimbursement from the responsible nation's treaty funds. Along the mountain route at an unspecified point along the Timpas or upper Purgatory in September 1837, Pawnees led by Big Soldier attacked a southbound company of traders, taking merchandize and horses valued at over $3,000 and possibly killing a traveler. In 1845, Congress denied a claim in this matter because the incident had occurred on Mexico soil. (White, 1:401-14)

The following year, Indian relations with the trail were about to turn for the worst. Beginning in May, Indians watched with great consternation as large columns of U.S. soldiers marched toward Santa Fe, long lines of supply trains moved in both directions, and travelers slaughtered buffalo for food and sport. Although numerous reports circulated telling of Indian depredations, there were relatively few actual cases of open warfare in that year. One incident happened, however, on October 28 about thirty miles below the Arkansas Crossing in which a Pawnee force struck a Santa Fe-bound U.S. government supply train, taking a large number of mules and supplies, killing a man, wounding four others, and burning a wagon. Comanches also received blame for a few raids occurring that autumn. (Chalfant, 44)

Seeking to defend their lands, buffalo, and life in 1847, Comanche, Kiowa, and Arapaho contingents struck the Santa Fe traffic along the Arkansas and eastern New Mexico settlements. Expressing a reason for his people's anger, an Arapaho declared that "bad" white men had "ran the buffalo out of the country, and starved the Arapaho." (Garrard, 106-09) Virtually any Plains Indians could have truthfully expressed the same feeling. Lives were lost on both sides as Indian raiders targeted livestock and property belonging to the intruders. As in the past, Cheyennes sought to remain neutral but the murder of one of their most respected peace chiefs, an elderly man named Old Tobacco, in May by a caravan member, plus other transgressions, seriously undermined, without nullifying, their policy of peaceful coexistence with the United States.

That spring, U.S. officials authorized the construction of a walled way station on the Arkansas where caravans could seek safety, rest, and repairs for their wagons. Located in the heart of Indian country, Fort Mann, as it was called, became a focal point of intense conflict. Facing an ongoing series of attacks, beleaguered employees abandoned the post within a few weeks.

In late July, Indian opposition along the Arkansas soared to an unprecedented level in response to the harm caused by an ever-increasing flow of trail traffic. Rather than taking steps to curtail the traffic, the U.S. war secretary upped the ante by authorizing the formation of 500 Missouri volunteers for service on the trail. Arriving there that fall, a portion of these soldiers occupied Fort Mann while others wintered at Big Timber (in southeastern Colorado) in an ill-conceived plan to awe Arapahos and friendly Cheyennes of the upper Arkansas into submission.

A bloody incident involving treachery erupted in November at Fort Mann. Soldiers lured about sixty members of a passing Pawnee party into a deadly ambush set inside of the fort's walls. Before springing their trap, the troops had feinted friendship by providing tobacco and food to their unarmed guests. With the sound of rattling sabers breaking the calm, the Pawnees, realizing the precariousness of their situation, fled toward the fort's gate. Commencing hostilities, the soldiers killed at least four of them, including a chief's son, and wounded fifteen to twenty others. Because the victims were Indians, the U.S. army did not press charges against any of the perpetrators. (Barry, 727, 755, 760)

In the aftermath of the Fort Mann tragedy, the frequency of Pawnee sightings along the trail and in New Mexico declined. A combination of factors impeded their independence. In 1848, the U.S. army constructed a fort on Grand Island near the Pawnee towns on the Loup and Platte rivers, which left their children, women, and men extremely vulnerable in the event that the occupying force decided to attack them. Another extenuating consideration was the Pawnees' precipitous population decline. By the late 1840s smallpox and cholera epidemics, hunger, and warfare had caused their numbers to fall to approximately four thousand people.

As Pawnees nearly vanished from the trail's scene, outbursts of periodic conflict involving other Indians remained the norm. As the violent winter of 1847 and 1848 came to a close, U.S. volunteers launched a series of largely ineffective search and destroy missions along the trail, in the surrounding area, and in eastern New Mexico against Indians deemed hostile. Using their mobility and tactics to evade pursuit, Comanches, Kiowas, Plains Apaches, and others suffered some losses despite glowing army reports indicating that the campaign had inflicted heavy casualties on enemy combatants. At the closure of the Mexican War, U.S. officials withdrew their troops from the Santa Fe Trail in Kansas.

With Fort Mann sitting abandoned once again and U.S. forces gone, the undefeated Indians sought to carry on their customary ways while continuing to face a precarious economic position. With basic subsistence continued to be a major factor threatening their lives and independence, some of them periodically raided caravans, chased intruders from the buffalo herds, and sought compensation for damages from travelers. (Barry, 755) Intermittent incidents of trade and cooperative relations also transpired amid the outbursts of violence. With military options failing to achieve the projected outcome of punishing defiant Indians, U.S. officials turned to diplomacy in an unsuccessful attempt to convince Comanches, Kiowas, and Arapahos to move away from the trail. (Berthrong, 112)

U.S. officials once again turned to the establishment of forts to protect the travelers en route to Santa Fe and the Pacific Northwest on the Overland Trail. In Kansas their army established Fort Riley in 1853, Fort Larned on the Pawnee River in 1859, and Fort Atkinson in 1860 near where Dodge City would sit several years later. Also in 1860, soldiers built Fort Wise, later renamed Fort Lyon, at Big Timber. Within the next few years, they erected Forts Zarah, Hayes, Harker, Wallace, and Dodge, along with numerous camps, on the Kansas plains to facilitate white American expansionism by controlling Indians.

Meanwhile, as warfare waned in Kansas during the late 1840s, New Mexico witnessed a sharp increase in violence as the U.S. government sought to establish its hegemony over Indians. Jicarilla Apaches and Utes, feeling the weight of the U.S. invasion and the springing up of new settlements in their lands, periodically skirmished with trail travelers, settlers, and soldiers. With a new set of occupation troops in place, they faced retaliation from detachments stationed at Santa Fe, Rayaldo, Las Vegas, and other posts. (Barry, 756-77)

U.S. troops, or some of them at least, seemed to be spoiling for a fight. On August 16, 1849, forty Jicarillas with their leader Lobo camped near Las Vegas to trade. On the outskirts of the town, soldiers commanded by Lieutenant Ambrose E. Burnside attacked them without provocation. The fight resulted in the death of sixteen Indians and the wounding of three soldiers, including Burnside. Additionally, the U.S. troops captured six Jicarillas, a man and five women including Lobo's daughter. (Howard, 30-32)

On October 24 or 25, Lobo and other Jicarillas, joined by Utes, retaliated by attacking James White party's near Point of Rocks, a Santa Fe trail landmark situated in an area considered safe from Indian strikes. The action resulted in the deaths of six or seven travelers and the capture of Mrs. White, her infant daughter, and her black slave. Pursuing U.S. troops later overtook the fleeing Indians near the present town of Tucumcari, but failed to recover any of the captives alive. Mrs. White died from an arrow wound to her chest at the onset of the soldiers' charge into the Indian camp. The fate of the missing infant and servant remains a mystery. (Barry, 885) Another detachment of U.S. troops had meanwhile traveled eastward on the Santa Fe Trail in hopes of recovering the missing people. This force took along Lobo's daughter so she could conduct negotiation with her people or be exchanged for the prisoners. Near Las Vegas, however, a soldier killed her, reportedly during an escape attempt. (Tiller, 35)

The Jicarilla's military resistance along the trail and elsewhere continued for a few more years. The strengthening of the U.S. military presence in New Mexico and Colorado, along with the construction of Fort Union in 1851 near the spot where the mountain and dry routes of the trail converged, made it untenable and too costly for them to fight back. Consequently, for the first time in their history, they slipped under the domination of colonization. It would not be until the 1880s, however, that the U.S. government would establish a reservation for them.

Although attrition ultimately wore down the Pawnees and Jicarillas, other Indians maintained the capacity and will to resist foreign domination. However, the U.S. Congress, with its Kansas-Nebraska Act of 1854, created unprecedented social, economic, and political problems for many Indians, irrespective of their political status, by opening the plains for white American settlement. With incoming homesteaders flowing into Kansas and gold seekers rushing into Colorado, demands echoed loudly, calling for the removal, if not extermination, of Indians. This phase of the white American invasion caused another downturn in the quality of Indian life as the newcomers ruthlessly slaughtered buffalo, occupied lands, and killed people. With emigrants bringing suffering, hardships, and even death to Indians, conflict erupted once again along the trail and elsewhere. In 1857, Southern Cheyennes, for the first time, briefly took up arms against U.S. expansionism in a move that reversed their longstanding policy of trade and peaceful coexistence with white Americans. In doing so, they faced the specter of injury and death common in warfare. Years later, George Bent, the son of a founder of Bent's Fort and a Cheyenne woman, explained the Cheyennes' disadvantage in terms of firearms: "The Cheyennes had very few guns in those days and most of these weapons were cheap, short-rage smooth-bores. Our warriors had never had a fight with troops, and now they were to meet more their own number of cavalry, all armed with carbines, pistols, and sabers." (Hyde, 102-03) More fighting erupted in subsequent years.

During the 1860s, Comanches, Kiowas, Plains Apaches, Cheyennes, Sioux and Arapahos united militarily in retaliation for the massacre of friendly Cheyennes, Arapahos, and Kiowas at Sand Creek. This fighting was an essential part of a large effort by them to maintain their freedom and ways of living. (Hyde, 137-222) As usual, the Santa Fe Trail became an epicenter of the warfare. With the fighting causing deaths, property destruction, and travel delays for their citizens, U.S. officials launched a massive military build up to protect their citizens and to squash Indian resistance. (Oliva, 161)

Facing overwhelming odds, these freedom fighters relied on their mobility to strike blows and evade pursuit, but the fighting took a heavy toll on them. In 1867, U.S. agents lured thousands of Cheyennes, Arapahos, Comanches, Kiowas, and Plains Apaches to Medicine Lodge Creek for a treaty council where they reluctantly agreed to remove themselves to reservations in Indian Territory. Although these people moved to the reservations, outbreaks of warfare continued until the mid 1870s when the combined weight of U.S. expansionism and military might not only have broken their resistance but also stripped them of their independence. Meanwhile, U.S. pressure had pushed the Pawnees, Kaws, and Osages onto reservations in Indian Territory. These southward movements virtually ended Plains Indian contact with the Santa Fe Trail.

The Pueblo Indians

In New Mexico, historical factors created another political reality for the Pueblo Indians in terms of their relations with the Santa Fe Trail. Living along the Rio Grande and its tributaries in several dozen towns on all sides of Santa Fe, these Indigenous peoples had varying degrees of contact with the trail. Given such names as Taos, Pecos, Santa Ana, Santo Domingo, San Felipe, Tesuque, San Juan, and Nambe, each of these Pueblo towns was in reality a distinct political entity with its own government, institutions, and lands. They shared a common culture. They had experienced the heavy hand of foreign domination since the late 1500s. Under these circumstances, they mostly experienced a cooperative association with the trail and its travelers. An exception to this general rule is the participation of Taos Indians in an 1847 uprising against U.S. domination.

Accounts indicate that the crews of some caravans, whether originating in New Mexico or Missouri, included one or more Pueblos. (Gregg, 206-07) At times, some of them participated in trail activities in the capacity of military escorts in conjunction with Mexican soldiers. Perhaps more commonly, Pueblos were also an agricultural people who supplied travelers with fruits and vegetables in Santa Fe. They also sold pottery and woven blankets. (James, 110-11; Gregg, 183-84) Perhaps because so many of them spoke Spanish in addition to their native tongues, white Americans often referred to them as Mexican Indians.

Situated about twenty-five miles from Santa Fe on the banks of the Pecos River and east of the Sangre de Cristo Mountains, Pecos Pueblo was the only pueblo located directly adjacent to the trail. For centuries, Pecos, the eastern most pueblo, had been a prominent trading center that linked the pueblos with the Plains Indians. However, because of the destabilizing effects of Spanish colonialism and disease, its inhabitants would not become central participants in the Santa Fe trade.

Four U.S. travelers made written reference to Pecos people during the 1820s and 1830s. While en route to Santa Fe in November 1821, Becknell's party passed through the town, which he referred to as St. Baw. (White, 2:65) In a brief journal entry, Becknell merely indicated that Mexican Indians had built it. Later that month, another Santa Fe bound party including Thomas James stayed overnight within the deteriorating walls of the old pueblo. Recalling this experience about twenty years later, he declared that the town, which he called *Pecca*, stood as proof of the Indians' advancement "in the arts of civilization before the Spaniards came among them." (James, 80-81) Referring to the reception his party received, he stated: "The inhabitants, who are all Indians, treated us with great kindness and hospitality." (James, 81) James also noted the repressiveness of the Mexico's law on them:

> "In the evening, I employed an Indian to take my horses to pasture, and in the morning when he brought them up I asked him what I should pay him. He asked for powder and I was about to give him some, when the Spanish [Mexican?] officer forbade me, saying it was against the law to supply the Indians with ammunition. Arms are kept out of their hands by their masters who prohibit all trade in those articles with any of the tribes around them." (James, 81)

James's account indicates the fear held by Mexican colonizers for armed Indians.

In 1834, Albert Pike, a traveler in a caravan under Charles Bent, made one of the last written records of an inhabited Pecos Pueblo. His description tells of a town standing on the verge of extinction. "In the Pecos tribe," Pike wrote, "there were not more than fifteen to twenty men." (Pike, 152) In 1838, the nineteen survivors moved westward, taking up residence at Jemez Pueblo. Although incorporated into Jemez society, the descendants of Pecos Pueblo continue to acknowledge a connection to their ancestral home through family genealogies, oral histories, and ceremonies.

Six years after the Pecos's move, in *Commerce of the Prairies* Josiah Gregg, who had visited the pueblo on several occasions when its population ranged from fifty to a hundred individuals, offered a terse, if not romantic, view of its inhabitants. He asserted that travelers often saw them "standing here and there like so many statues upon the roofs of their houses, their eyes fixed on the eastern horizon, or leaning against a wall or a fence, listlessly gazing at the passing stranger." (Gregg, 180)

Standing empty and deteriorating from the twin effects of the weather and scavenging travelers and settlers, Pecos became a famous trail landmark that evoked speculative assertions about its origins. A commonly held misconception among trail travelers and New Mexico residents alike held fancifully that the former inhabitants were descendents of Montezuma and they had a spiritual obligation to keep their sacred fire burning until his return. (Gregg, 178-80) Travelers echoed versions of this mythology for several generations.

Meanwhile, situated in north-central New Mexico west of the mountain branch of the Santa Fe Trail, Taos Pueblo provided participants in various trail activities. Their experiences included danger, conflict, and death. In June 1822, two of them accompanied James' westbound caravan. At Cow Creek in Kansas, a thousand Pawnees confronted James' party. Describing the encounter, James asserted that the Pawnees wanted to scalp the "Mexican" Indians but that the Pawnee "chief" used his influence to safeguard the endangered men. This unnamed leader, perhaps Saritaris's brother, also protected other members of James's party from harm by upholding a promise of peace his brother had given to the Great Father the previous year. (James, 110-11) Although James did not acknowledge it, this incident demonstrates that Pawnees did not share a common attitude about how they should deal with intruders.

Several years later, New Mexico officials wanted to end their war with Pawnees. In particular, the expansion of Mexican settlement into the Pecos River valley sparked bouts of violence with these plains peoples. In Santa Fe, New Mexico governor José Antonio Vizcarra, lacking the manpower to deploy a large military force against them because of his province's warfare against Navajo resisters, turned to a diplomatic solution in hopes of stopping the Pawnee raids. Accepting a U.S. government invitation to attend a peace council with Pawnee leaders, a delegation of fourteen Mexicans and twelve [Pueblo?] Indians departed Santa Fe on August 11, 1824, en route to a U.S. military post named Fort Atkinson situated on the banks of the Missouri River near the mouth of the Platte River. On September 12, chiefs from the four-confederated Pawnee nations apparently consented to live in peace with New Mexico and not to interfere with the flow of trail traffic.

The supposed feelings of peaceful co-existence stemming from the peace council and treaty passed quickly. Several weeks later a Pawnee force overwhelmed and disarmed a small group of New Mexico hunters who had apparently encroached on Pawnee hunting lands. Before releasing their prisoners, the Pawnees returned the weapon of a man who had been present at the Fort Atkinson treaty council. It is unclear if this man was a Mexican or an Indian.

Meanwhile, Mexico occasionally pressured Pueblos into active military service, placing them in harm's way without adequate arms and training. In 1829, Lieutenant Colonel José Antonio Vizcarra, the former New Mexico governor, led a

Mexican army with forty Taos Indian allies eastward over the Santa Fe road en route for the U.S. border. Along the way, a force of Indians engaged the encroaching army, killing several soldiers. Among the dead was a Taos man who reportedly took a bullet meant for Vizcarra. In October, the Mexican army crossed the Arkansas and joined the U.S. troops for several days. Using stereotypical terms to describe the Taos men, Second Lieutenant Philip St. George Cooke wrote that "they resembled demons rather than men" and that one displayed grief "howling like a famished wolf." (Cooke, Scenes, 86-88) A career soldier, Cooke spent numerous years seeing duty on the trail.

In 1843, New Mexico's effort to repel a Republic of Texas plan to expand its borders into New Mexico in the early 1840s fell heavily on Taos Indians who were impressed into service to ward off the Texas invaders. A key phase of the Texan's initiative called for plundering a Mexican caravan en route to Missouri in the spring of 1843. In June, a detachment of Texans attacked an advance Mexican guard consisting of about a hundred men, mostly Taos Indians. In the ensuing route, the Texans killed twenty-three members of the Mexican force while wounding thirteen others. (Cooke, "Journal" 231, 238)

At Taos Pueblo, friends and relatives of the deceased viewed several neighboring white Americans with suspicion, believing them to be aligned with the belligerent Texans. Those lingering feelings, along with new resentment toward the U.S. invasion of New Mexico in August 1846, most assuredly encouraged many of them to participate in a popular rebellion against U.S. rule. At Taos on the morning of January 19 of the following year, a group of Indian and Mexican freedom fighters assassinated Charles Bent, the U.S. territorial governor, and other supporters of the U.S. occupation.

U.S. troops and civilians dispatched from Santa Fe and other places rushed to the scene. They planned to forcefully end the uprising, to avenge the American deaths, and to send a bloody message about the harsh consequences of armed resistance to the U.S. occupation of New Mexico. Having been routed in several battles, five hundred or more insurgents made a stand behind the walls of Taos Pueblo. Members of the punitive expedition besieged the town with barrages of cannon fire, destroying a thick-walled church holding many of the resisters and killing more than a hundred people and capturing about four hundred others. The assailants also cut down many of those who tried to reach the safety of the nearby mountains.

Justice was swift and unfair for many of the captives. In a martial law tribunal, U.S. authorities tried and convicted a number of them on the charges of treason or murder. At least twenty-eight condemned men died in a series of public hangings in the Taos Plaza. While incarcerated, Tomás Romero, a Taos Pueblo leader who had played a key role in the assassination of Bent and his cronies, lost his life to the hands of a murderous U.S. soldier who entered New Mexico with the Army of the West. (Gómez, 30-41)

Conversely, other pueblos of New Mexico mostly accepted life under U.S. domination. W. W. H. Davis provided his biased view of their adaptation, writing: "Since the close of the war with Mexico they [Pueblo Indians] have remained at peace with our government, and seem pleased with the change of masters. They are friendly in their feelings toward the Americans but have always manifested hostility to the Mexicans." (Davis, 138)

The Santa Fe Trail brought increasing numbers of white Americans into Pueblo country. Although unable or unwilling to challenge U.S. rule, notwithstanding the Taos Rebellion of 1847, the Pueblos steadfastly refused to abandon their revered values, beliefs, and customs in favor of those of the new colonizer.

The Displaced Indians

Living on conjoined reservations in eastern Kansas, Shawnee and Delaware peoples had extensive contact with the traffic. The trail, established a few years before the arrival of these peoples, transected Shawnee territory. Situated above the Shawnees' territory, Delaware lands were touched by the Overland Trail, a route that reached from Missouri to California and the Pacific Northwest that was founded in the early 1840s. Both of these peoples had previously been overwhelmed and lost their ability to resist white American expansion before their removal in the mid 1820s. In Kansas, economic and geographic considerations encouraged many of them to ally themselves with the United States. In doing so, they cooperated with U.S. officials, travelers, and traders and participated in various capacities involving the spread of U.S. hegemony over the land and its inhabitants.

On the reservation, some Shawnees reaped economic benefits from the dramatic increase in trail traffic that occurred in 1846. Apparently oblivious to the fact that a significant portion of the Shawnees sought to live a customary life, an observer described them as an industrious people who enjoyed the luxuries of "civilized" life. (Hughes, 30) Others used racial language to depict them as being half-civilized. Interestingly, the free and independent Pawnees considered them to be half white. Despite these unflattering characterizations, some Shawnee families sold the soldiers and other travelers en route to New Mexico such items as corn, potatoes, meat, and prepared meals. Pascal Fish owned a hotel and a ferry that transported wagons, property, supplies, and people across the Kansas River.

Shawnee and Delaware men often accepted employment as guides and hunters for wagon trains, exploratory parties, and the U.S. army. Some found work as teamsters while others made a living as independent hunters and trappers who traveled onto the plains and into the mountains to sustain themselves and their families by selling hides and pelts. Some worked at Bent's Fort on the upper Arkansas River. Delawares in particular served as guides and scouts with U.S. army units during the 1850s, occasionally fighting against the independent Indian nations on behalf of the colonizer. Some of them accompanied John C. Fremont and his expeditions to the far west in the 1840s and 1850s.

Yet, one should not get the erroneous impression that Shawnees and Delawares lived in perfect harmony with the trail and Euro-Americans. On occasion, travelers created conflict on the reservation by cutting timber and not preventing their livestock from invading the local inhabitants' cornfields. Travelers periodically transmitted such highly infectious and deadly diseases as smallpox and cholera to Indians. Fear of contacting these germs occasionally created panic among the Shawnees and Delawares. In 1847 at Taos, a Delaware known as Big Nigger supposedly sided with the Indian and Mexican insurgents who battled the occupying U.S. force sent to put down the rebellion.

Despite their service to the U.S. government and Santa Fe traders, the days of the Shawnees and Delawares in Kansas were numbered because of racial attitudes among the Euroamericans pouring into the region. Shortly after Congress opened Kansas for non-Indian settlement in 1854, incoming white American homesteaders began to advocate Indian land cessions and removal. By 1870, U.S. officials had removed the Shawnees and Delawares to Oklahoma.

Conclusion

Contrary to an axiom found in the master narrative about the hands of Indians being bloodied by the commission of senseless acts of violence against unoffending white Americans, Indians who had contact with the Santa Fe Trail were rational humans who had been pulled into a vortex of colonialism from which there was no escape. This setting brought Indians and non-Indians together in a series of contacts ranging from warfare to cooperation. Those Pueblos, Shawnees, and Delawares, who had previously lost their independence and ability to militarily resist foreign domination, generally had cooperative relations with the trail. Conversely, Pawnees, Comanches, Cheyennes, Jicarilla Apaches, and others who had possessed their freedom had mixed relations with the trail. As implied by Saritaris, this road (which was part of a larger process of expansionism) severely harmed Indian land tenure and life. By the late 1860s, U.S. expansionism had literally cleansed the trail of its surrounding Indian populations, with only the Pueblos retaining the ability to live on parts of their dramatically reduced homelands. These facts are the legacy of the Santa Fe Trail of Tears.

References:

Alvarez, Manuel. "Report of Manuel Alvarez, 1842." In *On the Santa Fe Trail*. Ed. Marc Simmons. Lawrence: University Press of Kansas, 1986, 6-10.

Barry, Louise. *The Beginning of the West: Annals of the Kansas Gateway to the American West, 1540–1854*. Topeka: Kansas State Historical Society, 1972.

Berthrong, Donald J. *The Southern Cheyennes*. Norman: University of Oklahoma Press, 1963.

Cooke, Philip St. George. "A Journal of the Santa Fe Trail." *Mississippi Valley Historical Review* 12 (September 1925): 227-55.

———. *Scenes and Adventures in the Army: or Romance of Military Life*. Philadelphia: Lindsay & Blakiston, 1857.

Chalfant, William Y. *Dangerous Passage: The Santa Fe Trail and the Mexican War*. Norman and London: University of Oklahoma Press, 1994.

Davis, W. W. H. *El Gringo; or, New Mexico and Her People*. New York: Arno Press, 1973.

Ferguson, R. Brian and Neil L. Whitehead. "The Violent Edge of Empire." *In War in the Tribal Zone: Expanding States and Indigenous Warfare*. Santa Fe: School of American Research Press and Oxford: James Curry, 1992, 1-30.

Garrard, Lewis H. *Wah-to-yah and the Taos Trail; or Prairie Travel and Scalp Dances, with a Look at Los Rancheros from Muleback, and the Rocky Mountain Campfire*. Norman: University of Oklahoma Press, 1973.

Gómez, Laura E. *Manifest Destinies: The Making of the Mexican American Race*. New York and London: New York University Press, 2007.

Gregg, Josiah. "Commerce of the Prairies:" *The Journal of a Santa Fé Trader*. Dallas: Southwest Press, 1933.

Hyde, George E. *Life of George Bent: Written from His Letters*. Ed. Savoie Lottenville. Norman: University of Oklahoma, 1968.

James, Thomas. *Three Years among the Indians and Mexicans*. Philadelphia and New York: J. B. Lippincott Company, 1962.

Howard, Bryan. *Wildest of the Wild West: True Tales of a Frontier Town on the Santa Fe Trail*. Santa Fe: Clear Light Publishers, 1988.

Hughes, John T. *Doniphan's Expedition on Account of the U.S. Army Operations in the Great American Southwest*. Chicago: Rio Grande Press, 1962.

Kappler, Charles, comp. and ed. *Indian Treaties, 1778–1883*. New York: Interland Publishing Inc., 1972.

Oliva, Leo E. *Soldiers on the Santa Fe Trail*. Norman: University of Oklahoma Press, 1967.

Morse, Jedidiah. *A Report to the Secretary of War of the United States on Indian Affairs*. New Haven: S. Converse, 1822.

Pike, Albert. *Prose Sketches and Poems Written in the Western Country*. Ed. David J. Weber. College Station: Texas A&M University Press, 1987.

Tiller, Veronica E. Velarde. *The Jicarilla Apache Tribe: A History*. Revised Edition. Albuquerque: BowArrow Publishing Company, 2000.

White, David A. *News of the Plains and Rockies, 1803–1865*. Vols. 1 and 2. Spokane: Arthur H. Clark Company, 1997.

6

"The Porch"
by
Kim Suina
Pueblo of Cochiti

Santa Fe's 400-year anniversary signifies the mark that Pueblos have made on the city's aesthetic and cultural ambiance—in fact, it is these characteristics that have attracted tourists for over one hundred years. Less explored is the integral role that Pueblos, especially those from villages in proximity to the city, have played in shaping the economic and social fabric of Santa Fe, and in turn, the city's impact on these villages as a source of economic subsistence and a place of cultural exchange. My grandma's story is but one of many stories of Pueblos, who ventured into Santa Fe with wares in-hand to earn a living.

One of my fondest childhood memories is sitting at my maternal grandma's house in Cochiti stringing corn necklaces. Barely old enough to wield a sewing needle between my tiny fingers, I would sit at the kitchen table with a cookie-sheet full of brightly colored corn kernels as the voices of Paul Harvey and other AM radio regulars heard during the late seventies and eighties resonated in the room. I would alternate between bright fuchsia and turquoise corn beads: "two pinks," "two blues," "two pinks," "two blues," and so on; other times I would stick to plain pink, blue, or any other color we had to choose from. Corn had to be punctured in just the right place, the tender spot near the center of the kernel, or we'd end up with wasted beads—the thread would rip right through the kernel if placed too close to the edge. Fingers colored by dye and sore from an occasional needle prick, I would inevitably turn to grandma for help upon completing a strand; I could not quite push the needle through the leather straps that would tie each end together, but grandma could. My brother, sisters, and I passed our summer days this way, making corn and other types of necklaces to sell under the

'Porch'—what is formally known as the *portal* at the Palace of the Governors in Santa Fe.

Grandma kept the bead supply constant. Like Easter eggs, corn kernels steeped in pots filled with various colored dyes on grandma's stovetop. For pigment she used Rit-brand dye or crepe paper streamers, the kind you see hanging at birthday parties. When she placed the crinkly streamers in hot water, the colors bled until the bottom of the pot barely remained visible. Blue streamers resulted in the truest version of turquoise blue, the quality of the precious stone we tried so hard to imitate. "Beads" included a rainbow of dyed corn kernels, melon seeds, and glass beads that she picked up from Santa Fe, Albuquerque, or Bernalillo—three cities within an hour drive of Cochiti, a Keresan-speaking village along the Rio Grande. Grandma usually bought a twenty-five pound sack full of dried white corn from the feed store in Bernalillo. Sometimes we alternated melon and glass beads, while other times we simply used glass beads in alternating colors to make long necklaces and chokers. We also made corn beaded bracelets, a favored item because they took so little time to make. When our hands got tired or when we decided it was time for play, we placed the colored corn into plastic bags for storage in the refrigerator.

For sale at the Porch, grandma also made pottery as well as beaded leather baby booties and purses, some with metal jingles. For consumption by other community members, she made shawls, traditional Indian dresses, and beaded leather pouches. I never asked her, but grandma likely learned to make all of these things from her mother or from other women in the village. The style of necklaces we strung depended on availability of supplies and demand from tourists in nearby Santa Fe. Sometimes chokers sold better than long necklaces and others times hot pink sold better than purple. We adjusted our output accordingly. At times, I wondered who bought our necklaces. When assembling beaded chokers, I usually envisioned young girls about my age as the target audience. As for the long necklaces, I assumed old Anglo ladies wore these things. I recall only a few occasions when grandma wore a corn necklace herself and my sisters and I never wore the chokers—we made these necklaces with tourists in mind.

The Porch played an important economic role in my grandma's life. Grandma sold on-and-off there throughout her life, until the 1980s when she was well into her seventies. When she started selling there is unclear; however, she had mentioned helping her own mother, notable watercolor painter, Tonita Peña, sell paintings at the Porch and to nearby galleries, likely during the 1920s or 1930s. Other members of her family also sold at the Porch.

Grandma's sister, who married a man from nearby Santo Domingo, sold jewelry and bread, and grandma's mother-in-law, who had developed quite a reputation as a trader, worked at the Porch and went on trading trips hundreds of miles away to

Gallup and beyond.[1] In addition to tourist dollars, grandma periodically brought home wages from babysitting and house cleaning for Santa Fe families, working in a curio shop and as a seamstress sewing fiesta dresses for Santa Fe girls and women. Meanwhile, grandpa worked as a taxi driver, deliveryman, tour guide, and silversmith. Grandma and grandpa lived in Santa Fe throughout the fifties and into the early sixties until community obligations called them back to Cochiti.

Grandma's day started early on the days she worked at the Porch. She would head up to Santa Fe before sunrise from her modest house overlooking the fields in Cochiti. Seating was assigned on a first come, first served basis so getting there early was important. Because she did not drive she had to catch a ride from other people in our village or from my mom. Cochiti is about a thirty-minute car ride to Santa Fe highlighted by a drive along the Bosque, a place that, if you catch it at the right time, before the winter frost sets in, glows with brilliant oranges and yellows. The trip also features a climb up La Bajada Hill, the imposing geographical landmark designated as the boundary separating the *Rio Abajo* (upper river) and the *Rio Arriba* (lower river) by the Spanish, who considered these two distinct regions. Depending on the era, grandma utilized multiple types of transportation, including horse and wagon, community-operated public transportation, and private vehicles. For those Pueblos who lived further from Santa Fe, especially in the years before technological improvements in travel, stints at the Porch were likely less frequent, if at all. In contrast, today Santa Fe is a place where many Pueblos work, buy their groceries, cash their checks, and visit the doctor.

Once grandma arrived in Santa Fe—however she managed to get there—she wasted no time securing her place at the Porch. She carefully displayed the items she and her grandchildren had hand made on a cloth in front of her, and rested on a milk crate or wooden stool with her back rested against the white washed walls. Alone, or sometimes with mom, she sat next to other Indian women and men, Pueblos and Navajos most commonly, hoping to sell a necklace here, a beaded coin purse there. As they do today, vendors sold a wide variety of art work, crafts, and food: pottery, shell and silver jewelry, a variety of beaded necklaces, leather items, woven items, sand paintings, drawings, paintings, drums, oven bread, pies, biscochitos, and tamales. The portal overhead offered solace to grandma and other vendors nestled below from relentless summer heat, summer cloudbursts, and winter snowfalls that are common to Santa Fe, a city cradled by the Sangre de Cristo Mountains.

The Palace of the Governors, aka "The Porch," has a long and colorful history. Dating back to the early 1600s, the Palace is the oldest continuously occupied public building in the United States and is listed on the National Register of Historic Places. Originally an outpost for the Spanish colonial government, the historic building is now part of a museum and educational complex dedicated to New Mexico history and culture, with the New Mexico History Museum being the most recent addition. Whether the *portal* was part of the original structure is unclear. Currently, the Palace of the Governors is a Pueblo Revival style building occupying an entire block on the north side of the Santa Fe plaza. Each end of the portal overlooking the plaza is anchored with bastions and built-in adobe *bancos* or benches and interspersed with wooden posts. For Pueblos, the significance of the Palace of the Governors shifted over time. Although now a place of economy, in the past the Palace served as a stronghold for an, at times, oppressive Spanish colonial regime. Pueblos defiantly occupied and transformed the building and its surroundings into a "pueblo" after ousting the Spanish in 1680 during the Pueblo Revolt. They remained there until 1693 when the Spanish took back the building, punished Pueblo resisters, and reasserted their authority.[2]

The Palace of the Governors has been a central meeting place for Pueblo vendors and tourists alike. In the late 1800s and early 1900s, cultural tourism emerged as a viable source of income as Pueblo farming communities faced the impacts of drought, land dispossession, and the transition from barter to a cash economy. The federal government recognized the importance of this industry to Indian livelihood with the passage of the *Indian Arts and Crafts Act of 1935*, a measure regulating the production and sale of Indian arts and crafts. Historically, the vendor population had been comprised of members primarily from New Mexico's nineteen Pueblos, with those from villages closer to Santa Fe dominating in number. At first glance, tourists, and perhaps even locals, might have felt sorry for grandma and others like her, as they sat on the sidewalk peddling their wares, but earnings from the Porch have been an invaluable source of income for Pueblo families throughout much of the twentieth century. The venue offered grandma and others direct access to tourists and the informal nature of such a vocation allowed for flexibility in schedule that other jobs did not, an important requirement for the average Pueblo person whose life is dominated by a calendar full of activities and celebrations that help maintain group cohesion and make us unique as Pueblo peoples.

Although informal in some respects, trade at the Porch does have its rules and regulations. The Porch has operated as an all-Indian marketplace since its inception. All items sold there are Indian handmade, with stricter criteria now requiring vendors to demonstrate their craft for program organizers to verify knowledge of technique and use of materials. Current rules also forbid vendors from wholesaling their work. Before such rules were put into place, grandma sold corn necklaces for wholesale to curio shops around the plaza even though she did not earn nearly as much as she did when she sold directly to tourists. Her own young children, including my mother, helped her string corn necklaces. One exceptionally large order required that she and the kids string thirty-six dozen corn necklaces. As kids do, they turned the monotonous task of filling wholesale orders into a competition, racing to see who could complete the most necklaces.

Despite changes in rules governing the program, throughout its existence the basic setup of the portal market has remained remarkably consistent. Vendors still sit lined up against the Palace walls with their wares placed on the ground in front of them, while customers still stand, separated by an ocean of cloth dotted with islands of turquoise and coral. Any romantic notions that tourists might harbor about Native Americans are likely dashed when they arrive at the Porch to find Pueblo vendors wearing T-shirts, jeans, and sneakers, with the glimpse of an occasional *chongo* (traditional Pueblo hair bun) wearing or moccasin-clad vendor in the mix. Grandma went to the Porch wearing one of her usual selections of calico printed dresses bound by a traditional red, green, and black woven belt as well as a folded bandana tied at the nape of her neck covering all but a few strands of hair. She usually topped off this look with a checked apron. For grandma, an apron was not only for cooking, but a great place for storing Kleenex, a spare safety pin, or an orphan button.

Grandma left us kids at home where we eagerly anticipated our earnings from her day at the Porch. We did not get to go with grandma because by this time, sadly, kids were restricted. In previous years, grandma and mom bundled up my then baby brother to sit at the Porch, but by the late 1970s a new rule requiring vendors to be at least eighteen years of age meant that children could no longer go.[3] Up until then, the multi-generational makeup of the Porch population included children entrusted with the grownup task of attending to customers and closing sales. When grandma and grandpa lived in Santa Fe they sent their own three youngest children to the Porch while she stayed home cranking out items to sell the next day. For extra money, the two boys also shined shoes. At lunchtime, she usually sent grandpa to deliver homemade tamales, fried potatoes, tortillas, or any other foods rounding out her repertoire. On rare occasions grandma and grandpa allowed the kids to indulge on a "twin-cronies," a grilled hotdog cut in half, placed in a hamburger bun and smothered with red chile, or a Frito pie, a favorite New Mexican dish consisting of red chile beans, cheese, and corn chips. Generally, however, every penny had to be saved.

By the time the Porch started operating as a regular market in the 1930s under the direction of the Museum of New Mexico, Pueblos had been selling to tourists for years. On well-traveled pathways, at railroad stops and on the shoulders of the highway, vendors sought face-to-face contact with buyers. Beginning in the 1880s, Pueblo vendors set up shop at train stops hoping to catch the eye of tourists in search of keepsakes from the Southwest. Tourism in New Mexico expanded and flourished with the construction of Route 66 in 1926. In rare cases, Pueblos became the tourists themselves, visiting World's Fairs and expositions in cities like Chicago and San Francisco to demonstrate the arts and crafts of their supposedly perishing cultures. Selling at the Porch during popular multicultural gatherings, like the Santa Fe Fiesta and during weekend fairs, provided grandma and other Pueblos opportune moments to supplement the village economy. The Fiesta was, and remains, one of northern New Mexico's more popular cultural events. The first modern-day Santa Fe Fiesta, a three-day event commemorating Diego de Vargas's 1692 reconquest of New Mexico, took place in 1911. The Museum of New Mexico established the Indian Arts and Crafts Fair in 1922, to coincide with the Santa Fe Fiesta, an event that drew Pueblo artists and laid the roots for the modern day Santa Fe Indian Market. After the Fair took a hiatus for a few years, vendors resumed selling under the Porch during the 1936 Fiesta, the same year that a writer for the New Mexico Association of Indian Affairs, Maria Chabot, inspired by Mexican open markets, organized a series of Saturday markets at the Porch featuring the works of artists from different Pueblos each week. Support from the Museum of New Mexico for a full-time portal program where vendors could sell their wares occurred sometime in the 1930s.[4]

The Porch's popularity as a workplace for Pueblos fluctuated throughout the years. A noticeable boom in the number of vendors vying for limited spaces occurred at the height of the Santa Fe Fiesta and again during the late 1970s and the early 1980s when the demand for Indian arts and crafts experienced an upswing. Vendors slept under the Porch to reserve highly coveted spaces for the next day. The Museum of New Mexico addressed this issue by assigning spaces and later implementing a lottery program to assure their orderly assignment if the number of vendors exceeded the number of spaces.[5]

Time spent at the Porch was not all work. Vendors passed the hours socializing with other vendors, locals, and tourists. In addition to locals, grandma met people from other parts of the country. Some of these relationships continued beyond the world of the Porch and in her usual gesture of friendship, she invited these people to eat at her house on Cochiti feast day and other celebrations throughout the year. One woman from Missouri, who grandma and mom met at the Porch in the early 1970s, became a dear family friend and still visits Cochiti once a year. Grandma also utilized time at the Porch to run errands while my mom or a neighboring vendor watched her spot. Sometimes she'd run to the Five and Dime to check something off her shopping list or to La Fonda, an historic hotel in downtown Santa Fe, to use the ladies room.

When she finally got home from the Porch, she'd unpack her tote bag. Out of it came those items that had not sold that day, and more importantly, a plastic sandwich bag filled with coins, dollars, and a steno pad or scrap piece of paper penciled with a meticulous accounting of sales. In scribbled cursive she kept track of what she had sold that day. She used to sell corn necklaces for a few dollars or less depending on style. After she handed us money, we usually made a beeline for the only store in the village, a few thousand dusty steps away from grandma's front door. There, we lined the store owner's pockets with the few coins and dollars we had received from grandma, while our pockets overflowed with hastily unwrapped Bazooka Joe bubble gum wrappers and comic strips. Allowed to keep most of our profits, we weren't burdened with financially supporting our family as had generations of children before us. By this time, grandpa had passed and grandma relied on income from social security and earnings from her arts and crafts sales.

In her late nineties, grandma took to stringing various colored plastic pony beads onto precut leather straps, a "hobby" that she had picked up at the elderly center. No corn to be colored, no needles to be maneuvered, and no earnings to be made, but with crooked yet determined hands she earnestly strung beads. After spending a lifetime doing so, I assumed it brought her comfort in her old age.

Grandma, like other Pueblos, toiled away at her craft and sat for countless hours at the Porch to support her family. Creative and innovative, these Pueblos followed the market and paid close attention to trends, catering their arts and crafts to appeal to buyers while maintaining traditions integral to their communities for hundreds of years.

"A Living Exhibition"
Labor, Desire, and the Marketing of American Indian Arts and Crafts in Santa Fe
by
Matthew J. Martinez
Pueblo of Ohkay Owingeh

This chapter discusses the producing and selling of American Indian art to better understand how artists negotiate their position as laborers in a sea of tourism. As the oldest capital in the United States, Santa Fe, New Mexico is steeped in history with the plaza being the focal point for both commerce and social life. Despite its status as producer and vendor of art, the tourism industry in Santa Fe continues to market American Indians in the plaza as "living exhibits." Multiple publics and spaces provide a unique site of analysis for interpreting labor and contemporary experiences of indigenous peoples as producers and vendors of art.

Introduction

Studies of North American Indian[1] economic life have largely ignored the participation of indigenous peoples in the labor market.[2] This essay examines a contemporary example of American Indian labor through interviews conducted with American Indian artists at the Santa Fe plaza. The study of labor provides a unique site of analysis for understanding American Indian communities not commonly captured in the stereotypical image making of the Southwest. This analysis also examines a paradox: American Indians on the one hand are encouraged as individuals to be part of the entrepreneurial spirit in being self sufficient by making a living, while at the same time, policies are crafted so that

American Indians and their artwork are marketed to perpetuate a notion of a "living past." Natives of the Southwest continue in the nation's imagination as artisans, as living relics of the past, and as performers of spiritually authentic rituals. In fact, the New Mexico Board of Tourism continues to market the state as "America's Land of Enchantment" and tourism materials continue to feature stereotypical images of dancers in traditional "Indian" regalia. (Martinez, 2008)

This research draws upon the emerging literature of global ethnography as presented in Michael Burawoy's *Global Ethnography (2003)*. Burawoy's work discusses the dynamics of local struggles and global forces. The examination of local struggles, undertaken by American Indian artists as laborers, brings a new understanding of global forces that are transcended in tourist markets. Through the process of this research I explore the impact of tourism on indigenous art markets and the role local American Indian artists facilitate as laborers. In addition, a central question guiding this work is how can the study of everyday life, through work, provide an understanding of processes that transcend national boundaries? My project is grounded in local communities, but with a lens toward examining international art markets and federal policies. My task is to assemble a picture of American Indian labor by recognizing diverse perspectives and forces through connected sites. As someone who grew up in northern New Mexico, I have always been interested in how our pueblo communities and people interact with the traffic of culture. The goal of this essay is to present a greater understanding of the role Indigenous peoples play as laborers in a sea of tourism, which has not been documented in the larger discussion of Santa Fe's historical place.

Travel and Desire in the Southwestern Imagination

American Indians have always been central to the imagining of the Southwest. To visitors over the last century, Pueblos, Navajos, and Apaches seemed to be "exotic, primitive people" who lived sufficiently in a harsh but beautiful and captivating landscape. This image making in the Southwest was promulgated by social scientists, in the fields of anthropology and history to capture the experiences of a vanishing race, as well as by entrepreneurs of the tourism industry. The iconography of representations presented images of Natives as ruins, ritualists, and artisans; that is, American Indians were represented as people doomed to vanish or as living relics of the past, as performers of colorful ceremonies, and as makers of pots, baskets, and jewelry. (Dilworth 1996; Lyman 1982)

Leah Dilworth's *Imagining Indians in the Southwest (1996)* examines this phenomenon of how Southwestern Indians evolved into the non-Indian American imagination from a "vanishing race" into the ideal American artist. *Imagining Indians* attempts to understand the cultural circumstances that made this transformation possible and shows that "cultural primitivism," as practiced in the Southwest by non-Indians at the turn of the century, has had lasting social and cultural implications. Dilworth marks the 1880s as the starting point of Euro-American migration to the Southwest. The interest in the region increased due to the development of the railroads such as the Atchison, Topeka and Santa Fe. Travel entrepreneurs made it their business to represent indigenous cultures to people outside of the region. The Southwest became known as a place of the unique, the handmade, the rural, and the authentic. (Weigle and Babcock, 1996)

In tourist literature, as well as the early ethnography of the region, the Southwest was often compared to the biblical Orient. (McLuhan, 1985) Americans were told that they need not journey to distant lands when ancient ruins, magnificent landscapes, and exotic peoples existed within their nation's own borders. (Lummis, 1893) This regionalist, and nationalist, rhetoric was often similar to the discourse of Oriental-ism. Barbara Babcock *(1990)* has written that "the Southwest is America's Orient," and Marta Weigle *(1990)* has called the development of the region's cultural distinctiveness "Southwestern-ism." Both scholars identify conceptions of the "primitive" as crucial to constructing and maintaining the Southwest as an "Other" to the nation.

By 1885 the pueblos[3] were accessible by rail from both coasts. Before the mid 1890s, tourism was not a major concern. Soon, at the turn of the twentieth century, cash economies developed on all the southwestern reservations. Apaches worked for wages in the mines and for the railroads. Also, many Navajos and Pueblos worked for the railroads since the 1880s and at other wage-labor positions in towns such as Albuquerque and Santa Fe. Laguna Pueblo is perhaps the best known pueblo for its contribution to railroad history and their role as laborers in the development of the Southwest. (Peters, 1996) The rise of arts and crafts coincided with railroad history. Soon markets developed for crafts such as silver work, basketry, pottery, and blankets. Before 1890, Navajos did not make silver for sale to travelers. (Adair, 1944) The Fred Harvey Company got into the business of providing precut turquoise stones and silver to the traders, who then gave it along with design specifications to Navajo silversmiths to make into jewelry. By the 1920s the manufacture of "Indian" jewelry was a huge business and was conducted by non-American Indians in Gallup, Santa Fe and other surrounding travel destinations. To meet the demand and to earn wages, Navajo women began to make silver jewelry. The Pueblos along the Rio Grande learned silversmithing from the Navajos, but it was not commercialized to the same extent among the pueblos until well after the 1920s when demand for silver jewelry increased. (Adair, 1944)

In the 1920s guidebooks began to include information on how to find and appreciate the pueblos. (Martinez, 2008) Representations of American Indian life in the Southwest began to appear in all of the railway's promotional literature. Increasingly, American Indian crafts appeared not only in museums and at exhibitions, but also in department store windows, train stations, and in homes across the nation. Outside markets began to determine the sorts of American Indian crafts that were produced. Baskets, pots, rugs and silver jewelry were by far the items most in demand. This was perhaps due to the fact that they could easily find a place in American households as utilitarian as well as decorative items. (Dilworth, 1996)

The introduction of tourist markets changed the production of Pueblo pottery. Traditionally, Pueblo potters did not sign their pots. It is known that pottery makers did not sign their work until after 1920. The first potter to do so was Maria Martinez of San Ildefonso Pueblo (Ibid). Maria Martinez quickly became known as *the* Pueblo potter who traveled extensively demonstrating her artwork to American audiences. As pottery became more valuable, buyers and collectors wanted to know who made the artwork. The identification of some artisans as especially talented made their works more valuable in price. Maria Martinez, it is said, would sign the works of other potters in her village because having her signature on pottery brought higher prices. (Marriott, 1948)

When non-American Indians began collecting indigenous made items, it was generally enough for collectors to be able to identify them by the tribal group. But gradually, collectors demanded to know which individuals made each item and signing became necessary. As the ethnic market developed, quality could be assured by "buying a brand name." Signatures lent authenticity to objects, and American Indian artisans began to be recognized as individual artists. (Dilworth, 1996) This was a significant paradigm shift in the way American Indian families and individuals viewed artwork. For Anglo American desires, the historical practice of signing and ownership was secondary in nature.

The process of signing a name on an object, therefore signifying a sense of ownership, quickly became the norm regardless if the labor involved more than one person. This was usually the case among the Pueblos. For example, one family member would be responsible for gathering and straining the clay and another would mold the clay in a bowl or vase formation. At times, several family members may put their designs on the pot. And firing the pottery was almost always a communal effort. Another dramatic change among the pueblos was the practice of pots and baskets becoming less utilitarian. No longer were pots quite as common to cook and store food. The increasing trend toward the marketing of "Indianness" to be displayed in galleries and homes across the country created the contemporary fine art industry. Tessie Naranjo writes that "Western economics (money) determines, more and more, why and how pottery is made." (Naranjo, 1996, p.195)

In addition to women laborers who were hired to be Harvey Girls, the 1920s and 1930s marked a dramatic increase of East Coast women who migrated to Santa Fe. Artists such as Georgia O'Keeffe became influential figures who carved out artist colonies in New Mexico. In addition, elite East Coast women turned to the Southwest in search of an alternative to European-derived concepts of culture. Women such as Elizabeth White, Mabel Dodge Luhan and Margretta Dietrich had a major hand in creating American Indian art markets, fairs and festivals in Santa Fe. (Mullin, 2001)

Contested Policies and Spaces

With the above -described historical backdrop, Santa Fe, New Mexico is a prime location for understanding contemporary tourism and its impact on indigenous communities. As one visitor stated, "[T]he city's economy feeds an unending diet of traditional Indian and Hispanic art, architecture, food, and ceremonies. This gives the place a sense of colonial Williamsburg or Disneyland. I feel downtown Santa Fe is like a theme park" says Lee More, 26, an executive assistant. (Clifford, 1997, C2) Comments like these by this visitor to New Mexico are quite common. Travelers to New Mexico want to get away and explore the out of the ordinary of their daily life routines. Even more importantly, buying artwork becomes essential as souvenirs and memories of travels to the Land of Enchantment.

Within the last century, American Indian art and culture have taken on new transformations in style and imagery and have become increasingly popular items in the international market and mass media. Santa Fe is a city that thrives on Indigenous culture for the sustainability of the economy and the proud promotion of the trendy art capital of the Southwest that captivates over 2 million visitors each year. The Santa Fe plaza attracts tourists because of its multiple venues available to buy indigenous art, food and style. Santa Fe is more than a place to buy and sell indigenous art but an economically important workplace for indigenous peoples as it supports hundreds of families throughout New Mexico. (Hoerig, 2003)

According to a report by the U.S. Department of the Interior, in 2000 the Indian arts and crafts industry became a billion-dollar industry in the United States. As a result of this profitable industry, the rise of fake and imitation art has become an epidemic. The U.S. Customs and Border Patrol (CBP) has estimated that an average of $30 million in Indian-style arts and crafts is imported annually from countries such as the Philippines, Mexico, Thailand, Pakistan, and China. These imports, combined with domestically produced imitations, represent an estimated $400 to $500 million in revenue. *(U.S. Department of the Interior 2005)* As one artist states, "[T]here is a huge demand for Native American arts and crafts, but you try and sell your work, it's difficult because you're competing against all these cheap fakes—it's frustrating". (Gibson, 1990, p.16) So says Loren Panteah, a jeweler of Zuni, New Mexico, where up to 85 percent of the working population rely on arts and crafts as their primary or secondary incomes. Furthermore, "of the estimated $1 billion annual Indian arts and crafts market in the United States, up to half of the products being sold are believed to be fakes or illegally reproduced works". (Gibson, 1990, p.17)

The rising popularity and economic benefits of American Indian art is apparent when, for example, a United States manufacturer set up a factory in the Philippines in the 1980s and persuaded the locals to rename their village Zuni, after the Zuni tribe in New Mexico. *(Deutsche Presse-Agentur 1998)* Appallingly, factories in the Philippines are now able to stamp their imitation American Indian art as "Made in Zuni." Developing nations are continuously setting up factories to cash in on "Indian" arts and crafts. For example, the Brazilians, Nigerians and Pakistanis weave copies of Apache, Navajo and Pima baskets. Mexicans weave imitation Navajo blankets. Chinese carve Zuni-type animal fetishes. Thai workers make imitation jewelry by sometimes using blue plastic instead of turquoise stones. Filipino workers specialize in Hopi kachina dolls as well as Zuni inlaid jewelry. (Brooke 1997; *U.S. Department of the Interior Office of Inspector General 2005*)

To alleviate such problems of misrepresentation, the Indian Arts and Crafts Act of 1990 was signed into law. The goal of this act was to provide hefty financial and criminal penalties for fake American Indian art. (*U.S. Department of the Interior Office of Inspector General 2005*) However, enforcement of the Act is problematic because of vague policy wording and the lack of support from government agencies. The federal law designed to protect American Indian artists is practically unenforceable. Since the 'Act' first passed in 1935, the law has only been used to bring indictments in the past 70 years; and, there has never been a civil or criminal conviction. (Ibid) The Act *(1990)* also defined an Indian as "any individual who is a member of an Indian tribe, or for the purposes of this section, is certified as an Indian artisan by an Indian tribe." The term "tribe" includes those recognized federally or by state legislature. In short, an American Indian artist is mandated by federal law to provide proof of tribal enrollment in order to market art made by the individual. An American Indian artist can only make the type of art of a tribe in which he or she is an enrolled or recognized member.

This Act further established the Indian Arts and Crafts Board with the power to determine who is and who is not an official American Indian artist, which makes the misrepresentation of oneself or one's art as "Indian" a criminal offense. (Josephy, Nagel, and Johnson, 1999) The passage of the Indian Arts and Crafts Act had some dramatic results with artists panicking to find or rediscover their tribal identity.

American Indians are the only ethnic group in the United States who are mandated by federal law to "prove" their identity. By not proving their identity, American Indians are easily dismissed from participating in art shows, educational benefits, health care, and various other governmental programs. The process of defining Indianness varies from tribe to tribe. There is no uniform policy. Furthermore, the majority of American Indians are participating in exogamous marriages and this further problematizes identity since tribes and the federal government continue to restrict tribal enrollment through a certain percentage of blood quantum. (Wilkins, 2002) The complexity of American Indian identity is much too lengthy for a thorough analysis to be included in the scope of this essay. Suffice it to say that indigenous identity is ever evolving in relation to federal government policies.

A Living Exhibition

The Native American Vendors Program art market at the Palace of the Governors is Santa Fe's most popular tourist attraction. Known as the Portal Program for its location under the front *portal*, or porch, the program is under the direction of the Museum of New Mexico. Here, the Portal Program supports hundreds of American Indian artists who sell to millions of visitors each year. (Hoerig, 2003) Because of the program's high profile, it is familiar to almost everyone who has visited Santa Fe. Images of the portal along with the vendors appear on postcards, T-shirts, and in tourist literature. All of the tour buses stop in front of the portal to purchase artwork. This also gives tourists a prime opportunity to photograph "real" American Indians in public.

The display of indigenous peoples by imperial powers was practiced in the nineteenth and twentieth centuries, forming a basis for many of the world's great museums. Living displays found their widest expression in the World's Fairs. Historically, American Indians were central to World's Fairs and staged as tributes to industrial progress and celebrations of power. The placement of indigenous peoples in displays located them at various points down the "evolutionary ladder" of social and racial progress. According to Benedict (1983), the display of people has much to do with power relations between the displayers and the displayed. The Museum of New Mexico's Native American Vendors Program is not all that different from conventional museum practices—the exception being that now American Indians have the opportunity to interact and converse with the public. In the Portal Program, American Indian artists are readily accessible to tourists who can purchase directly from the artists. The Portal Program thrives on the notion that tourists can be confident in their purchase of handmade American Indian arts and crafts. The vendors are also strong advocates of rules protecting their artwork. The task for the

Portal Program is to maintain traditional American Indian art that is also guided by federal policies—an added strain when confronted with the influx of imitation Indian art.

To be a vendor in the program, American Indians must be from a New Mexico tribe[4] or have some other connection (such as being married to someone enrolled from a New Mexico tribe), provide a Certificate of Indian Blood and have gone through an artist demonstration. The artist demonstration consists of showing the program that an individual actually does make the artwork, and uses "authentic material." Authentic in the program's vision is the use of actual turquoise stones, sterling silver and clay that is gathered locally. In addition, all artists must stamp their art with a unique maker's mark or sign their work. The vendors constantly undergo inspection for poor or questionable material. In addition, artists can only sell what they make and must display a permit with their name, tribal affiliation, and identification number while vending. (Palace of the Governors, 1999)

For most of the artists in the plaza this is a full time job. A lot of artists also send their family members to sell for the day (they too must go through the process of demonstrating their work) while some artists stay home and work on jewelry. This is not uncommon. I interviewed a husband and wife team who told me that she sells during the week and he stays home to work at the shop cutting stones and polishing. They switch on weekends and he goes to sell in Santa Fe, while she stays working on jewelry. This was a common practice among a lot of the artists to form a sort of "tag team" of vendors. Everett, a young Navajo man, and his mother took turns vending in the plaza and working at home on jewelry. This also occurs with potters. A Santa Clara vendor told me that he and his wife took turns going for clay, mixing, and polishing while one of them went to sell. The "tag-team" efforts are quite common and seem to be very successful for artists selling at the plaza.

Prior to the mid 1970s and 1980s there were no formal rules governing the sale of art in the Portal until the Supreme Court case *Livingston v. Ewing (1979)*, which challenged the idea of "Indians" vending in the plaza. The case involved Anglo immigrants from New York, Paul and Sara Livingston, who wanted to profit from the booming popularity of Indian arts and crafts. On numerous occasions, museum officials enlisted the aid of the state police to remove the non-Indians who would continuously return. The conflicts between vendors, Indians and non-Indians, led to a series of lawsuits and complaints. The museum and the program eventually prevailed in these suits; in the process an informal market became the Portal Program. (Hoerig, 2003) The case ultimately ruled that the Museum of New Mexico can be selective in permitting only American Indians because they are "protecting a valuable state interest, that of acquiring, preserving and exhibiting, archeological and ethnological interest in fine arts . . . It is thought that only Indians can make

Indian goods and therefore that is in the public interest to allow Indians to do it". (Livingston v Ewing, 1979)

In addition to vendors in the Portal Program, there are several American Indian artists and vendors set up around the plaza area who also travel to Santa Fe every day to work. These individuals are not connected with the Portal Program, and do not abide by the same rules and regulations as those in the program. They are often set up in front of hotels, galleries or the Cathedral area. The only requirement is that they need a city permit and permission from owners if they set up in front of a gallery. They mostly sell jewelry, such as silver bracelets, necklaces and earrings. Also, worthy of mention, in the context of global workers, is the rise of Mexican nationals who gather in the early morning off the plaza area in search of employment. It is common for construction companies, hotel and resort owners, and home owners in Santa Fe to pick up a day laborer. The plaza not only caters to high-end art buyers, but with the economic downturn in 2010, it continues to serve as a major work site for Indigenous peoples (American Indians and Mexicans) in search of earning a living wage.

Most of the Portal vendors have basically the same daily agenda. Each morning starting at 7:00 a.m., vendors begin to arrive at the plaza. They mark their space by putting down a cloth along the sidewalk in front of one of the 64 numbered spaces that line the wall of the Palace of the Governors. These artists come to the plaza from their homes in the surrounding pueblo villages, the Navajo reservation or from Albuquerque and Santa Fe for the opportunity to sell their artwork. It is not uncommon for artists to travel over an hour each way to Santa Fe. There are a total of 1002 enrolled vendors in the program. Not all artists choose to sell continuously but may only wish to sell during peak seasons such as Christmas or during summer months. If there are more vendors than spaces, which usually happens, then the program utilizes a lottery system. Each vendor then draws a number to get a space. Those who draw a number get to sell for the day and the others either go home or put their name on the waiting list to see if someone will leave by noon. Regardless of traveling to Santa Fe and passing a demonstration, vendors are constantly reminded that the committee does not guarantee them a space. Once vendors arrive at the plaza and get a space, they begin carefully unpacking and placing each piece of work on their rugs or blankets and polishing last minute silver pieces. Oftentimes some artists gather for morning coffee at a nearby coffee shop or the Five and Dime store. I have run into quite a few of the artists at these places where I met and talked with them about their work experience.[5]

The Portal vendors must set up their pieces on the brick surface, usually on a blanket or cloth, while other surrounding vendors in the plaza use a small table stand. The Portal Program prohibits "tables or elevated stands" for displaying of jewelry. (*Palace of the Governors, 1999*) The vendors now get to bring in their own chairs, which were previously prohibited by the program. Vendors also get to wear shorts in the summer, since this too was not allowed. Formerly, they could only wear jeans or dresses.[6] Artists usually sell until about 4:00p.m., depending on sales, while some go home by noon and give others a chance waiting to sell. Once they get home, most vendors continue to do some work whether that is polishing, beading, or firing pots in preparation for the next day. Most of the artists sell in the plaza full time, and at times participate in various markets throughout New Mexico and surrounding states. The largest and most prestigious art market is the Santa Fe Indian Market held annually in August which brings an estimated 80,000 visitors in one weekend. (Bernstein, 1993; Gibson, 2000)

The items sold in the Portal Program range widely from "traditional" forms of art such as silver and turquoise bracelets, necklaces, rings, small pottery, sand paintings, carvings and weavings, to not so traditional items such as sterling silver golf tees, guitar picks, money clips, and pink and turquoise tomahawks. Items also change themes depending on the time of year. Artists are well tuned to the pulse of the tourist season and items made are dictated by what is popular. For example, Christmas season is a prime opportunity to find clay style tree ornaments in the shape of reindeers or Santa Clause figures. Silver crosses are also common during the Christmas holiday season. And, during Easter season some vendors commonly make designs in bunny or holiday basket imagery.

The interview questions for American Indian vendors in this project were designed to inquire about everyday experiences selling in the plaza and the labor process involved in producing and vending art. In total, 25 interviews were conducted with artists and vendors at the plaza as well as with Museum of New Mexico staff.[7] Questions focused on the daily experiences of selling art in the plaza, the types of preparation involved for producing and vending in Santa Fe, interactions with tourists and reactions to state institutions and policies. Essentially, the image of the "Indian" sitting in the plaza is not generally viewed in the public's eye as a form of work. In contrast, the interviews conducted present a much different perspective. Artists who create their pieces do very much see their creation as work. In addition, vending in the plaza is very laborious. Postcards and tourist guidebooks negate the intensive physical and emotional labor that is involved with the producing and vending of artwork in the plaza. Despite the fact that American Indians have always been involved in Santa Fe's travel industry, this history is hidden in the world made visible to tourists because it is symbolically unmarked and outside of the role in which the travel media has cast Pueblo people. (Martinez and Albers, 2009) The following interview excerpts convey a snapshot of labor experiences that are not commonly captured behind the stereotypical image making of the Southwest.

Working in Santa Fe: American Indian Responses

My initial approach with artists was to gauge a sense about the work of being an artist and understand why they got into the business. Not surprisingly, almost all artists responded that this has been a family affair. Either their parents sold in the plaza or another relative had a connection with selling in Santa Fe. Making pottery or jewelry has been handed down from previous generations. In addition, the children of the vendors in the plaza hold an annual fair to display and sell their artwork. This too ensures continuity of indigenous artwork. This event is sponsored by the Museum of New Mexico and often includes food and traditional Pueblo performances from the surrounding villages. For safety reasons, children are not allowed under the Portal while vendors are selling and this is the only day in which children are welcomed and encouraged to be part of the entrepreneurial spirit.

I asked vendors what they thought of the lottery system and how this has worked for them. Most vendors believed it was fair so that everyone got a chance to sell. One vendor, Mitchell, said "it gets rough at times when I draw a blank 10 times in a row without selling. There is no guarantee for a space and so we have to budget our time and money because we never know when a space will come up for us." A few of the vendors also sell out of their homes in the pueblos but they mainly utilize their houses for making pieces and not selling. Vendors constantly need to prepare for times when they may not get a space to sell or find a way to make other sales. Those not in the Portal Program, who set up around the plaza, have a "safe space" as long as they have a city permit or a gallery owner or hotel allows them to set up. One Jemez woman, who sells baked bread off a side street in the plaza, said she had to constantly ask permission to set up and promise storeowners something:

> "Usually they require 10% of what I make; sometimes I do not make much. One time I was selling bread, and was making bread to show how it is done and a lot of people dropped in to watch, but didn't buy much. I had a lot of people asking questions about how I made the bread, what kind of ingredients and things like that, but not many sales. I got into it with the store people since they thought I was making a lot of sales because they always saw people around me. I gave them 10% of what I sold, and told them that was all I sold that day. I never went back there. Now I don't sell for them. I have my own [city] permit and can sell where I want as long as I get here first. Sometimes it is hard with my daughter so I come whenever I can."

Selling food is not as common as jewelry and other artwork. Her husband sells artwork in the Portal Program and she accompanies him to Santa Fe when both their schedules allow.

When I asked vendors about the rules and regulations they need to abide by to be part of the program, all seem to endorse the idea of the program checking for the quality of materials. This assures the participants that they are part of a unique community of artists unlike other vendors who are not monitored. One vendor, Letty, stated about those not in the program:

> "They can sell whatever they want, nobody checks on them, and if buyers do not know the difference they are caught buying fakes. Some of them don't even make the jewelry they sell or they sell for commercial business using plastic instead of turquoise stones or liquid silver that fades. They may sell jewelry for cheaper, but you get what you pay for. Here, our work is authentic and real. They [Portal Program] make sure we have authentic material and that we personally make all the items we sell. They are always checking on us to make sure we sell real Indian jewelry that is handmade by us and nobody else."

From talking with Portal vendors, there seems to be a general sentiment of "fake vendors" against those not in the program. The American Indian vendors not part of the Program contend that they *do* make their own jewelry. I asked one vendor who sells in front of the Cathedral why he wasn't in the Portal Program. He stated "too many rules and regulations, here I can come and go as I want . . . I'm able to fluctuate between materials using plated nickel silver and sterling silver, I have more space to spread out my work and I'm not cramped in the Portal competing for tourists." The flexibility is evident among artists who do not sell as part of the Portal Program. Items on the display table, whether made by the individual artist or not, range from silver jewelry, bead work, to coffee mugs and key chains. Vendors who are not part of the program are allowed more physical space to get up, walk around, stand and converse with people rather than being situated in one confined space like those under the Palace Portal. One Portal vendor, Marvin, expressed his concern about the rules:

> They don't allow us to have a radio or headphones while we are sitting here. It gets boring sometimes and we just read and share the newspaper. I would like to have my headphones. They don't even allow pagers or cellular phones either. I guess they just want us to sit here and look pretty.... And no credit card machines, too. So many tourists want to buy with credit cards and we can't make a sale. I think we would sell more if the program allowed a credit card machine so tourists can buy whatever they want on their card.

According to the guidelines governing the program, "The use by Portal Program participants of televisions, radios, tape recorders and players, binoculars, cellular phones, cameras, credit card machines, *and other modern appliances or equipment not essential to participation in the Portal Program shall not be permitted*" (emphasis mine). (Palace of the Governors, 1999) With this stated, it is important to convey that the Portal Program is an official program operated under the Museum of New Mexico where artists agree to such rules and regulations. When I asked the Director about not having "modern appliances," she responded that this was in place to keep uniformity and less distraction from vendors and the public. Another main reason given for the prohibition of cameras among vendors is that the Portal is a place of business and the devices would be distracting and improper. However, tourists who approach the Portal to photograph are not prohibited from recording or photographing within this place of business. In contrast, the vendors who are not set up in the Portal Program frequently do use credit card machines for sales. And at times I have noted vendors around the plaza who have a small radio usually tuned into the news or a sports station.

On several occasions I have witnessed tourists photographing vendors in the plaza and asking inappropriate questions. Some tourists seem to be surprised that venders speak and understand English. Most of the time tourists are merely curious about the piece of artwork they are buying and tend to inquire about the process that it took to make the pieces and the designs. I asked vendors about their experience when dealing with tourists. The general response was that for the most part vendors do enjoy talking with people about their artwork. What I did get from interviews was that tourists constantly take pictures of vendors without permission and assume that they negotiate their prices. Mable, a jewelry maker who is Yakima Indian from Washington but married to a Santo Domingo man, stated the following:

"One thing is that people want souvenirs, and I don't consider my artwork as souvenirs. I hear all the time that they want to buy a souvenir from a Santa Fe Indian to take back to their family members. I work as an artist and every piece that I make is special with different styles. I don't push my art; if people choose a bracelet, then that was meant for them to take. Another thing that tourists do is that they can buy a $1,000 art piece from a fancy gallery and then want to bargain down a price for a $10 bracelet that I made. I say no way. Each piece is priced and I do not bargain because I feel the prices are reasonable and someone else will pay that price so I do not have to bargain. Do they go to a gallery and bargain there? The mentality of consumers is that we're Indians and are not taken seriously as artists or people trying to make a living. They see us sitting down laughing and talking with people. I guess we look cute to them."

For most of the vendors there is an economic incentive based on what tourists buy that often drives the production of artwork. The artists I interviewed do, at times, make specific items for vending in the plaza. One jeweler, Mitchell, mentioned his bracelets with intricate designs and earrings do well during the Christmas season, but the summer months are prime for selling larger pieces such as belts and necklaces. Another vendor, Everett, mentioned that at times he does make extra items when he anticipates something will sell more than usual:

> "For the last couple of years, every summer there has been this Christian group who has a conference or camp out in Glorietta and every Wednesday they bring the bus and drop them off in the plaza area. They buy all my necklaces with crosses. I caught on to this and started to make more silver crosses with turquoise stones and they just bought them all every time. I always know when to expect people like them who visit the porch [Portal area] to buy just one type of jewelry."

Lastly, I inquired about the Museum of New Mexico marketing the Portal Program, which describes that "Native Americans selling their traditional arts and crafts on the Portal of the Palace constitute a living exhibit of the Palace". (Ibid) One vendor, Marvin, stated the following:

> "Well, we are a living museum. We are in one location, very unique in one place selling our artwork. Where else can people see Indians from many different pueblos in one location? Our work reflects where we come from… Here, tourists get to talk with people and we get to explain to them about our work and our backgrounds. Our work is traditional and should represent the people and the tribe. We are also an educational program, to educate the public about our artwork and being Indian."

This response was somewhat unusual as most vendors do not buy into the notion that they participate in a living exhibit. When asked the same question, most artists viewed themselves as hard working people trying to make a living.

The Portal Program guidelines are based on the notion that the presence of American Indian artists is an integral part of New Mexico history. Moreover, the Museum of New Mexico established the program and determined the following:

> "Reserving the Portal for the display and sale of New Mexico Indian crafts would not only help to preserve traditional aspects of New Mexico Indian culture but would be of educational value to the visiting public by providing the opportunity for contact with New Mexico Indian artists and artisans in a historically relevant context." (Ibid)

This is the fundamental belief of the Portal Program—to preserve Indigenous culture that would be educational to the public. It is unclear how "traditional" culture is determined. In fact, most of the vendors are constantly grappling with the idea of what constitutes traditional American Indian art. There are a wide variety of items sold in the plaza from those that are passed from family generations to some more of the recent inventions of popular tourist items like dream catchers and silver toe rings. On the one hand, the Museum of New Mexico encourages the entrepreneurial spirit of vending art in the Plaza, while at the same time American Indians are staged, positioned and marketed as remnants of a "primitive past" through the prohibition of modern appliances in the plaza.

The guidelines further stipulate that sales in the program shall be "conducted on the brick surface; no tables or elevated stands are permitted". (Ibid) The Portal Program is also influenced by a lengthy history of federal policies that function to promote the development of American Indian arts and crafts. This was the initial intention of the Indian Arts and Crafts Board urged by John Collier in 1935. According to the Act (1935), the function of the Board is to "promote the economic welfare of the Indian tribes and Indian wards of the Government through the development of Indian arts and crafts and the expansion of the market for the products of Indian art and craftsmanship"(Section 2). With the influx of imitation Indian art, federal and local policies have proven inadequate for promoting the economic welfare of American Indians and instead, much like postcards and tourist guidebooks, perpetuate a distinctive and romantic visualization of the Southwest. (Martinez, 2008)

Conclusion

This chapter attempts to understand the process of labor involved among American Indian artists in a tourist economy. What has been discussed offers insight into the working dynamics of American Indians producing and vending artwork in one of the nation's most premier travel destinations. Much to the contrary of stereotypical image making in the Southwest, the workday of an artist does not end with vending but continues at home in preparation for the next day. Labor is often a "tag team" effort and not solely an individual practice. This helps ensure that artwork is being produced and sold simultaneously in order to make a living in an unpredictable tourist market. Nothing about indigenous art is individual. Furthermore, American Indians experience a great deal of emotional labor while vending in the plaza. The constant gaze and questions from tourists adds to the unsettling feeling for those in the Portal Program or surrounding plaza area who are not guaranteed a space to vend.

As Santa Fe begins to celebrate its 400th anniversary in 2010, we must be reminded that since the beginning of travel to the region indigenous peoples have played an integral part in building and promoting the city. This essay represents a step to further understanding contemporary Native experiences through the lens that labor plays in a tourist economy. Local indigenous people are competing with state, federal and international interests and markets. Federal policies and local museum policies may have been well intended to protect American Indian artists but for the most part they have been crafted by Euro-American desires to define indigenous identity and culture. Policies governing the sale of American Indian art need to be critically evaluated and formulated in order to *not* perpetuate notions of a living past; but, much to the contrary, that American Indian art is complex and ever evolving. In order to ensure that indigenous art, artists and communities are adequately reflected and valued in Santa Fe's history, polices and practices governing the sale of artwork need and must seek alternative NATIVE approaches.

Acknowledgments

I am very grateful to the many vendors who took the time to talk with me about their work and experience at the plaza.

—*Kúdaawóháa.*

References:

Adair, J. (1944). *The Navajo and Pueblo Silversmiths.* Norman: University of Oklahoma Press.

Babcock, B. (1990). 'A New Mexican Rebecca': Imaging Pueblo Women." *Journal of the Southwest* 32:400-437.

Benedict, B. (1983). *The Anthropology of World's Fairs: San Francisco's Panama Pacific International Exposition of 1915.* London and Berkeley: Lowie Museum of Anthropology in association with Scolar Press.

Bernstein, B. (1993). *The Marketing of Culture: Pottery and Santa Fe's Indian Market.* PhD Dissertation. The University of New Mexico.

Brooke, J. (1997). "Sales of Indian Crafts Rise and So Do Fakes" *New York Times*, August 2, Section 1, Page 6, Column 5.

Burawoy, M. et al. (2000). *Global Ethnography: Forces, Connections, and Imaginations in a Postmodern World.* University of California Press.

Clifford, H. (1997). "Disney-fying Santa Fe; Tourists drive prices up, native charm out," *The Boston Globe*, December 28, C2.

Deutsche Presse-Agentur. (1998). "Tourists often misled on Indian crafts-market flooded with fakes" August 28.

Dilworth, L. (1996). *Imaging Indians: Persistent Visions of a Primitive Past.* Smithsonian Institution Press.

Gibson, D. (1995). "Copycats Try to Corner Native Arts and Crafts," *Native Peoples Arts & Lifeways*, Vol. XIII, No. 5, 16.

———. (2000). "Going to Indian Market: Santa Fe event largest of its kind" in *Native Peoples Arts & Lifeways*, August 22.

Hoerig, K.A. (2003). *Under the Palace Portal: Native American Artists in Santa Fe.* Albuquerque: University of New Mexico Press.

Indian Arts and Crafts Board (1935). August 27, Section 2.

Josephy Jr., A.M. J. Nagel, and T. Johnson, (1999). "Indian Arts and Crafts Act" in *Red Power: The American Indian's Fight for Freedom.* University of Nebraska Press: Lincoln. 245-250.

Littlefield, A. and M.C. Knack (1996) *Native Americans and Wage Labor: Ethnohistorical Perspectives.* Norman: University of Oklahoma Press.

Livingston v Ewing (1979). 601F. 2d 1110, 1114.

Lummis, C.F. [1893] (1952). *The Land of Poco Tiempo*, Reprint, with a foreword by Paul A. Walter. Albuquerque: University of New Mexico Press.

Lyman, C.M. (1982). *The Vanishing Race and Other Illusions: Photographs of Edward S. Curtis.* New York: Pantheon Books.

McLuhan, T.C. (1987). *Dream Tracks: The Railroad and the American Indian 1890–1930.* Random House: New York.

Marriott, A. (1948). *Maria: The Potter of San Ildefonso.* Norman: University of Oklahoma.

Martinez, M.J. (2008). *Double Take: Tourism and Photography Endeavors Among the Northern Pueblos of the Rio Grande.* PhD Dissertation. University of Minnesota.

Martinez, M.J. and P.C Albers. (2009). "Imaging and Imagining Pueblo People in Northern New Mexico Tourism" in *The Framed World: Tourism, Tourists and Photography.* M. Robinson and D. Picard (Ed). Ashgate Publishing Company. 39-62.

Mullin, M.H. (2001). *Culture in the Marketplace: Gender, Art, and Value in the American Southwest.* Duke University Press.

Naranjo, T. (1996). "Cultural Changes: The Effect of Foreign Systems at Santa Clara Pueblo" in M. Weigle and B. Babcock, editors, *The Great Southwest of the Fred Harvey Company and the Santa Fe Railway.* The Heard Museum: Phoenix, Arizona. 187-196.

Palace of the Governors. (1999). *Guidelines, Rules, and Regulations Governing the Portal Program at the Palace of the Governors,* Adopted 05-30-99, MNM Rule 57.

Peters, K.M. (1996). "Watering the Flower: Laguna Pueblo and the Santa Fe Railroad, 1880–1943" in *Native Americans and Wage Labor: Ethnohistorical Perspectives* edited by Alice Littlefield and Martha C. Knack. University of Oklahoma Press. 177-197.

U.S. Department of the Interior Office of Inspector General (2005). *Indian Arts and Crafts: A Case of Misrepresentation* Report No. E-EV-OSS-0003-2005, June.

Weigle, M. (1990). "Southwest Lures: Innocents Detoured, Incensed Determined." *Journal of the Southwest* 32:499-540.

Weigle, M. and B. Babcock. (1996). *The Great Southwest of the Fred Harvey Company and the Santa Fe Railway*. The Heard Museum: Phoenix, Arizona.

Wilkins, D.E. (2002). *American Indian Politics and the American Political System*. Rowman & Littlefield Publishers.

Regarding Ethnicities and Cultures
by
Diane Reyna
Pueblo of Taos/Ohkay Owingeh

The news of the commemoration of the 400th anniversary of the founding of Santa Fe filled me with all too familiar feelings of apprehension, dread, and resignation. How could such intense feelings result from the word "commemoration"? My misgivings about public historical commemorations in New Mexico are based on my life experience in New Mexico and because I was raised within a Pueblo community, I have an allegiance to a Pueblo worldview. People like me who carry the bloodlines of two cultures and ethnic groups, the Pueblo and the Nuevo Mexicano, contradict and are challenged by the reticence of individuals to examine their origins and impact of long held beliefs and behaviors. My uneasiness increases when public commemorations are used to express a cultural or ethnic superiority and stature over another based on notions of pure ancestry. People like me observe and live on the frontier of both cultures.

I am a woman born from distinct ancestors whose lives first intersected approximately 400 years ago in this land now called New Mexico. My relatives can be found within several Pueblos and Nuevo Mexicano villages in Northern New Mexico. People like me are intimately cognizant of the complex historical and cultural dynamics that emerge when public events like the commemorations of the founding of Santa Fe are celebrated. I am challenged during these types of events by those who have insisted on imposing notions of superiority by refusing to acknowledge their own integrated heritage in order to claim pure ancestry.

My Nuevomexicano great-grandmother, Martina Martinez, spent her childhood at Taos Pueblo. She was one of many Nuevo Mexicanos who were born and raised within Pueblo communities around the late 1800s and early 1900s. She spoke fluent Tiwa as well as Spanish. She married, settled and, with my great grandfather, managed a sheep ranch in the community of Pilar, south of Taos. On my father's side, my grandmother, Crusita Mondragon Reyna, was born to a Taos Pueblo mother and a Nuevomexicano father.

One morning in 1962, I left my home at Taos Pueblo to begin my ten-minute bus ride into the town of Taos, New Mexico to attend my third grade classes at St. Joseph Catholic School. The transition point between home and town was a worn gunmetal cattle guard that marked the place and moment where the people of Taos Pueblo exited and re-entered their community.

"You stupid Indio!" There she was—towering over me. Disgust and condescension in a guise of holiness left me stunned to tears in that third grade classroom. Her brown face, half-haloed by a stiff sliver of white cotton, and her tall thin body draped by an imposing darkness of black pressed wool, were highlighted only by the shine from the large black rosary beads that hung from the side of her waist. Shaken by the trauma, humiliation, and laughter of my classmates, I tried to hold back the tears by pretending to look for my books underneath my desk. I was trying to find a place of refuge from the stares, the voices, and the laughter.

There it was—the moment, at which this eight year old from Taos Pueblo and a Hispanic nun and teacher re-enacted centuries-old dynamics of contrasting histories, ethnicities and cultures of Northern New Mexico.

Later that afternoon, I crossed that familiar cattle guard once again, this time with shattered assumptions and illusions of life in Northern New Mexico as I had known it. The rumbling of rubber bus tires across the twelve steel bars incised in worn pavement announced my return to the safety and understanding of my family and community.

My parents crossed that same cattle guard later that afternoon as they rushed to meet with the parish priest and nuns. The outcome of the meeting was a denial by the nun that the incident happened. My mother eventually enrolled me in public school.

I believe my parents' immediate response to my circumstance was based on their own experiences with racism and marginalization. For example, staff at the Santa Fe Indian School had made my father carry a heavy plank of wood on his shoulders for speaking his language. New Mexico State University would not accept my mother unless another Santa Fe Indian School graduate accompanied her so together they could provide mutual support against the prejudice that existed on campus in the

1940s. My mother's stubborn determination to attain a college education convinced the university officials to relent and allowed her to attend NMSU on her own.

"Our forbears referred to themselves as Españoles Mexicanos (Spanish Mexicanos), which resolves the very basic question of how Spanish or how Mexican we are."—Mary Montaño

I grew up hearing townspeople refer to themselves as "Spanish." At Taos Pueblo, I heard people refer to townspeople as "Mexican." I developed the habit of referring to Spanish-speaking individuals as "Spanish." I would describe my paternal and maternal grandmothers as being "half-Spanish" or being "Spanish." The term became so ingrained that today I still find myself using the "Spanish" description before catching myself and replacing it with the term that brings contentment and relief; that term is "Nuevomexicana" or "Nuevomexicano" because it is an acknowledgement of Mexico in the history and relationships of those who lived and died on this land since the Spanish arrived in the 1600s.

In reviewing the records of Taos County from the 1910 Federal Census, I found that the majority of Spanish speaking residents described themselves as New Mexicans. A few respondents used the word "Spain" or "Spanish" to denote themselves. The resurgence of the Spanish identity occurred during the territory of New Mexico's quest for statehood. Upper class "Hispanos" and "Anglo" Americans worked to restore the legacy and lineage of Spain in the minds of members of Congress in order to alleviate their misgivings of granting statehood to a mix-blood Mexican population; "…to change the way outsiders, and they themselves, imagined New Mexico society." (Montgomery, 2002)

"I am the same distance from the conquistador as from the Indian. Righteousness should not come easily to any of us."—Richard Rodriquez

In 1990, I attended the Santa Fe Fiesta for the first time. I had avoided attending this event because of the organizer's stated purpose that Fiesta was the celebration of the reconquest of the Pueblo People in 1692. On the Santa Fe Plaza, I watched the *Entrada,* which is the re-enactment of the surrender of the Tesuque Pueblo people to Don Diego de Vargas. A group of Hispanic men, women and children dressed in wigs, gunnysacks, war paint and dime store war bonnets portrayed the people of Tesuque. In contrast, the actors portraying de Vargas and his conquistadores were attired in polished armor and accompanied by the historically accurate blue robed Franciscan friars. Several of the "Indians" beat on drums with rhythms reminiscent of old television westerns. Imitative singing and war cries added to the voice of the narrator who guided the audience through the play. At its conclusion, the narrator spoke to the crowd saying, "You have just seen re-enacted the dramatic and transcendental re-entry of the immortal hero Don Diego de Vargas, the peaceful conquistador."

Behind the scenes, drama and upset prevailed. The audience was unaware that the young man who portrayed the leader of the Pueblo of Tesuque was devastated to tears by the narrator's callous proclamation. Randy Kanitobe, a tribal member of the Kewa (Santo Domingo) Pueblo, had carefully selected his attire to respectfully and authentically represent his Pueblo and was shaken by the demeaning and offensive dress of his "people" who joined him on stage. My own eyes were blurred with tears of remembrance and empathy as I watched this young man and his younger nephew struggle to cope with the effects of a public commemoration of ethnic pride and identity.

> "The conquests never really succeeded, and the days of attempted conquests are, or ought to be, over and done. The memories of those failed attempts remain, and their trappings, made by the passage of time to seem more glorious than perhaps they ever were originally, are brought out for celebration from time to time. They delight the eye and enchant the mind for a while, and they are put away until the next time." (Sprott, 1989)

In 1998, two commemorative projects to honor Don Juan de Oñate, who, amongst several atrocities toward Pueblo peoples, ordered the severing of a foot of all male captives over twenty-five as punishment for the Acoma Pueblo rebellion of 1598, were the focus of controversy in New Mexico between two opposing groups representing specific points of view on history, memory and culture. The first of the two controversies erupted when activists severed the bronze foot of a statue of Oñate in Alcalde, New Mexico, in January of 1998. Cutting off the foot of the Oñate statue in Alcalde demonstrated:

> "...the emotional and political energy that resides in memory, and its potential to magnify longstanding ethnic tensions and ideological fissures in society. Debate over such monuments

brings to light deep-seated assumptions, beliefs, and perceptions regarding the past, and provides a venue and a specific moment at which they might be contested. As tensions escalate, public spaces themselves often become sources of contention and disputed terrain. When spaces and landmarks are contested, so are the histories they consecrate and the community values or identities they symbolize; so, too, are the social relations of power which give them emotional meaning and political value." (Nieto-Phillips, 2004)

The second controversy surfaced as public furor erupted in Albuquerque in 1998 over plans to erect a commemorative statue to Don Juan de Oñate. The Oñate Cuarto Centenario Project was to coincide with the 400th Anniversary of the founding of Santa Fe. On one side, individuals from nearby Pueblos and their supporters from the Chicano community in Albuquerque, attacked and opposed the project based on Oñate's and Spain's role in the deaths and punishment of resisting Pueblos in the 1600s. "Spanish" or Hispanic individuals counter-attacked with equally passionate responses to the honoring of Oñate. The rancor that was created by the two opposing groups caused the project to stall. Participants in the controversy:

"...claimed that an objective look at history would reveal the truth. But clearly, collective memory, if angry in particular, is selective remembrance shaped preeminently by group loyalty. Differing outlooks on the same facts served to mobilize the civic warlords and foot soldiers of the present." (Gonzales, 2007)

The Albuquerque Public Arts Program, responsible for implementation of the project, responded to the stalemate by initiating a process that would begin to address the underlying historical and cultural tension behind such public commemorations. Individuals from the Pueblo and Hispanic communities participated in a series of year-long mediated dialogues. The group consisted of artists, historians, educators and public servants. The time consuming and, at times, uncomfortable process allowed each of us to speak candidly to and with each other. I was able to listen with difficulty but openly to those who expressed personal, cultural and historical views contrary to mine. I was allowed to speak without interruptions about the Oñate project and its relationship to my experiences with racism and marginalization in Northern New Mexico. An unexpected and significant outcome of the dialogues was the recognition that my mixed ancestry held the memory of two enduring cultures that possessed the spirit to persist and survive throughout the past 400 years. This personal revelation reflected the group consensus at the end of our process.

We recommended that the commemorative sculpture express "…inspired respect for ancestors, evoke the spirit of community and coexistence of distinct cultures, underscore family roots and values, unique heritage, and create a life affirming, emotionally engaging and spiritually uplifting atmosphere." (Ibid)

The mixed ethnicity and ancestry of northern Nuevomexicanos reflects a more realistic and authentic history that is worthy of a public celebration. A celebration that honors the survival and memory of Pueblos and Nuevomexicano people, whose ancestors lived, survived and died as neighbors, compadres, comadres and relatives in Northern New Mexico over the past 400 years. This honoring and celebration could begin to create the needed shift to new directions toward inclusion of everyone who chooses to call Santa Fe home. Creating a true community celebration will begin to weaken and change the current dynamics of cultural and ethnic resentment exasperated by current exclusionary public celebrations such as the Santa Fe Fiesta.

"We of the twenty-first century may be headed for a desire for cleansing, of choosing, of being one thing or another. The brown child may grow up to war against himself. To attempt to be singular rather than several. May seek to obliterate a part of himself. May seek to obliterate others."—Richard Rodriquez

To create new celebrations or commemorations, we as members of the Santa Fe community must first assess our own behavior in regard to other ethnicities and cultures that live among us. We must also assess how each of our communities and families regards other ethnicities and cultures. We must practice skills of observation and listening. We must be more observant to the stereotypical and harmful behaviors of members of our communities who label and thus mistreat others who are not members of their community.

We can learn to shape Santa Fe's public celebrations and commemorations by continuously seeking to understand the complex history of northern New Mexico. Only by understanding the experiences of each other can we begin to eliminate knee-jerk responses to injustices experienced in this community. Change involves shared leadership from many members of the community in planning truly inclusive public events.

As Santa Fe community members, each of us bears the responsibility, regardless of our ancestry and ethnicity, to actively advocate for such celebrations. We must do this on behalf of our children and grandchildren who rely on adults, youth, elders, civic and religious leaders. We must create a respectful community that prepares and mirrors for them a place in a global world that needs to rely on human interdependence and cooperation for its survival.

References:

Gathering Up Again: Fiesta In Santa Fe. Co-dir. Jeanette DeBouzek. Diane Reyna. Quotidian Independent Documentary Research, 1992

Gonzales, Phillip B. *Expressing New Mexico: Nuevomexicano Creativity, Ritual, and Memory.* Tucson: The University of Arizona Press, 2007.

Montano, Mary. *Tradiciones Nuevomexicanas: Hispano Arts and Culture of New Mexico.* Albuquerque: The University of New Mexico Press, 2001.

Montgomery, Charles. *The Spanish Redemption: Heritage, Power, and Loss on New Mexico's Upper Rio Grande.* Berkeley: University of California Press, 2002

Nieto-Phillips, John M. *The Language of Blood: The Making of Spanish-American Identity in New Mexico, 1880s–1930s.* Albuquerque: The University of New Mexico Press, 2004.

Rodriquez, Richard. *Brown: The Last Discovery of America* Viking, 2002.

Sprott, Robert, O. F. M. *Address.* Santa Fe Fiesta. Santa Fe, New Mexico. 10 September 1989.

9

Grounded in Faith
by
Carol Harvey
Diné

I am very grateful for having been raised in Santa Fe, The City of Holy Faith—the City Different. It gave me the opportunity to fully experience my Navajo and Hispanic cultures. It gave me the opportunity to be 'Grounded in Faith'.

As a daughter of a Navajo father and a Northern New Mexican Hispanic mother, my life has been blessed with the best that each culture has to offer. In commemoration of the founding of Santa Fe, which has experienced profound historical and cultural development over the last 400 years I offer up the following humble vignettes, inspired by my family, my Navajo and Hispanic cultures, and my city, Santa Fe—my home, my sanctuary, my retreat, my most beloved birthplace.

The Sacred Trust

1618 Second Street

Our Santa Fe home, made from adobe with the dirt from our yard, looked smaller to me as if it was settling back into the Earth—reclaimed. With our help, Daddy made the adobe bricks. We mixed the dirt together with water and straw, sloshing around in it barefoot and breaking up the dirt—feeling the wet mud squish between our toes. The chocolate like batter was then poured into wooden rectangular frames, holding four adobe bricks at a time. The sun was then left to do its job. By the next week, the adobes were ready to be stacked under a tarp in the empty lot, standing on their sides eight high. Each one was different—the straw and the dry cracked dirt mingling together as they chose to.

Supper

While we worked outside, Momma made our usual dinner—beans with chicos, chile, and tortillas. She sorted the pintos to remove any small rocks and *frijoles viejos* (old shriveled beans). She then rinsed the pintos in cold water, added chicos, a little bacon, and cooked them all day in a Picuris pot made of mica clay. At the end of the day she made gravy (for thickening the beans) from flour, bacon fat, and bean juice, using a small black cast iron frying pan. Sometimes flames jumped out of the pan as she poured in the bean broth! *Aya!*

Momma also roasted green chile, turning each piece evenly on the grill to brown all sides. She popped them with a sizzling swat if they started to swell so they wouldn't cook unevenly. After the chile was roasted, she steamed the fragrant pods in a hot, wet tea towel. Peeling the toasted skin away and yanking the stem off the tops with the *semillas* (small seeds) still clinging, Momma squished the soft strips through her fingers, eventually combining them with mashed garlic. The garlic prevented anyone getting an upset stomach.

As for making tortillas, Momma knew the recipe by heart. She mixed the dough in a ceramic bowl adorned with blue Navajo crosses encircling the rim—scooping flour in by the handful, sifting in baking powder and salt, spooning in lard by the finger full, and adding warm water with Pet evaporated milk to soften the dough. Next, she rolled small balls of dough, patting them with her fingertips as she lined them up next to the rolling board. Dusting the board with flour so the dough wouldn't stick, she rolled the dough balls out into perfect circles. She flipped them really fast between her hands to stretch them out and then threw them on the grill. Coming off the hot grill, the tortillas were thick and soft and we buttered them with melted lard.

The Turquoise Room Expanded

Daddy added on to the house as money was available. Our house started off as a single turquoise room with my crib next to the wood stove. Later, a kitchen and a bathroom with indoor plumbing were added—no more using the outhouse or heating water by the bucket and filling up the grey metal wash tub for a bath. He put in hardwood floors with two inch planking, which he leveled and blind nailed. He then sanded, stained, filled, varnished, and buffed the floor with oil. On the ceilings, he used *vigas* with uneven knots in the wood creating imaginary 'eyes'. Between the vigas were small, narrow slats of grainy, lacquered wood. The outside of our house was stuccoed in gold.

The Navajo Carpenter, Nalwood

Daddy hand carved most of our furniture, which was adorned with a radiant sun on each piece—warming the wood. As he drew his design on a piece of wood, using the curve of his hand as a guide, he teased out the hiding sun. Cutting from the center out, the sun was eventually revealed. Each ray was separated with the precise cutting and leaning of a v-parting tool. Daddy then tapered the design with a file creating sinuous curves. Using a veneering tool, small concave cuts were made around the sun as if its light had escaped, dappling the wood. He 'eyed' his work frequently—sawdust filling his work room.

Daddy raised and sanded the grain on each piece until it was smooth to the touch, gently dusting off the surface of the wood. Applying the varnish across the grain, he intermittently tapped his bristled brush on the inside of the varnish can and then glided his brush with the grain. He used a pickstick, a cotton swab rolled in cooled varnish and rosin and molded to a point, to lift up stray lint or dust. After the cool air dried the varnish, he smoothed the wood with fine sandpaper and shined it with a paste of powdered pumice and machine oil. For a higher gloss finish, he used rottenstone and oil. Daddy's style changed over time, and he later told me that he no longer wanted to use shellac, varnish, or lacquer preferring to leave the wood in its natural, roughhewn state. I sometimes imagine him polishing his furniture with boiled linseed oil and gum turpentine and then adding a coat of beeswax to make it glisten.

Indian Art

An image of a lone Navajo man driving a wagon along an empty road near the Chuska Mountains hung in our living room connecting Daddy to his ancestral home. We knew so little of his past or his family that any insight loomed large. I wanted to capture my ancestral past and hold it close and tight.

I recall a tempera painting hanging in the living room, done by one of Daddy's friends, of my sister, Mary, dressed Navajo style in midnight blue velveteen and wearing a silver squash blossom necklace, sitting in front of a hogan holding a lamb. Next to her, my sister, Cordie, in the colors of Indian paintbrush to match her auburn hair, stands framed against the sandstone cliffs of Arizona wearing a woven sash around her waist with an 'eye-dazzler' blanket draped across her shoulder. Daddy and Momma's coarse, plain, red, grey, black, and white striped Navajo blanket, so tightly woven that it deflected rain, lay on the edge of a chair. Their black Santa Clara wedding vase, a San Felipe *awanyu* pot, and a geometrical Jicarilla Apache pot, stood on a voluted shelf.

Fusion

Daddy's Navajo roots mingled comfortably with Momma's northern New Mexican, Spanish, Catholic traditions. St. Anthony wearing a scapular, the baby Jesus in an ivory, satin, embroidered dress that Momma made, and religious candles stood on the mantle. A mosaic crucifix hung on the door. A braided rag rug, from the scraps of our childhood dresses, lay on the floor. Momma sewed those dresses on her Singer—enveloped in the dusty haze from the cotton fabric, a light film on her and the furniture—as she embellished each dress with scalloped hems and bell-shaped sleeves, bric-a-brac, eyelet lace, or pearl heart-shaped buttons. A shiny, copper lamp that I had polished with toothpaste, after Momma bought it, tarnished, at a flea market, gave a soft glow to the living room. The Sacred Heart quietly watched over the dining room. Outside of the porch's weathered, wooden posts, and carved corbels, Momma's favorite blue morning glories lay underground, waiting for spring.

Little Daddy

We used to stand at the mailbox waiting for Daddy to come home from work at the Indian Hospital. When we saw him, always wearing his sharply creased khakis, we'd yell, "Little Daddy, Little Daddy." While he soaked his feet in a pan of hot water, I hung on the edge of his chair waiting to dry them off so I could feel his tough, black nails. Riding horseback on a freezing day, his feet had gotten frostbitten when he was eight years old out herding sheep.

I traced the tattoos he got in the Army—a fierce eagle tattoo and a tattoo of an Indian chief in full war regalia with Daddy's name underneath—and he traced my blue veins that sat on top of my skin telling me the 'H' my veins formed was for Harvey. Because we were Harveys, we had an 'H'.

To assure a quick mind, his ears had been pierced at birth with a sharp stone; the long, creased lines lay flat.

The Homecoming

When I was nine we got a used yellow Pontiac and Daddy was now able to take us to visit his family on the Navajo Reservation. We had never been past Albuquerque, so we were excited. We camped along the way! It was a chance for

Daddy to go home to visit his aunt who had raised him. He taught us to say '*yá át ééh*' (hello).

We left for the reservation in August, leaving Santa Fe early in the morning. We drove along the Blue Mother River (Rio Grande) that fed the crops of the Cochiti, *Kewa* (Santo Domingo), San Felipe, Santa Ana, Sandia and Isleta pueblos. The laughter of the *Koshares* (Pueblo clowns) could be heard as we journeyed to our land—their blackened faces peering at us—teasing and joking—scaring us! The beat of cottonwood drums sounded every time we drove onto Native land marked by highway signs.

As we drove past Acoma, I imagined the Eagle Dancers soaring off the White Rock Mesa; their full, grey and white feathered wings keeping them aloft as they gently rode on the wind between the Pueblo and Enchanted Mesa—their golden beaks glistening in the late afternoon sun, their shrill cries drifting on the wind. Daddy said Acoma is 365 feet above the dusty sage strewn land and if you think of it as a year you can remember the height.

Acoma thin-walled pottery is white with black geometrical designs or polychrome that is white, black and clay colored. My favorite was the Storyteller with all the children sitting on her lap.

The Sky City *Ako* People did not look kindly upon the Spanish who, in 1598, violently raided the Pueblo. The "People of the White Rock" defended themselves and many Spanish soldiers were killed. In retaliation, Juan de Onate, sent a force to Acoma and over took the Pueblo by force, killing hundreds of men, women, and children. It is said that captured men, women, and children between the ages of twelve and twenty-five were sentenced to hard labor. Men over twenty-five had a foot lopped off as a warning to the other Pueblos who opposed Spanish rule. Children under twelve were given to the Church. How this could happen I don't know. Acoma Pueblo seems so impenetrable even today.

In Grants, Daddy got a speeding ticket. We had to go to kangaroo court. Even though we knew that we were coming close to our demarcated land, we were scared. He paid them what they asked and we went on our way.

Within the confines of the Four Sacred Mountains, we were safe, in Daddy's cradle of origin. These Mountains are Holy Places. One's spirit can travel beyond each Mountain and it is there that one can be healed. Mount Blanca, decorated with white shell and covered with a sheet of daylight, is the eastern boundary of *Dinétah* (Navajo land). Mount Taylor, decorated with turquoise and covered with blue sky, is the southern boundary. The San Francisco Peaks, decorated with haliotis shell and covered with a yellow cloud, are the western boundary. Mount Hesperus, decorated with cannel coal and covered in darkness, is the northern boundary.

As we drove deep into Dinétah, I fell asleep. I dreamed that Daddy held my hand, and took me to the foot of Mount Taylor. He walked with me a short distance and then said, "This is as far as I can go with you Carol." I walked further up the mountain alone. I knew I could make it to the summit because of all the running I did. Suddenly, I was at the top, transported, without feeling any passage of time, space or effort. I was just there.

A turquoise hogan stood before me. Inside were two wrinkled, aged women, dressed Navajo style. A loom stood off to the side. They welcomed me in, and I stood next to the fire burning low in the center—Navajo tea brewing in a kettle. I imagined them to be Spider Woman and Changing Woman.

I said, "I'm looking for an altar and a Holy Book buried underneath to guide me." Without speaking, they told me, "We have no book, we do not write. We have no altar." Spider Woman said, "I will give you a gift, instead—the gift of silence." I saw in front of me a pond. A fish swam effortlessly before me in the clear, greenish water. I heard its fins. I saw a small red ant crawling along on a green leaf. I heard it walking. The forest I was sitting in was alive with sound. "You don't have to speak to fill the silence, Carol. It's already full. You can learn from it." I felt myself waking up, but Changing Woman, said as I was drifting away, "Here is a ring for you, Carol." It was silver with coral, stamped with an ant, a spider and a cockroach.

I heard a voice from the 'Other World' saying, "Each Mountain has a lesson for you, Carol. You will visit each one when it is time. You were born Navajo, no one can take it away. It is not something you learn or acquire. It is something you just are."

A rodeo and dances were being held at the Gallup Intertribal Ceremonial. We watched the rodeo from a hillside with many other Navajos while eating mutton stew and fry bread. In the evening, under distant, twinkling stars, we watched the tribal dances. Most of the women wore broom skirts and velveteen blouses with old nickels or dimes sewn all over the front and down their sleeves. Some had the old brass or aluminum tokens used by the trading posts. Their finery included turquoise and silver necklaces, earrings, concho belts and bracelets. Their hair was pulled back and tied with yarn. The men sat on their haunches, dressed in velveteen or flannel shirts, their long hair tied back with bandannas across their forehead.

We camped at Window Rock. We climbed to the window in the rock, worn through by the wind and rain, and it was very scary sliding down. It was like winter sledding except we were out of control. We hit the bumps in the sandstone as we slid down, speeding like rockets. We flew through the air only to land again against the sandstone—careening downward. That night, my sister, Jeanie, slept on the picnic table and kept the fire going all night. My sister, Cordie and I slept in the trunk of our car. We got to see the Tribal Council building and the government offices that Daddy painted when he was eighteen. Daddy said someday I could be a council member like Annie Wauneka. We went to see the educational displays at the Tribal fairground building and saw ourselves on TV.

We drove to St. Michaels, Arizona where Momma had the priest bless our car, then to Fort Defiance, and then to Ganado. It was caterpillar season and there were thousands of them on the roads. When we honked the car they would freeze and lift the front end of their bodies momentarily. I was glad when we left them behind—I was afraid to get out of the car and step on them.

When we got to Daddy's aunt's home in Round Rock, no one was there. The hogan was empty. The hogan was made from juniper, mud and rock. Just as we had built our home from the soil in our yard, her hogan was made from the resources at hand. Six strong juniper poles formed the outer circle, which was filled in with juniper logs then topped with a juniper log roof. The logs were crisscrossed, interwoven and covered with juniper bark, wood chips and mud. The dry caked mud on the roof and the mud filling the cracks between the posts matched the dry Earth. The wooden door faced east so she could come out to greet Dawn Boy and Dawn Maiden each day.

At first the Navajos had no homes; they lived out in the open. It was decided by a Council that they needed a dwelling within which to hold their sacred rites, so a hogan was made in the East for the God of the sunrise and a hogan in the West for the God of the sunset. They were consecrated in prayer and song with holy corn pollen.

We made ourselves at home under the lean-to. Using the juniper from the Chuska Mountains, four strong poles with v-shaped tops had been dug into the Earth, their bark stripped. Smaller poles lay across them forming a roof, with boughs of fresh juniper lain across. More poles extended outward from the sides holding more boughs in place for shade. An empty loom was at one end of the lean-to. The juniper boughs smelled fresh and we could see the Milky Way.

Later that evening we saw lanterns coming across the field and it was her. Without a sound, she gently shook Daddy's hand. They spoke softly. A few minutes later, Daddy turned and walked over to our car. He looked out over the dark valley and kicked the left front tire. Since we couldn't speak Navajo we didn't know what was wrong. We found out later his father had died a month or so earlier. Daddy had once told us that it wasn't dignified to cry over death and that when he died, he wanted us to be still and silent, to accept that he had lived his life, and that there would be no reason to be sad. That night he sat still and silent, his face worn and tired in the lantern light.

On an oil drum stove that stood in the middle of the hogan, Daddy's aunt made coffee, Navajo tea, mutton stew and fry bread. We sat on sheepskins on the floor while she cooked. She was tiny. Later we slept in the lean-to. I dreamed of sitting at the foot of the sun, of a brilliant temple, of God and of a humble atom telling me I was a miracle, magical, unique and unrepeatable. I asked, "Why are you only an atom?" He replied, "It is the only matter I needed to sustain myself; the rest I gave to Man."

In the morning, I stared up at the forest green boughs, the berries still clinging to the branches, the sky pale yellow in the northeast and fuchsia in the south. We left after breakfast and never went back.

The Foreman

I remember the summer day Daddy came home for lunch, sat down on a chair in the kitchen, and said to Momma, "I didn't get the promotion. Mr. Barnes did." Daddy's weathered face reminded me of a lake bed—dried up—the caked mud cracked in a million pieces. I wanted time to go in reverse and for the decision to be different. I wanted to cry out, "It isn't fair! You put the star at the very top of the Christmas tree every year. Mr. Barnes would never even climb up there. It wouldn't even be important to him!" I wanted to hug Daddy but the distance was too great. The cataclysm loomed in front of me and I couldn't cross. With venom and disgust, Momma stared right at Daddy and then turned away as if it was his fault. The subject was never brought up again.

Coyote

On our way to Momma's home in Coyote, we stopped at Echo Canyon for a picnic. The sandstone rocks rose out of the ground straight up from the sagebrush and juniper. Tall, erect pine trees grew right up against the rocks and sometimes right out of them. In the bowl of the canyon, streaks of red paint cascaded down the chipped wind shorn sandstone—waterfalls frozen in place. The painter had boldly stroked against the rock, streaking thickly here, timidly there—fine trickles of paint against the sheer stone. We called out our names and they reverberated throughout the canyon.

I climbed on the rocks and sat looking out over the Rio Chama Valley—the cholla cactus, vegas de coyote (candles of the coyote), and sagebrush marching across the floor. Piñon bushes, renowned for their fragrant firewood, dotted the landscape, their nuts long squirreled away by wood rats. Their forest green needles contrasted against the red of their bark. The Utah juniper's branches drooped so low that birds could fly by and grab its blue berries. Vistas were carved out by openings in the black jack ponderosa pines—their long needles serving as kindling for fire—their seeds eaten by the Ancient Ones or made into bread.

The rocks loomed high above the valley floor like Viking ships traveling to a new world—sailing uncharted seas. Their masts, etched in stone, are furled in the eroded stone marked by wind, rain and snow—frost cracking the stone. Testing the wood, solid waves undulated over and across the ship's boughs as clouds hustled past on the grey cloudy day. In other parts of the sandstone, a carpenter had gouged out the wood, the waves of the sea sequentially rolling in and out, capped with froth.

On the way, the waters of the Chama River glistened blue in the late afternoon. The river flowed gently in the autumn afternoon past golden groves of cottonwood and yellow snakeweed. Here and there clusters of logs formed small dams, creating a small flurry as the river shifted its course. We drove further into the forest. The piñons and junipers were replaced by pines and Gambel oak, then by Douglas firs and aspens. The road wound higher and higher. At last we came to a clearing and stopped.

Momma's usual beans with chicos were cooking on her aunt's wood stove. Green chile peppers were being roasted as flies swarmed around the kitchen. Although there was a screen door, it was impossible to keep the flies out. For a while we swatted at them and then just ignored them.

I peeled chile with my cousin. We didn't speak to each other, only smiled. She learned English at the local school but at home everyone spoke Spanish. Somehow it didn't seem right to speak anything else, so I was quiet. I was welcomed and it was enough to just be there.

After we ate, we went to visit another home. There they were preparing hamburger and fried potatoes—another Harvey family special. I helped dice the potatoes. They made coffee with the rain water they caught on their roofs. The water was stored in wood barrels and boiled for drinking. That night they turned on kerosene lamps and we ate supper together.

I never learned these people's names.

The Sangre de Cristos

We chased each other in a game of freeze tag deep in the pine, aspen clad Sangre de Cristos. Dusk came upon us, hiding behind the thick circumference of the tall, ponderosa pines. The layered bark of the trees, like tributaries of the Pecos and Rio Grande, merged into each other, their descents not yet complete. Transparent bees and other insects—their insides sucked out, caught in spider webs, still clung to the bark. Colonies of lichen and moss carpeted the damp areas lending a velvet pall. Beneath the shallow top layer of the forest floor, its debris lay decomposing, commingling—unrecognizable. The sound of our feet, crackling on the dry leaves and pine needles reverberated throughout the forest—the decibel range magnified as the sound spread, bouncing between pines, threatening to reveal our hiding places. We learned we could never really hide.

Towering above us stood Daddy and Momma, transformed into trees of the uppermost, canopy layer. Their needles, abundant and full, lush and deep-green, filled each twig and branch with long shoots. We watched, frozen in place, comical, grotesque statues, as ivy began to slither up Daddy's trunk, grafting itself to his bark, feeding off of him. Eerie and haunting moss hung from Momma's branches—entangled her—cutting off her circulation. The needles of both trees began to yellow—the area behind each twig barren—and seedless cones fell to the forest floor—their leading shoots died back, their growth stunted. Spores settled on their branches.

Bit by bit, the trees surrendered, sealing off rotten branches, relinquishing damaged heartwood. The weight of the falling branches tore away strips of bark, creating holes where pools of water could collect—giving fungi a perfect place of attack, to canker their insides. The sound of the cracking wood echoed through the forest, soughing, moaning a sorrowful, grief-stricken dirge. Stag beetle larva fed off their disintegrating wood; lice fed off the fungi.

We sensed the coming collapse of the trees, but didn't know how to protect them, how to treat their exposed wounds, how to make them resistant to the blights preying on them, how to save them. The deterioration and the destruction continued, unabated, in front of us, as we stood paralyzed, trapped in our game. Each fallen needle, cone, twig, and branch left a track on the forest floor of the diseases killing the trees, a web of their fragile lives, a trail for the tracker.

The Amphitheater

Pecos

We packed Momma's tackle box with small, barbed hooks, weights, fishing line, pliers, and a knife, and climbed in the back of our green GMC truck—rain or shine. As we drove past Glorieta, Daddy said, "The Earth's skin is red here from the Indian blood spilled in the fighting with the Spanish." The wind whipped our hair and deposited a layer of powdered dust on our faces.

Driving over metal roofed bridges, the Pecos River flowed noisily below us, as we traveled deep into the faulted, limestone Canyon that was Momma's home—past the man-made lakes. Momma's sister had drowned in the Pecos, carried off by the strong, swift current. (Her Dad had died in the nickel mine at *Terrero,* the birthplace of the Pecos. She quit school then to help raise her four younger brothers).

We parked where the river wasn't too high. We dug for yucky, brown earthworms—coiled on top of each other—which I hated to hold. I squirmed and shook as I picked them up and Momma eventually waded off in the river with them and her rod.

Navajos don't fish. When their comfortable Fourth World was flooded by Water Monster out of fury at the theft of his babies, those lost in the flood became Water People. Daddy didn't want to be a cannibal, so he hung out with us, and we built dams and played—looking for the mermaid Momma had seen. The salty water was cold, and the rocks were slippery from the larva that lived on them.

Momma kept the trout she caught on a sharpened willow branch, shoving it through their mouth and chin, laying them in shallow water along the embankment—cautious not to lose them to the river. When she came back to camp, she put them in a metal bucket filled with river water.

Since the Pecos was her home, she only had to drop her line for the trout. Like a magnet to steel, they were drawn to her. A ghost—she was invisible to the trout until she reeled them in.

Momma got mad at us for playing with their slippery, slimy bodies after she caught them, which splintered their bones and made them harder to clean. It had no effect because we still *had* to peer into their gold-rimmed, dead eyes, open their mouths wide, move their gills and pet their sharp fins and tail. We pretended they were leaping, flying upstream through riffles to spawn, or hiding, buried in the gravel in the river, or suspended in a deep, dark pool, refusing to take any bait. After slitting their bellies and gutting them, we fried them over an open fire using a corn bread coating.

Survival

In the Autumn we went piñon picking south of Santa Fe in the amphitheater of the Sangre de Cristos, the Sandia and the Jemez Mountains. Daddy gave us our annual eye exam, "If you can see the Sandias, you don't need eyeglasses." We shook the trees, and caught the piñons in coffee cans—chewing the brown, sticky pitch for gum. Once I saw a tarantula hobbling across the piñon needles on the ground.

Daddy, whistling like the eerie Taos flutists and Kokopelli, the premier Anasazi flutist, foraged along with us. His plaintive notes hung on the wind, haunting us, traveling in slow motion, fusing the gap between the Ancient Ones and us.

We roasted the piñons at home on the wood stove, turning them for even browning. Eating them the right way took patience because the nuts were small and you had to crack the brown shells to get the nuts inside. I just ate them, shell and all!

Daddy told us, "When I graduated from high school I only had a quarter. Someday you might be in the same boat. I was able to get a job painting the blue trim on the government offices in Window Rock. You need to know you can survive without money, without food, without water." So we went without food and water.

We idealized Daddy's life of hardship—patiently sitting on his haunches, taking snow baths, throwing rocks right-handed with his left hand tied behind his back so he wouldn't be left-handed, losing his dog, Blackie, who fell off a cliff and onto a ledge. Daddy was kidnapped from home by a man on horseback who found him hiding in a water trough, taken to boarding school at the age of eight, alone, without his brother or sister.

He never complained when he relayed these matter-of-fact fragments of his past. Instead, he tried to pass on to us what he learned and mastered along the way: "Be good, be quiet, keep to yourself, don't say anything bad about anyone else, and do what you're told." He told us, "When I'm tired, the small part of my neck, just below my hairline aches. I talk to it, I tell it to relax and it does. When I'm sore, I use the heat from my hand to ease the pain." Also, "If anyone says anything bad about you, just say a prayer for them. Don't say anything back to them."

Bandelier

The long ladder led to the caves at Bandelier located on the Pajarito Plateau in Frijoles Canyon west of Santa Fe, in a vast piñon, juniper and sagebrush caldera with Indian ruins recessed in red, volcanic cliffs. The ancient Pueblo Indians lived in the caves and worshipped in subterranean, ceremonial *kivas*, with *sipapus* (small holes in the Earth), connecting them to the spirit world. They built elaborate multi-storied talus brick villages.

In the early morning, meandering clouds hung low in the canyon and it seemed as if we could reach them—touch their wetness—as we sat deep inside the caves, waiting for the sun to melt away the mist. Then, we climbed down to run in the snow-fed stream rambling through the canyon, the *El Rito de los Frijoles*, headed for the Rio Grande, the 'Blue Mother River' to the Indians. We searched for small brown trout, but never saw any.

The rocks at Bandelier are pockmarked where air bubbles formed while the lava cooled and hardened. They smell dusty, erode with just a touch, and taste flat. We traced over the pictographs left by the Ancient Ones, membrane to membrane—erasing time.

The Park Service Museum displayed old Indian bones, pottery shards with simple geometric shapes and painted with black, carbon paint, spiral-coiled willow baskets, murals showing the Indians hunting and cooking and fluted tips of arrowheads meticulously carved.

We imagined climbing, and slipping, at night over loose, treacherous lava rocks, to the top of the volcano—exhausted, pushed to our limit, cold—peering into the fiery red, bubbling, boiling, molten lava, warm sulfur steaming from the Earth around us, eerie, frozen rock sculptures exhaled by the volcano. Hiding in basaltic niches, we perched on tuff overhangs so we wouldn't be sacrificed at sunrise.

Daddy said being around these places wasn't good, "The Ancient Ones might not want us here." He hummed to let them know we were approaching.

The Indians left Bandelier—*hohokam*.

Tesuque

On Sundays, when Momma got off work, we drove on the winding, curving, back road to Tesuque, north of Santa Fe—the hot wind pollinating our faces with a cloud of golden grain. Tesuque was how the Spanish said the Tewa words, *Te Tesugeh Owingeh*, the "village of the narrow place of the cottonwood trees" or perhaps *Tatunge*, the 'dry, spotted place.' Part of Tesuque was dry—yucca, chamisa, sagebrush and cactus dotted the banks of the dry, sandy arroyos—barren mesas loomed in the distance, canvas-covered by scattered piñon trees. The other part of Tesuque was green and lush, a small farming community fed by snow from the Sangre de Cristos.

We stopped at 'Tesuque Lakes' desert picnic area to eat watermelon. Daddy said, "When I was little, we bottled watermelon juice, and pretended it was Coca-Cola." We'd tap the watermelons before we chose one to make sure that it was red and juicy inside. Sometimes, the stand owner would take his knife and cut out a little chunk for us to sample.

Getting into the picnic area meant climbing through a barb wire fence, but that didn't stop us. Momma warned us to keep away from the far lake. "It's dangerous." We pretended the Water Monster lived in the murky, brackish, still swamp.

While Momma and Daddy rested we hunted for wildflowers, gently studying them on their stems, their structure, colors, and patterns—counting the hundreds of little flowers making up the cone of Mexican hats, with their drooping, dark red and yellow petals—the bright red-orange, pale green, ivory and yellow petals of the parasitic Indian Paintbrush.

We mimicked dragon flies, practicing their maneuvers, flying low, hovering, gliding sideways and backwards, relying on their instinctive, autorotation techniques to avoid crash-landing—pitching downward and forward, then pulling up at just the right moment.

We chased yellow butterflies with small, almost invisible, black dots on their wings along with amber leopard-patterned ones and orange ones too! All with black '*ojos*', all with soft, veined, fringed wings, all more fragile than ashen paper.

Serpentine whirlwinds chased us, caught us, spinning us around and around then spitting us out as their energy dissipated. We reeled, and fell to the ground, breathless, and sandlogged.

Aya! Cordie sat on a devil cholla cactus once and had to go to the hospital to get all the spines taken out. Momma said, "They do that, they jump out, and pull you down."

Chimayo

Chimayo was another favored watering hole in the farming region of the Rio Grande Valley. All along the winding road following the Rio's branches, we saw adobe houses, trimmed in Taos blue, standing right up against the street, the local families selling fresh green chile in different sized baskets, strands of *ristras* and dried corn. We bought green chile by the bushel, picked Bing cherries in June, and peaches and apples in the fall.

Here and there in the arroyos, old cars or trucks sat abandoned, rusting, wrecked, stripped, sometimes filled with water after a heavy rain. We played in the warm, muddy, brown water of the labyrinth of *acequias*—the red slick, slippery clay sticking to our shoes and clothes.

At the *Sanctuario*, crutches, casts, and nasty stuff covered the walls, left behind by those healed by faith. At the back of the church was a hole filled with holy dirt, to rub on or take home in a jar. Wooden statues of *santos* enshrined in niches awaited entreaties, dark, red blood dripping from them, some lying in wooden coffins. Painted *retablos* peered from behind burning candles, whispering to us to come.

Nambe

Nambe Pueblo was Daddy's favorite. We'd all squish in the front seat of the truck, to avoid the fine, white dust raised by our truck. One of the local families had to open and close the entry gate. We got in free because we were Indian.

The cottonwoods along the Rio Nambe created a natural shade. A narrow trail curved high against the hillside to the double waterfall. Once, Jeanie got us to climb to the top of the waterfalls and then we didn't know how to get down. We inched down the rock, clinging to any crack or raised surface as a handhold, until we reached the basin of the falls. None of us knew how to swim so we never tried the clear, cold, deep pool.

We dreamed we rode on a cirrus cloud down the meandering Rio, our gossamer canoe steered by an ancient, tall Indian man, standing in the back, still and quiet, guiding us on our journey.

Sunday Excursions

We'd play at St. Francis playground while we'd wait for Momma to get off work. I got motion sick a lot and I'd still ride the merry go round and end up nauseous. Momma worked for the Sisters of Charity at St. Vincent Hospital. I don't know what she did but she wore a white uniform and very, very clean white polished nurse's shoes. After we picked her up, we'd drive along Canyon Road to the Santa Fe River and play in the small waterfall.

The river ran fast in the spring, but by the end of the summer it would be practically dry. Along the upper river, the dense brush hampered our access. Closer into town they had widened the banks and put rock walls along the sides. Momma would bring us leftovers from work, like chicken, for a picnic.

Sometimes, we'd go out to Camel Rock. We'd park, eat watermelon, climb on the red sandstone camel's head or run down its back at full speed. Catching ant-eating, blood-spraying horned toads with a mysterious third 'eye,' we would check each toad's belly, convinced that if it was yellow the toad was poisonous. Sometimes we caught little bitty babies. Wandering through the dry arroyos, we'd speed up the erosion, sliding down the treacherous banks, the soft dirt tumbling behind.

The Carmelites and their convent were Momma's solace. Their chapel was plain, without statues or an altar. I liked that you never got to see them, and that all they did was pray. When we talked to them (sometimes on Sunday) they would be behind a dark screen.

Sunday drives were Momma's favorite. She loved to tour expensive homes under construction so that's what we'd do—surveying the rooms and inspecting the wiring, the lighting, the plumbing, and the fixtures, breathing in the dust from the framing and the insulation. Elegant courtyards, patios, clerestories, and large windows merged with the vistas before them. Like the Pueblos, they used the texture of the land—the rivers, streams, canyons, mesas, mountains, piñons, junipers, rocks, grasses, wildflowers, and the natural fiery hues of New Mexico. And so the craftsmen continued the legacy of the ancient Indians, balancing art and utility—simple, straight, broken, horizontal, vertical, diagonal and curved lines; round, square, and triangulated shapes; planes in the forefront and background; repeating, patterned, rhythmic, using the light from the front, the back, the side—revealing, silhouetted space, now shallow, now deep.

The River

> In the Sangre de Cristos during the Winter, an unformed mass of ice and snow lies in a deep, tranquil sleep—a River waiting to be born.

The warming sun of Spring, melting and breaking up the snow pack, creates a trickling, hungry newborn.

Cradled by the Earth, its course determined in part by ancient forces, and in part by the meandering, scrolling, shearing, scouring, icy spring water, the River carves its own unique path.

Tumultuous and turbulent in its Spring giddiness, it prances and pulls, galloping head-ward, downstream over sheer bedrock, unrestrained.

After the Equinox, its energy diminished by the heat, the River reluctantly slackens off to a canter, drifting like quicksilver down a sluice.

Then slowing to a restful trot, it cascades gently past aspen and goldenrod, gleaming in the chill of Fall.

Then lying ostensibly dormant, frozen to a trickle, at a standstill, the snow-mass again waits for Spring.

The Designer

My Sister Jeanie

Her real name wasn't even 'Jeanie.' When she was three, my sister assumed her turquoise, papoose doll's name. Her doll was the size of an adult's hand, made from soft fleece, with a sienna face, brown squares for eyes, a single, red stitch for her mouth, small balls of fleece for fists, buttonhole stitching around her face, and a simple, straight stitch and French knot design in fuchsia and gold on her hooded blanket. Jeanie carried her against the back of her neck, tucked inside her dress. She made her dance, singing "la-la-la-la-la-la-la."

The Weaver

We stalked flowers, leaves, bark, berries, and wild grasses, picking them at mid-day so the sun would have dried up the dew. We hung them from their stems on the clothesline to dry or put them on a piece of mesh window screen set on bricks. We then stored them in brown paper bags until we were ready to make dye for embroidery thread. Yellow Sweet-Clover made a pale yellow color; Snakeweed made medium yellow; Globemallows and Golden Rod, brilliant yellow; Indian Paintbrush, dull orange; Brown Onions, rust; Violet Penstemens, khaki; Scarlet Buglers, Bluebonnets, and Wild onions made varying shades of tan; Sage Brush, light brown; Red Onions, light medium brown; Juniper Mistletoe, medium brown; Chamiso, dark brown; Piñon sumac and ocher, black.

We shredded the leaves and blossoms, cut any twigs or bark into small pieces, then wrapped the material in cheesecloth. In a big, enamel pot, we cooked the dye material for an hour until the water became the color we wanted. Then, we strained the liquid dye through a sieve. Adding cold water, we simmered the thread for two hours; stirring with a wooden spoon so the dye would penetrate evenly. After the thread cooled, we rinsed it and hung it to dry, turning the skeins regularly so they would dry evenly. To set the dye, we boiled the thread for an hour in a mixture of alum and water.

Each dyed skein was wrapped in homemade wax-paper envelopes and organized by shade like a color wheel. From this thread, Jeanie embroidered Globemallows, Larkspur (*Espuela de Cabellero* or horseman's spur), Penstemen, and Scarlet Buglers in their natural, muted tones. She also embroidered Daffodils, Roses, and Tulips, using many different, ingenious stitches such as the chain, feather, single feather, long feather, long armed feather, parallel feather, fly, star, spider web, herringbone, lazy daisy, chain scroll, chain ring, picot, straight, satin and, my favorite, the French knot—her textile strands of color overlain and interwoven.

The Traveler

Off the wrapper advertisement of a Milk Nickel (a five cent ice cream bar), Jeanie ordered a telescope to see Cassiopeia, the Queen of Ethiopia, and Orion the Hunter, Poseidon's son.

Jeanie keyed off the Big Dipper, which to Navajos is a family around a hogan fire. Peering at the wintry Milky Way, and galaxies far removed, we were pulled by gravity's force, thrust out into the universe's cold, vast, outer space, weightless, drifting, floating, tumbling, turning, endlessly orbiting the earth.

Apache Canyon

We rode our bikes on the Santa Fe Trail to Apache Canyon, fifteen miles north of Santa Fe, past piñons and junipers that witches could not pass unless they knew the exact number of needles on the trees.

Traversing the rutted, scarred route, the *cordillera* into Santa Fe, we entered our private, secret retreat—a steep walled canyon trodden over time by the Llano,

Folsom and Plano ancestral Indians, the Anasazi and Mogollon ancient Indians, and Pueblo and nomadic Plains Indians. The canyon floor was also traversed over time by helmeted Spanish conquistadores on horseback, Anglo merchants, and Union and Confederate forces that skirmished in the canyon.

Tired, we ate cold red chile sandwiches and drank bottled watermelon juice while breathing in the canyon's piñon scented air and dreaming away the day.

The Designer

In high school, Jeanie studied design at the Institute of American Indian Arts. She liked drawing in charcoal, pen and ink. She blended the charcoal as she chose, tracing over it at will, with fine lines of black ink undulating across the page—the black dust and ink smudging and staining her face, her hands, her nails, and her clothes.

At first, silhouettes were captured fleetingly—the curve of a face, a breast, a hip, a thigh. Eventually she produced page after page of elegant, lavish models, attired with the strict discipline of the day—fashion etiquette meticulously observed. Her sinuous, sumptuous, sultry models gazed to the right, to the left, in three-quarters pose, or straight ahead—all predicated on sharp, crisp angles, accentuated curves, elongated torsos, their faces shrouded in shadow. They sauntered out of their parched sanctuary, alert, dominant, proud, displaying their form, sashaying down the modeling runway, stalking the crowd, devouring the paparazzi, feeding on the frenzied excitement, then satiated, retreated to their portfolio preserve.

California Virus

After graduation, Jeanie came home and could only find work at White Swan, a laundry on Cerrillos Road. She schemed with her friend, Tracy, on how she would meet her in California.

Jeanie started running away, hitchhiking to Albuquerque. I wasn't supposed to say anything, but as soon as Momma got home, she smelled the fever luring Jeanie away. Slamming the door on her red Dodge, Momma would take off to Albuquerque to find her and bring her back home. Not even the devil-killer hill, La Bajada, deterring her. The last time though Jeanie got away.

Momma prayed that she would come home. After that failed, she hired a fortune teller, then a tarot card reader, (even though she knew it was so wrong for a Catholic), to tell her where Jeanie was, why she had left, and if she was okay. Seeking Jeanie's return, Momma hiked from Santa Fe to Chimayo—leaving early in the morning—taking only a canteen of water—her Requiem Marathon. None of it worked.

Hokam

From the whispered information I overheard at the hospital, it turned out Jeanie had been living and working in the garment district in Los Angeles. Her daughter, Kecia, was nine. A hospital employee there had tracked down Momma and said, "We think we may have your daughter."

As I sat near her, a tangle of tubes sustaining her, I said, "Jeanie, wake up. Come on, let's go to Apache Canyon. We'll climb the long hills without walking our bikes. We'll beat the wind this time. Come on. Let's go. We'll spend the day." I heard no answer.

A nurse came in, and said, "The only voice she probably recognizes is your Momma's."

Jeanie was '*hokam*,' the Pima singular word for 'all used up'. The plural of hokam is '*hohokam*' and describes why the ancient Indians left an area. The ancient Indians for us, the Anasazi, had made tools and weapons, decorated their pottery with geometrical shapes, weaved willow baskets for which they were renowned, built villages of tiered masonry, carved mysterious, haunting petroglyphs, left behind their handprints emblazoned on their cave walls—then they had vanished—disappeared—*hohokam*.

The Pristine Rivers

The ancient Anasazis inhabited Colorado, New Mexico and into Arizona, nurtured by the Rio Grande (the "Blue Mountain") and Pecos Rivers. The Rivers flowed southward, commingling at Amistad, and then coursed onward to the Gulf of Mexico. Over time, the rivers that fed the thirsty families and crops of the Anasazi were transfigured.

Hot dog wrappers, potato chip bags, candy wrappers, styrofoam cups, soft drink and beer cans, tangled fishing line, dirty diapers, animal carcasses, rusting cars and trucks, toxic pesticides, metallic waste, industrial chemicals discharged from factories and plants, raw sewage, and human and animal fecal contamination converged in their attack on the rivers before they ended their journey—comatose, at the Gulf of Mexico —*Hohokam*.

Jeanie had been caught up in this onslaught. Her blood, the same blood in the veins of our rivers—poisoned—the pollution and stench unabated—her arteries choked. As she lay in front of me, her moaning echoed to me from the cesspool she had fallen into —alone.

She lived like this for eight years. She lost weight, her body curled up into a fetal position, and she never regained consciousness.

The Quest

The day of the funeral it snowed—dry, blowing, hissing snow—snowflakes like sharp discs. Momma was running around at the last minute, as usual, fifteen minutes before Mass, taking a bath in a thimbleful of water, trying to find her clothes, and getting dressed. I thought, We're going to be late, and I'm the driver—Great.

St. John's Catholic Church was dark and cold, and so empty it echoed. No sunlight reflected through the stained glass. The only light came from candles flickering in front of hand-carved *bultos*—bleeding, weeping Mary, grieving as she held her Son—St. Michael trampling on Satan—Jesus clasping the Orb, rising into Heaven.

Particles of dust encircled the brocade-stoled priest as he prayed and lifted his gold-plated chalice high—singing the Gloria. He blessed us with Holy Water. Momma continued to cry. From Daddy, we had learned that it wasn't dignified to cry over death. We stood still, silent and composed.

We drove to the National Cemetery in even heavier, blinding, piercing snow. We moved as fast as the tectonic plates of rock grinding against each other, deep beneath us. Still, Momma gripped the back of my seat, all the while crying, and begged me, repeatedly, "Please, Carol, please, slow down, please, slow down for the love of God and Jesus, Mary, and Joseph—*Dios mio*." If I had been hopping on one foot, in the snow, racing the car, I would have won handily. I told her again, though, "Momma, I'll try." I drove even slower.

When we got to the cemetery, we gathered under a solitary, tarp shelter. Around us, piñon and juniper trees, laden with snow, stood out against the still and silent landscape. As my younger brother read a prayer, Daddy stood next to him, he was smaller now, his brown, creased face, placid. Momma was still crying. I wished she would just stop. It seemed so inappropriate. I couldn't look at her, afraid to see the cracked, convulsed Earth in her face.

I wanted to run away, taking Jeanie with me, to Apache Canyon—to trudge through the deep snow with her—to make angels, in the fresh, fallen, feathery down snow—dance like blue, Spring butterflies, laugh as pine cones from the forest canopy twirled around us, spiraling downward, destined to feed the microbes buried deep below us. Instead, her coffin, with a single bouquet of white lilies, was lowered into her grave.

The Blue Mother River carved its crescent meandering scrolls in the alluvial plain in front of us, etching its course in the earth's skin. Gleaming snowflakes covered Momma's black mantilla. Each intricate, delicate, hexagonal, frozen crystal burst forth from its nucleus, repeating its symmetrical harmony, trying with all of its might to transcend its structure, to explode, hurling its dust particles back into space. Instead, they finished their journey, gently melting on Momma's grey hair.

The City of Holy Faith Is Ever Alive

Frost glazed the sage bushes along El Camino Real. Clumps of grama grass salted with frozen ice stood sentinel. Yucca pods encased in glittering solid ice witnessed the Winter Solstice. Icicles hung from the needles on piñon trees. Aspen leaves not yet fallen reflected the sunshine in the delicate, thin slices of ice enveloping their golden sheen. Milkweed competed with the brilliant white of the silky snow lacing the pods. Red berries covered with hoarfrost signaled the birth of Christ whose blood would be shed for us. Columnar ice marched across the cholla cactuses. Cattails lay strewn across the snowfall like pixy sticks from a child's game. Abstract six-sided crystalline snowflake patterns accentuated the sunlight streaming through the window of our rental car.

Tracks of birds and wildlife invited us to follow into the nests and dens and burrows sheltering them from the cold. For them the snow was a ladder to reach berries and branches, insulation, and material for underground homes. Breaks in the snow evidenced where chirping birds that had not migrated south burst out after spending a night blanketed under its warmth. Rodent droppings gave away to elaborate underground tunnels. New fallen snow provided added height to reach piñon nuts not yet fallen. Insects and reptiles lay asleep, hibernating until spring. Elemental, cellular microbes continued their process of breaking down the detritus of the forest floor buried deep under the mantle of snow.

A white-tailed deer peered out from behind a grey stark elm, its brown, still eyes mesmerizing. Its coloring, its protectorate, blended in with the forest. Its hideaway—disclosed only by its lack of movement and its direct stare—offered a seducing invitation to a muffled, serene spell of solitude broken only when the deer gracefully glided away.

An abandoned anonymous farmhouse, banished to survive in the winter alone, clattered with life as a Cardinal Oracle predicted an end to the storm. Mourning Doves pecked in the snow—scavenging for grain from the past harvest not yet devoured by the magpies. A red fox or a coyote, too stealthy to be identified, hid in its holy habitat—stalking any prey that might come across its path.

Although it was the dead of winter, the animated spirit of nature could not be halted. The brisk, fresh, alpine air breathed forth across the autonomous landscape. The coma of the earth existed only in fiction life scurried over, under and throughout the diaphanous down covering her. The sunlight, emerging from the overcast sky, promised a festival of light—dancing, dashing, dazzling, flashing, frenzied, frolicking, furied, galloping, gliding, glittering, glistening, gleaming, prancing and pawing, sparkling, and twinkling.

Sustaining the Revolution: Adaptations and Transformations in New Mexico State-Tribal Relations
by
Alvin H. Warren
Santa Clara Pueblo

It has been four hundred and sixty-eight years since the encounter between Native Americans and Europeans in New Mexico, and all twenty-two Tribes, Nations and Pueblos located in the state continue to reside on our ancestral lands, speak our languages, maintain our distinct cultures and traditions, and exercise our right of self-government. That this remains true, despite the superimposition of three separate national governments, is a testament to the resiliency of our core values as well as our unwavering commitment to maintaining our inherent sovereignty. Yet, it is also an indication of both the Tribes' extraordinary ability to simultaneously adapt to and transform these successive governments as well as the maturation of national and state governments in their relationships with tribal governments and Native people. The story of Santa Fe is, inextricably, the story of this evolutionary process. Since 1610 it has served as the capital of the Province of New Mexico under Spain, the territory and then department of New Mexico under Mexico and finally the territory and now State of New Mexico under the United States. As such, it has been the focal point of interactions that defined the relations between the governments of New Mexico and of the twenty-two Tribes, Nations and Pueblos. Over time these relations have experienced significant challenges with profound implications for both Indians and non-Indians. Yet, where we were in 2010 demonstrates a profound and hard-fought shift in relations toward one based more on mutual respect and intergovernmental cooperation that, ultimately, benefits all of the people in our state.

Using Spanish Law to Defend Pueblo Land Rights

Land, water and natural resources are a core value of the Tribes, Nations and Pueblos in New Mexico. As indigenous peoples our languages, cultures, histories, identities, and economic prosperity are inextricably interwoven with our ancestral lands. Our territories abound in Native place-names and habitation sites that span millennia and provide the foundation for our continuity as distinct and self-governing nations. The City of Santa Fe, for example, will always be known first to the people of the Pueblo of Tesuque and other Tewa Pueblos as *Oga Pogeh* and as a part of Tesuque's ancestral homeland. Archeologists, for their part, are now coming to determine that the indigenous history of Santa Fe is complex and extensive and that, by 1300, the Pueblo in present-day Santa Fe was one of at least 10 significant settlements and may have included 3,000 to 5,000 inhabitants. During the time that New Mexico was part of Spain and Mexico, the practice of awarding *Mercedes*, land grants to colonists, was used to establish colonial settlements. According to the 1680 *Recopilacion de Leyes de los Reynos de las Indias*, however, the governor was to ensure that the lands used and occupied by sedentary Indians was protected from encroachment by such grants. In reality, these laws were often disregarded, resulting in vast tracts of indigenous land being converted into town lots, farming lots, irrigation systems known as *acequias* and communal grazing lands.

Nevertheless, Pueblo leadership became increasingly sophisticated at using these laws and working with key Spanish officials to protect our land rights. One example occurred in the 18th century with Santa Clara Pueblo. In 1724 Juan and Antonio Tafoya of Santa Cruz sought a grant in the Santa Clara Canyon to establish a settlement. The Pueblo protested but was willing to allow the brothers to use the land for grazing livestock. Repeatedly, from 1724 until 1763, the Tafoyas violated this agreement by building a ranch house and diverting the Santa Clara Creek to irrigate their crops, which prevented vitally needed water from flowing to the Pueblo. Aware of their rights under Spanish law, the Pueblo petitioned successive governors in Santa Fe beginning with Governor Gervasio Cruzat y Gongora in 1733. He and his successors repeatedly sided with the Pueblo; directing the Tafoyas to abide by the original agreement with the Pueblo. Santa Clara also pursued remedies through the local courts, resulting in the imposition of a fine in 1757 by the Chief Magistrate of Santa Cruz, Captain Francisco Gomez de Castillo. When it finally became clear that the Tafoyas would never cease in attempting to take possession of the Pueblo's land, the Pueblo enlisted the support of the Catholic priest assigned to the Pueblo, Fray Mariano Rodriguez de la Torre. With Fray Rodriguez de la Torre's assistance, the Pueblo petitioned Governor Tomás Velez Cachupín in 1763 and—upon review of the history of ingressions—the governor annulled the grant given to the Tafoyas and granted the entire Santa Clara Canyon to the Pueblo for "cultivable and common lands of the said pueblo for their flocks and horses with all its pastures and waters...."[1]

While these laws protecting Pueblo land rights remained in effect after Mexico's independence from Spain in 1821, in practice—according to Pueblo historian Joe Sando—"corrupt administrators and politicians falsified documents, produced fraudulent titles to land owned by Indians, and were able to alienate Pueblo land, often without the Indians even knowing about it."[2] Mexican governmental officials were often lax and sometimes colluded with settlers to obtain Pueblo lands. And all this despite the fact that Indians were considered Mexican citizens.

It is not surprising, then, that many Pueblos welcomed the possession of New Mexico by the United States. In fact, in August of 1846 a delegation of Pueblo Indians met with Brigadier General Stephen Watts Kearny to request that the American government assist with restoring land they saw as stolen from them. They found a powerful ally in John C. Calhoun, who served as both the first Territorial Governor and the Superintendent of Indian Affairs. Governor Calhoun ensured that the Office of Surveyor General acted quickly to affirm the Pueblos' rights to their core lands, pursuant to the Treaty of Guadalupe Hidalgo between the United States and Mexico. This resulted in the issuance of patents in the 1860s by President Abraham Lincoln to the Pueblos for a portion of our lands. At the same time, the Navajo people were forcibly removed to Bosque Redondo, in southeastern New Mexico, not to return to their homelands until the Treaty of 1868 was executed. The Jicarilla Apache, by contrast, had entered into a treaty with the United States in 1852, which established the core of their current land base.

Disempowerment Under the New Mexico Territorial Government

Tragically, the responsiveness and collaboration demonstrated by the approval of the patents were quickly undermined by a territorial government aligned against the Pueblos. In particular, Pueblo Indians quickly learned that the patents did not guarantee the protection of the vast majority of our landholdings. First, the patents did not include the full extent of the Pueblos' traditional lands. Second, they only served to relinquish all title and claim of the United States to this land and would not affect any "adverse valid rights," if they existed.

Soon, Pueblo land rights became entangled in the growing scandal known as the "Santa Fe Ring"—a political machine of powerful lawyers, businessmen, judges, politicians and speculators that quickly worked to consolidate control over land in the new territory. In fact, members of the Santa Fe Ring had a key role in removing federal obligations to protect Pueblo landholdings based on the Territorial Supreme Court's decision in the 1869 *US vs. Lucero* case and the U.S. Supreme Court's ruling in the 1876 *US vs. Joseph* case. The elimination of federal protection would have dire consequences for the Pueblos. After the territorial court decision, the federal Special Agent for the Pueblos, John Ward, ominously predicted that, if allowed to stand, the decision would mean that "7000 honest and industrious Indians, living quietly in their villages, cultivating the soil for their sustenance, with very little aid from the government or any other source whatever, and in every respect self-supporting… will, in the course of years, [be] reduce[d]…to poverty and ruin."[3]

These cases forced Pueblo people to turn to the local governments and territorial courts to protect our land rights, which were often biased against them. First, in 1854 the Territorial Legislature and governor enacted a law disenfranchising Pueblo Indians. Thus, elected officials were unlikely to support Pueblo concerns over those whom they saw as their constituents. The same prejudice was imbedded in the territorial court systems, as noted in 1904 by Territorial Supreme Court Associate Justice John R. McFie: "[Pueblo Indians] are at a disadvantage in our courts, as I have reason to know by ten-year experience on the bench of the Territory. I have seen their testimony disregarded utterly although clear and convincing in my own mind, and it is difficult to secure any other result."[4]

As a result, by the 1920s non-Indian encroachment on Pueblo lands had reached epidemic proportions, amounting to more than 3,000 claims. By one estimation, Euro-American lawyers and settlers came to posses over 80% of the patented land grants and the United States gained 52 million acres of New Mexico as public domain. Pueblo people struggled to meet bare subsistence needs as our lands and waters were taken over without recourse. Even our ability to enjoy a fundamental American value—the free exercise of religion—was disrupted by the *Religious Crimes Code* and Interior Department circulars that made the practice of Native religions illegal.

Resurgence of Self-Government and Building of State-Tribal Relations

Yet, in the midst of these desperate circumstances, the seeds were sown that would transform the relationship between Tribes and first the Territory and then the State of New Mexico. It began with three events that took place in the first two decades of the 20th century. First, after the federal government finally began to assume its fiduciary and trust responsibilities to the Pueblo Indians around the turn of the century, the territorial government was compelled to accept language in its *Enabling Act* (36 Stat. 557, chap. 310) that both recognized that the terms "Indian" and "Indian Country" applied to the Pueblos and their lands as well as disclaimed all right, title and jurisdiction to Indian land in the proposed state. Second, in 1913 the US Supreme Court essentially reversed its decision in *US vs. Joseph*, deciding in *US vs. Sandoval* that the Pueblo Indians met the criteria to be considered 'Indians' as defined by the laws of the United States.

Perhaps the most decisive action taken by the Pueblos was the resurgence and reorganizing of the All-Indian Pueblo Council in the 1920s as a powerful voice on behalf of the unified Pueblos. The catalyst was a bill introduced in Congress in 1922 by New Mexico Senator Holm O. Bursum to *Quiet Title to Lands Within Pueblo Indian Land Grants*. True to its title, the bill sought to quiet the furor over rampant trespassing onto Pueblo lands by issuing patents to non-Indians for vast tracts of Pueblo land; extinguishing Pueblo titles and awarding minimal compensation to the Pueblos. The Pueblos felt that this bill would "complete our destruction…, deprive us of our happy life by taking away our lands and water and…destroy our Pueblo government and our customs."[5] The All-Indian Pueblo Council, embodying the same ancient alliance that successfully conducted the 1680 Pueblo Revolt, engaged a variety of supporters, conducted a public relations and lobbying campaign and were successful in preventing the Bursum Bill's passage. The result was a more-balanced "Pueblo Lands Act" enacted in 1924, which created a three-member board to examine all adverse claims to Pueblo lands, restore Pueblo title in those instances where claims were baseless and award fair compensation to the Pueblos where the board determined that claims were legitimate.

Even as the State of New Mexico came to terms with the reasserted sovereignty and advocacy of the Tribes, it would take decades for it to accept the reality that tribal members are also full citizens of the state entitled to equal rights and protections. The moment of reckoning came when Valencia County Clerk Eloy Garley denied Miguel Trujillo, a former U.S. Marine and WWII veteran, the right to register to vote because Mr. Trujillo was from Isleta Pueblo, lived on the Laguna reservation and the New Mexico Constitution denied suffrage to those considered "Indians not taxed." Despite his service to the country and the fact that Congress had passed a law making all Indians citizens in 1924, Mr. Trujillo and other Indians living on reservations in New Mexico were not permitted even the most basic form of civic participation in state government. In response, Mr. Trujillo retained three attorneys and petitioned the Federal District Court in Santa Fe for an injunction. Indians around New Mexico, including my grandfather, Alvin K. Warren, organized in support of Mr. Trujillo's efforts, sometimes at great personal and professional risk. In a historic ruling, on August 3, 1948, the Federal District Court determined that the denial of the right to vote to Indians was unconstitutional, in part because Indians did pay taxes. Thus Indians in New Mexico became among the last people in the United States to win the right to vote in state and local elections. In 1953, the New

Mexico Legislature finally removed the words "Indians not taxed" from the New Mexico Constitution.

That very same year the legislature also took the first step in formalizing the state's relationship with the Tribes by creating the New Mexico Commission on Indian Affairs. Reflecting a growing concern with the impact that waves of federal and state policy were beginning to have on the long-term survival of Native languages and cultures, the advocates that pushed for the commission tasked it with recording and transcribing the legends of the Tribes and Pueblos for posterity. The Office of Indian Affairs, based in Santa Fe, effectively became the working arm of the commission and served as an intermediary between the governor and legislature of the state and the twenty-two Tribes, Nations and Pueblos. Over time, especially beginning in the 1970s, the Commission evolved into a body of current and former tribal leaders, including visionaries like Zuni Governor Robert Lewis, Mescalero Apache President Wendell Chino, Jicarilla President Leonard Atole, Santa Clara Governor Walter Dasheno and San Felipe Governor Frank Tenorio.

These tribal leaders were at the forefront of a new era in tribal governance. Beginning with the work of the American Indian Policy Review Commission, the federal government's policy in the late 1960s and early 1970s shifted to one supportive of tribal self-determination and of strengthening tribal sovereignty. Accordingly, tribal governments began to more-fully exercise a renewed power and authority. Increasingly, this led to conflicts with state and local governments over issues such as regulatory jurisdiction, taxation, land and water rights and law enforcement.

Yet, a new group of state and tribal leaders came to realize that more could be gained from cooperation rather than conflict between the state and Tribes. Partly this was due to the increasing participation of Native voters, particularly Navajos, in state and local elections. This resulted in a slowly increasing number of Indian legislators like John Pinto, a Navajo who has served as a member of the State Senate since 1977, and the late Representative Leo Watchman, Sr., as well as the election of supportive non-Indian legislators such as Representative (and now Speaker of the House of Representatives) Ben Lujan, Representative Nick Salazar and several others.

In addition, a shift in federal policy to a state's rights approach provided the impetus for Tribes and state agencies to work more closely with each other. Rather than Tribes receiving funding through a block grant, federal programs such as Medicaid, Medicare and Welfare (later Temporary Assistance to Needy Families) were entrusted to state governments. Suddenly, Tribes and state agencies were compelled to work together to ensure that these programs and resources would benefit Native Americans living on and off the reservation. Finally, the enactment of the Indian Gaming Regulatory Act in 1988 cemented the need for a more effective working relationship between Tribes and the state as Tribes were required to enter into compacts with the state to conduct certain forms of gaming and as the state began to receive hundreds of millions of dollars from gaming tribes in "revenue sharing" pursuant to those compacts.

For these reasons, the 1980s and 1990s become an era of many firsts. In the early 1980s, Governor Toney Anaya and Navajo President Peterson Zah decided to formalize a new working relationship by signing the first *State/Tribal Protocol Agreement*. At the same time, a group of Native women including Cora Gomez of the Jicarilla Apache Nation and Margaret Dosedo of the Zuni Tribe organized the Indian Area Agency on Aging. Eventually, this would establish a structure for capital outlay and program funding for senior citizen centers in tribal communities across the state. Furthermore, after initial resistance from Attorney General Hal Stratton, it became recognized that tribal governments were, in fact, eligible for capital outlay funding, resulting in state funding beginning to flow toward the dire infrastructure needs in tribal communities.

Gradually, state and tribal and governments began to tackle other challenging issues such as temporary foster care, comity and reciprocity between tribal and state court systems, dual-taxation, and tourism. To do so they ingeniously developed mechanisms that maintained recognition of the Tribes' sovereignty while ensuring the state abided by its responsibility to serve all of its citizens, including Indians who live on and off reservations. In some instances this led to state agencies deferring state regulatory processes as long as tribal institutions and regulatory approaches were used. In February of 1992 a *Policy and Principles Agreement* was created that, for the first time, laid out a protocol and process for state-tribal relations. As state-tribal interactions became more frequent some state agencies began to designate tribal liaisons. Concurrently, twelve Tribes negotiated gaming compacts with Governor Gary Johnson in 1996, which would revolutionize tribal economic development and create a significant revenue stream for the state.

Throughout these monumental developments the Commission on Indian Affairs and the Office of Indian Affairs provided consistent leadership and support. Though the Office enjoyed many effective leaders and staff, it experienced tremendous growth and influence during the term of Regis Pecos, a former Governor of the Pueblo of Cochiti and current Chief of Staff to Speaker Ben Lujan. Long-serving tribal leaders were joined by new leaders who reinforced and built upon this new working relationship with the state. And, at the same time, more and more individual Indian people began exercising our right to vote and participate in political and policymaking processes.

A Watershed in State-Tribal Relations

The election of Bill Richardson as Governor in 2002 marked a watershed in state/tribal relations. Tribal leaders astutely gained assurances during the campaign from candidate Richardson that, if elected, he would take several measures to continue strengthening state/tribal relations. In return, they and their tribal officials encouraged voter registration and get-out-the-vote efforts among their members and provided other support to assure his election. In response, one of Richardson's first acts as governor was to sign a *Statement of Policy and Process* by which the governor committed his administration to recognizing and respecting tribal sovereignty, working in a government-to-government manner with Tribes and bringing down barriers that prevented tribal members from accessing state services. Next, he signed *Executive Order No. 2003-022* in June, 2003, elevating the Office of Indian Affairs to a cabinet-level Indian Affairs Department headed by a cabinet secretary. House Bill 39, enacted in April, 2004, codified the elevation of the department. As stated by Governor Richardson at the time: "The elevation of the Office of Indian Affairs was one of the promises that I made to the Native American citizens of New Mexico to more effectively tackle the many pressing issues that affect Indian communities… New Mexico's Native Americans now officially have an equal voice and a permanent place in my Cabinet."[6]

Governor Richardson proceeded to appoint more Native Americans to key administration positions than any previous governor, including cabinet secretaries and deputy secretaries, his chief legal counsel, his communications director and numerous state boards and commissions—some of which had never had a Native person in that position. In 2005, Richardson signed *Executive Order 2005-003* mandating the creation of a cross-agency, statewide policy on repatriation and the protection of sacred places. This was accompanied by *Executive Order 2005-004* that required seventeen state agencies to develop pilot tribal consultation policies or protocols in one programmatic area. In cooperation with the legislature, over $120 million in capital outlay funding was appropriated for tribal projects from 2004-2010 just through the Indian Affairs Department alone, which doesn't account for significant funding through the Department of Transportation, Aging and Long-Term Services Department or Environment Department. Increasingly, barriers were brought down to Tribes directly accessing multiple funding streams in state government, including resources for culturally-appropriate behavioral health programs, tribal economic development programs, New Mexico Finance Authority loan and grant funds and the *Governor's Road Improvement Projects* (GRIP) funds. Three historic water rights settlements were reached, after decades of stalemate, affirming the water rights of the Navajo Nation, Jicarilla Apache Nation and the Pueblos of San Ildefonso, Tesuque,

Pojoaque, Nambe and Taos. More Tribes entered into tax sharing agreements with the state and the unique arrangements were codified to exempt tribal tobacco and gasoline sales from state taxation.

As a result of the effective advocacy of tribal leaders, Governor Richardson's administration, Indian advocates and legislators—more than seventy bills or memorials directly benefiting Native Americans were enacted or passed from 2003–2010, including: SB 115, *The Indian Education Act*; HB 868, *The Tribal Infrastructure Fund Act*; SB 172, *The Indian Water Rights Settlement Fund*; HB 151, *Adding Indian Appointees to the Interstate Stream Commission and the Water Quality Control Commission*; HB 73 / SB 581, *The Reburial Grounds Act*; HB 50, *The American Indian Post Secondary Act*; HB 37, *Amendments the New Mexico Subdivision Act* to allow Tribes to submit opinions on proposed subdivisions throughout the state; HB 162, *Severance Bonds for Tribal Infrastructure* and HB 90, *The Native American Schools Dual Credit Program*.

Perhaps the most far-reaching is SB 196, *The State-Tribal Collaboration Act*, enacted in 2009. This Act codified an effective structure for state-tribal relations, requiring: annual summits between the state governor and tribal leaders; annual reports from all thirty-three cabinet-level agencies on their work and funding related to Tribes and Native Americans; training to key state agency staff to enhance services to Native Americans; the adoption and implementation of tribal collaboration and communications policies by all thirty-three cabinet-level agencies; and the designation of tribal liaisons in all thirty-three cabinet-level agencies.

Local Transformations and the New Santa Fe Convention Center

Even as these monumental developments occurred at the state level, similar transformations were taking place at the local level. Most emblematic was the conflict and compromise that ensued over the building of the new Santa Fe Convention Center.

In 2005 the City of Santa Fe prepared to demolish the Sweeney Convention Center and construct in its place a new fifty-four million dollar Convention Center. Yet the proposed project unearthed a reality invisible to many that Santa Fe is—first and foremost—an ancient Pueblo settlement. For this reason, when the initial excavations at the Sweeney site encountered Native American, Spanish and American human remains, dwelling sites and other ancient objects, Tesuque tribal leaders—particularly then-Governor Mark Mitchell—voiced the Pueblo's strong opposition to the building of the new Convention Center on that site. "To remove those burials and artifacts would be to erase the footprints of our ancestors, which we could not allow," said former-Governor Mitchell.[7]

The City of Santa Fe was compelled to consult with the Pueblo because of the 1990 Native American Graves Protection and Repatriation Act but, initially, sought to proceed with the Convention Center as planned. The Pueblo's concerns expressed to the planning committee went largely unheard but received support from the state's Cultural Properties Review Committee (CPRC). The city had hired the Office of Archaeological Studies (OAS), which was required to obtain a permit from the CPRC. The CPRC urged the city and Tesuque to try to work out a solution to the stalemate. Both sides knew that delays to the project would increase its construction costs.

The turning point, according to both then-Santa Fe City Council member and current Santa Fe Mayor David Coss and former-Governor Mitchell, was when city leaders went to the Pueblo in their official capacity to negotiate a compromise. For the Pueblo, this action demonstrated a long-overdue recognition of their sovereignty and of their ancestral relationship to the land underlying Santa Fe. As for the city leaders, it affirmed a recognition that direct, honest communications were necessary to find a way for the Convention Center to proceed while addressing the Pueblo's concerns.

Instead of battling through lawyers and the media, the city and Pueblo leaders chose to meet face-to-face, both at the Pueblo and in Santa Fe, and work out an agreement. They agreed that the new Convention Center would proceed, but with an understanding that eighty-eight fewer parking spaces would be constructed underground in order not to disturb other human remains and artifacts and that all unearthed human remains would be reburied at the site and not subjected to scientific examination. In 2008 the impressive, Pueblo-styled Convention Center opened its doors, with city and Pueblo officials participating jointly in the ribbon cutting.

The Convention Center experience forever changed the relationship between Santa Fe and the Pueblo of Tesuque. "Relations between the city and the Pueblo never existed—we were always on the opposite side," stated former-Governor Mitchell. "A positive outcome of this situation is that we now have a relationship that is unique between Tesuque Pueblo and the City of Santa Fe. When it comes down to certain issues, now the Pueblo and the city have an ally in each other. Although we still have to look out for our own interests we now do this by sitting across from each other and negotiating rather than by filing lawsuits."[8] Mayor Coss added: "I realized that I had grown up over the hill but, except for a couple baseball games, had never been to Tesuque Pueblo. Now I go to Tesuque Pueblo Feast Day and people are happy to see me."[9]

As he reflects back, Mayor Coss is clear about the underlying motivations in seeking out a compromise with the Pueblo: "There's been a long cultural and historical struggle and it's important to come out on the right side of that…it's important to come out on the side of justice."[10]

Conclusion

Every year thousands of visitors come to New Mexico—Santa Fe, especially—because of Native American culture and traditions. Among these are individuals from countries such as Russia, the Netherlands, the Ukraine, and Pakistan who are fascinated by the ongoing vitality of tribal governmental systems and the increasingly positive and effective relationship between these governments and their people and the state and federal governments. It is hard to summarize the slow and arduous journey that has brought us all to this point from a time when federal, territorial and state policies and leaders sought the outright destruction of Indian governments, languages, cultures and land rights. It is now widely recognized that Tribes and Native Americans are an essential part of New Mexico's social, political, economic, environmental and cultural destiny. Tribal economic development is driving regional job creation in many parts of the state and Indian people are more prominently involved in the governmental, private and non-profit sectors than ever before. Tribal lands and natural resources figure significantly in solutions to transportation, growth and development issues throughout the state. All of these underscore the reality that New Mexico's future and the future of Tribes and Native Americans are intricately and inextricably bound together.

As a long overdue recognition of this reality, comprehensive policies and programs have been institutionalized in recent decades that respect tribal sovereignty, support state-tribal collaboration and encourage increased civic participation by Indian people. Some may view this transformation as a natural evolution of federal, state and local governments. However, visionary and astute tribal leaders and advocates have played a vital role in achieving these changes. While adapting to withstand a barrage of governmental policies and actions that threatened their communities' very survival, tribal leaders courageously and strategically set about transforming those governmental systems. In choosing to view the development of effective state-tribal relations as a way to exercise and, in fact, strengthen tribal sovereignty, tribal leaders, like the late-President Chino and Governor Dasheno, established a new paradigm that will not only benefit Native people but all people in New Mexico. State and local leaders like Governor Richardson and Mayor Coss, for their part, have wisely adjusted to the reality of tribal sovereignty and the dual citizenship of Native Americans by focusing on developing collaborative solutions to shared challenges.

As New Mexicans we all have a responsibility to sustain this momentum. We can recognize the importance of both the 400th anniversary of the Spanish settlement of Santa Fe and the enduring legacy of the Tewa people of *Oga Pogeh* that stretches back to time immemorial and lives on today in Tesuque Pueblo. In so doing, we can finally recognize that the continued vitality of tribal governments and cultures both benefits Indian people and helps sustain the unique values and character that distinguish our state.

Notes

Chapter 2

1. George Reid Andrews, *Afro-Latin America, 1800–2000* (New York, 2004).
2. The best source for the study of slavery among American Indians is Russell M. Magnaghi's, *Indian Slavery, Labor, Evangelization, and Captivity in the Americas: An Annotated Bibliography* (Lanham, MD., 1998). Other important works are: James F. Brooks, *Captives & Cousins: Slavery, Kinship, and Community in the Southwest Borderlands* (Chapel Hill, NC., 2002); Estévan Rael-Gálvez, *Identifying Captivity and Capturing Identity: Narratives of American Indian Slavery in Colorado and New Mexico, 1776–1934*, PhD dissertation 2002, University of Michigan; Barbara J. Olexe, *The Enslavement of the American Indian in Colonial Times* (Columbia, MD, 2005); Carl J. Ekberg, *Stealing Indian Women: Native Slavery in the Illinois Country* (Urbana, Il: University of Illinois Press, 2007); Robert H. Ruby and John A. Brown, *Indian Slavery in the Pacific Northwest* (Spokane, WA, 1993); Alan Gallay, *The Indian Slave Trade: The Rise of the English Empire in the American South, 1670–1717* (New Haven, Conn., 2002).
3. Joseph Jorgensen, *Western Indians: Comparative Environments, Languages, and Cultures of 172 Western American Indian Tribes* (San Francisco, 1980).
4. Orlando Patterson, *Slavery and Social Death: A Comparative Study* (Cambridge, MA., 1982).
5. The role of women slaves in Africa and its relationship to the demography of African slavery in the Americas is explored in Claire C. Robertson and Martin A. Klein, eds., *Women and Slavery in Africa* (Portsmouth, NH., 1997).
6. Pauline Turner Strong, *Captive Selves, Captivating Others: The Politics and Poetics of Colonial American Captivity Narratives* (Boulder, CO., 1999); Rebecca Blevins Faery, *Cartographies of Desire: Captivity, Race, and Sex in the Shaping of an American Nation* (Norman, Ok., 1999). For an actual captivity narrative from Texas and New Mexico see: Carl Coke Rister, *Comanche Bondage: Dr. John Charles Beales's Settlement of La Villa de Dolores on Las Moras Creek in southern Texas of the 1830s. With an annotated reprint of Sarah Ann Horn's Narrative of her captivity among the Comanches, her ransom by traders in New*

Mexico, and return via the Santa Fé Trail (Glendale, Ca., 1955).
7. On the prohibition of Indian slavery in the New Laws see Silvio Zavala, *Los esclavos indios en Nueva España* (Mexico City, 1967), pp. 107-14, 179-92, 223. The restrictions on Indian slavery in the 1680 Recompilation of the Law of the Indies can be found in Law I, Title 2, Book 6, and Laws 12, 13, 14, 15 of Book 6, *Recopilación de leyes de los reynos de las Indias* (Madrid, 1681).
8. George P. Hammond and Agapito Rey, eds. and trans., *Don Juan de Oñate: Colonizer of New Mexico, 1595–1628* (Albuquerque, 1953), pp. 427-466.
9. "Report of Fray Pedro Serrano, 1761," in Charles W. Hackett, ed. and transl., *Historical Documents Relating to New Mexico, Nueva Vizcaya, and Approaches Thereto, 1773* (Washington, DC., 1937), vol. 3, p. 487 [hereafter cited as HD]. Paul Horgan, *Centuries of Santa Fe* (Santa Fe, 1956), p. 88. Spanish Archives of New Mexico (microfilm edition), 1761, 9:410-44 [hereafter cited as SA followed by the microfilm reel and frame numbers]. SA 1761, 9:262-67.
10. For an extensive discussion of these statistics, see my *When Jesus Came, the Corn Mothers Went Away: Marriage, Sexuality and Power in New Mexico, 1500–1846* (Stanford, CA., 1991), especially pp. 153-54.
11. Governor Vélez Cachupín's remarks can be found in SA 1752, 8:1070-1105.
12. *Recopilación de leyes de los reynos de las Indias*, op. cit., Book VII, Laws 3 and 17.
13. "Report of Fray Pedro Serrano," 1761, in HD, p. 487.
14. My analysis of David Brugge's raw data complied in *Navajos in the Catholic Church Records of New Mexico, 1694–1875* (Window Rock, AZ.,1968).
15. Marc Simmons, *Little Lion of the Southwest* (Chicago, 1973), p. 34.
16. Fray Juan Agustín de Morfi, "Desordenes en Nuevo México," Archivo General de la Nación (México) Ramo Historia 1778, 25-8:147 [hereafter cited as AGN followed by the legajo, expediente, and folio numbers].
17. "Petition of the Residents of Abiquiu, 1820," SA20:419.
18. AGN-HIST 1707, 25-4:62-63.
19. Report of Fray Pedro Serrano, 1761, AGN, Ramo Provincias Internas 36-3:128-29.
20. Report of Fray Carlos Delgado, 1750, AGN, Ramo Historia, 25-2:31.
21. This ten percent statistic is my own estimation, based on the fact that out of the 13,204 persons who were married in New Mexico between 1693 and 1846, 997 of them said they were "children of the church".
22. Donald C. Cutter, trans., "An Anonymous Statistical Report of New Mexico in 1765," *New Mexico Historical Review* 50 (1975): 347-52.
23. Manuel A. Chávez as quoted in Simmons, *Little Lion of the Southwest*, p. 35.
24. The benevolence argument originates in Fray Angélico Chávez's essay "Genízaros," *Handbook of North American Indians* (Washington, D.C., 1979), vol. 9, pp. 198-200.
25. SA 1757, 9:130. SA1763, 9:524-26. SA 1765, 9:921.
26. SA 1762, 9:172-78.
27. León's testimony can be found in LeRoy R. Hafen and Ann W. Hafen, *Old Spanish Trail: Santa Fe to Los Angeles* (Glendale, CA., 1954), p. 274. See also Sondra Jones, *The Trial of Don Pedro León Luján: The Attack Against Indian Slavery and Mexican Traders in Utah* (Salt Lake City, 2000).

28. SA 1752, 8:1070-1105.
29. The price of female slaves is found in Eleanor B. Adams and Fray Angélico Chávez, eds. and trans., *The Missions of New Mexico, 1776: A Description by Fray Atanasio Domínguez* (Albuquerque, 1975) [hereafter cited as MNM], p. 252. Prices for female versus males slaves can also be found in SA 1762, 9:262-67; SA 1761, 9:410-44; SA 1761, 9:349-51; SA 1713, 21:285-86
30. SA 1748, 8:827-34.
31. MNM, p. 42.
32. Morfi, AGN, Ramo Historia 1778, 25-8:147-48.
33. MNM, pp. 42, 259, 126, 208.
34. Martínez as quoted in Steven M. Horvath, *The Social and Political Organization of the Genízaros of Plaza de Nuestra Señora de Los Dolores de Belén, New Mexico, 1740–1812*. PhD dissertation, Brown University, 1979, p. 78.
35. Frances León Swadesh, *Los Primeros Pobladores: Hispanic Americans of the Ute Frontier* (Notre Dame, ID., 1974), p. 45.
36. Florence Hawley Ellis, "Tomé and Father J.B.R," *New Mexico Historical Review* 30 (1955): 89-144, quotations from p. 94.
37. Delgado, 1744, AGN Ramo Historia, 25-25:229.
38. SA 1741, 8:68; SA 1761, 9:336; Archive of the Archdiocese of Santa Fe (microfilm edition) Diligencias Matrimoniales 1705, 60:376.
39. Delgado, AGN, Ramo Historia, 1744 25-25:229.
40. Morfi, AGN, Ramo Historia, 1782 25-8:147.
41. SA 1777, 10:925.
42. Manuel Antonio's commission is listed in AGN, Ramo Provincias Internas, 1768 102-7:256. The case of Marcos Sánchez is found in SA 1793, 13:346.
43. Morfi, AGN, Ramo Historia 1776, 25-8:147.
44. Virginia Langham Olmsted, trans. and comp., *New Mexico Spanish and Mexican Colonial Censuses 1790, 1823, 1847* (Albuquerque, 1975).

Chapter 6

1. For more on Tonita Peña, see Samuel L. Gray, *Tonita Peña: Quah Ah, 1893–1949* (Albuquerque, N. Mex.: Ayanyu Pub., 1990). Historian Marc Simmons provides a biographical sketch of grandma's mother-in-law in Buddy Mays and Marc Simmons, *People of the Sun: Some Out-of-Fashion Southwesterners* (Albuquerque: University of New Mexico Press, 1979): 11–14. One of her trading trips took here as far as Kingman, Arizona.
2. On the Palace of the Governors and the Pueblo Revolt, see Karl A. Hoerig, *Under the Palace Portal: Native American Artists of Santa Fe* (Albuquerque: University of New Mexico Press): 25–26, 28.
3. Hoerig, 77–78.
4. Hoerig, 41, 51.
5. Hoerig, 54, 73–75.

Chapter 7

1. American Indian is used to refer to the original inhabitants living within the boundaries of the United States since time immemorial. Indian and Native are terms used interchangeably throughout the essay as shortened informal versions of the more appropriate American Indian label. American Indian is an all-encompassing term to refer to the existing collective group of over 500 tribes located within the United States. Indigenous is a broad term to refer to peoples across U.S. colonial boundaries whose ancestry dates prior to European arrival.
2. For a more thorough discussion of American Indians and labor see Alice Littlefield and Martha C. Knack *Native Americans and Wage Labor: Ethnohistorical Perspectives.* Norman: University of Oklahoma Press. (1996)
3. Pueblo is the Spanish word for village or town that the Spaniards gave to the indigenous peoples inhabiting New Mexico. A Pueblo person today still uses this as an ethnic term interchangeably with the indigenous language version. Currently, there are 19 Pueblo nations within the state of New Mexico. The lower case version, pueblo, is used as a noun to signify villages where many Pueblo people live.
4. Tribes represented in New Mexico include the 19 Pueblo nations: Taos, Picuris, Ohkay Owingeh, Santa Clara, Pojoaque, San Ildefonso, Nambe, Tesuque, Jemez, Santo Domingo, Santa Ana, San Felipe, Cochiti, Zia, Zuni, Acoma, Laguna, Isleta and Sandia . There are two Apache bands, Mescalero and Jicarilla. In addition, the Navajo Nation is the largest tribe located partially in northwest New Mexico, which extends into the state of Arizona. For a historical overview see Joe S. Sando *Pueblo Nations: Eight Centuries of Pueblo Indian History.* Santa Fe, New Mexico: Clear Light Publishers. (1992)
5. A note on methodology: Karl A. Hoerig worked collaboratively with the program's participants since 1995 and documented his research in *Under the Palace Portal: Native American Artists in Santa Fe.* Albuquerque: University of New Mexico Press, 2003. Hoerig's work provides an in-depth look at the history of the program as well as interviews with program participants. This research was initially helpful for understanding some of the context. However, this essay is concerned with not only Portal participants but includes the experiences of other vendors in the plaza who are workers situated within a tourist site.

In 2000 I secured permission from the Director of the Portal Program. I explained that I was working on a project that consisted of researching work in Santa Fe and that I would like to speak with some of the vendors about their experiences. The director said this would not be a problem but wanted to notify the committee about me being around the Portal talking with vendors. In addition, I contacted family and friends who worked in the plaza. In total I conducted 25 interviews from December 2000 to June 2006. Interviews were conducted while I was home in New Mexico on leave from school in the summers and between semester breaks. Interviews varied from a single question lasting only ten minutes to more extensive four to five hours. The average interview lasted about half an hour when vendors were not busy with customers. The more in-depth interviews took place at the artist's home upon initial contact in the plaza. Only the first name of the vendors has been cited and, in some cases, I used pseudonyms to protect the anonymity of the artists.

For those vendors not in the program, I approached them individually and informed them of my work and asked their permission for an interview. Most of them did not seem to mind answering questions. I also mentioned if this was not a good meeting time that I could come back another time if they preferred. Interviews were not tape recorded but were conducted in conversational-type dialogues. I recorded responses in a notebook during the interviews. I felt American Indian vendors would be more open when talking about their experiences selling in the plaza if I kept the interviews informal in a conversational mode rather than asking a list of prescribed questions and using a tape recorder. This worked well since vendors seemed to enjoy talking about their work as vendors and artists. Some of the vendors also knew me as a familiar person in the plaza through some family and friends who worked at the Portal. I also had previous exposure with artists as a volunteer with some of the local arts and crafts fairs in New Mexico.

6. The conversation of dress was discussed extensively with Everett who was one of the vendors selling silver jewelry under the Portal. As a young child, Everett remembers accompanying his mother and told me the story of the type of dress code that was enforced. Many other vendors also confirmed this story regarding dress codes.
7. In addition to interviews with American Indian vendors, I talked informally with several non-American Indian vendors about their work and experiences in the plaza. I did not include the information in this essay as part of the interviews since these informal conversations were more for my personal use to get a better understanding about working dynamics in Santa Fe.

Chapter 10

1. "Letter from the Secretary of the Interior, Transmitting Reports of surveyors-general of New Mexico on private land claim Canada de Santa Clara, No. 138." *The Executive Documents of the Senate of the United States for the Second Session of the Forty-Ninth Congress. Volume I, Executive Document No. 56.* Washington: Government Printing Office, (1887), p. 18.
2. Sando, Joe S. *The Pueblo Indians,* San Francisco: The Indian Historian Press, American Indian Educational Publishers, (1976), p. 69.
3. Hall, G. Emlen. *Four Leagues of Pecos: A Legal History of the Pecos Grant, 1800–1933.* New Mexico Land Grant Series. Albuquerque: University of New Mexico Press, (1984), p. 92, 118-119.
4. Jenkins, Myra Ellen. *"The Baltasar Baca Grant: History of an Encroachment."* El Palacio. Vol. 68, Nos. 1 & 2, (1961), p. 100.
5. Sando, Joe S. *The Pueblo Indians,* p. 94-96.
6. Press Release, Office of Governor Bill Richardson, "Governor Bill Richardson Signs Bills Officially Elevating Veterans Services, Aging and Long Term Services, Cultural Affairs, and Indian Affairs Departments to Cabinet Level," February 28, 2004.

7. Author's Interview with Mark Mitchell on June 17, 2010.
8. Author's Interview with Mark Mitchell on June 17, 2010.
9. Author's Interview with David Coss on June 17, 2010.
10. Author's Interview with David Coss on June 17, 2010.

Contributors

Herman Agoyo (Ohkay Owingeh) earned his bachelors degree at Manhattan College and later a Masters degree from the University of New Mexico. As a former Governor of Ohkay Owingeh and as Chairman of the Eight Northern Pueblo Council and the All Indian Pueblo Council, Mr. Agoyo has selflessly spirited efforts to improve the quality of life of the Pueblo people. Mr. Agoyo has authored several publications as well as co-founded and actively served on various boards and committees, most notably heading the successful effort of the installation of the Statue of Po'Pay in the Statuary Hall in Washington D.C. in honor of the 300th Anniversary of the Pueblo 'Holy War' of 1680. For his efforts, in 1993 Mr. Agoyo was named by *Newsweek Magazine* as one of the fifty most influential people in America. Mr. Agoyo and his wife Rachel currently live at Ohkay Owingeh.

Greg Cajete, PhD, is Director of Native American Studies and an Associate Professor in the Division of Language, Literacy and Socio Cultural Studies in the College of Education at the University of New Mexico. Dr. Cajete earned his Bachelor of Arts degree from New Mexico Highlands University with majors in both Biology and Sociology and a minor in Secondary Education. He received his Masters of Arts degree from the University of New Mexico in Adult and Secondary Education. He received his PhD from International College—Los Angeles New Philosophy Program in Social Science Education with an emphasis in Native American Studies.

Ramón A. Gutiérrez, PhD, was born in Albuquerque, New Mexico, and attended the University of New Mexico as an undergraduate where he received a BA degree in Latin American History and Art. In 1973 he was awarded a Fulbright-Hayes Fellowship to study Quechua in Peru, and went on to earn MA and PhD degrees in 1980 from the University of Wisconsin in Madison.

Dr. Gutiérrez is the author of numerous publications. His is currently the Preston & Sterling Morton Distinguished Service Professor of History and the College at the University of Chicago, where he also directs the Center for the Study of Race, Politics and Culture.

Carol Harvey, JD, (Diné) was born and raised in Santa Fe, New Mexico. She completed her education earning a Bachelors Degree with a dual major in Economics and Political Science, a Masters in Business and a Juris Doctorate at The University of Denver as well as earning a BA in Spanish from the University of Houston. Dr. Harvey has practiced energy law for the past three decades. As an enrolled member of the Navajo Nation, Dr. Harvey is passionate about positively impacting the lives of Native Americans and their communities.

Evelina Zuni Lucero (Pueblo of Isleta/Ohkay Owingeh) attended Stanford University earning a Bachelors degree in Communications and later earning her Masters degree in English from the University of New Mexico in the creative writing program. Currently, Ms. Lucero is the chair of the creative writing program at the Institute of American Indian Arts (IAIA) in Santa Fe, New Mexico—and is working on a second novel, *Silicon Coyote*. Ms. Lucero, her husband and children live at Isleta Pueblo.

Matthew J. Martinez, PhD, (Ohkay Owingeh) was born and raised in Ohkay Owingeh. He earned a PhD in American Studies at the University of Minnesota. Dr. Martinez has served on the Ohkay Owingeh Tribal Council and school board as well as served as the Director of Indian Education for the New Mexico Higher Education Department. Dr. Martinez formerly was on the faculty of the Department of Indigenous Liberal Studies at the Institute of American Indian Arts (IAIA) in Santa Fe.

Navarre Scott Momaday, PhD, (Kiowa) earned his Bachelors Degree from the University of New Mexico, and went on to earn his Masters and PhD from Stanford University in 1963. Dr. Momaday's distinguished career and dedication to the perpetuation of Native American culture has earned him several national and international awards and honors—most notably the Pulitzer Prize for his first novel, *House Made of Dawn*. Dr. Momaday is the Regents Professor Emeritus of English at the University of Arizona and is the founder and current chairman of the Buffalo Trust, a nonprofit foundation for the preservation and restoration of cultural heritage to Native Americans, especially children, founded on the conviction that the loss of cultural identity—and the theft of the sacred—is the most insidious and dangerous threat to the survival of Native American culture in our time.

Diane Reyna was raised at Taos Pueblo and has strong ties to her mother's village of Ohkay Owingeh. Ms. Reyna graduated from the University of New Mexico in 1977. She served as director of the IAIA/KNME 1992 documentary, "Surviving Columbus," which was honored with a George Foster Peabody Award. Currently, Ms. Reyna is Director of the Learning Support Center at the Institute of American Indian Arts (IAIA), which provides students academic, creative and cultural support designed to help them persist through college and life.

James Riding In, PhD, is an activist scholar and a citizen of the Pawnee Nation of Oklahoma, currently serving as Associate Professor of American Indian Studies at Arizona State University. Dr. Riding In earned an Associate's Degree from Haskell Indian Junior College (now Haskell Indian Nations University), a Bachelor's Degree in History from Fort Lewis College, a Master's Degree in American Indian Studies and a Doctorate in History from the University of California, Los Angeles. In 2009 he completed an exhaustive study for the National Park Service about Indians and the Santa Fe Trail. As a Native American activist scholar Dr. Riding is committed to the development of American Indian Studies as an academic discipline.

Kim Suina (Cochiti Pueblo) received her Master's Degree in History from the University of New Mexico, where she worked as an editor at the *New Mexico Historical Review*. Ms. Suina currently is a freelance historical researcher and author.

Alvin H. Warren (Santa Clara Pueblo) is currently serving as Cabinet Secretary of the New Mexico Indian Affairs Department, ensuring the department's central role in facilitating communication and collaboration between the Governor's Office, thirty-two cabinet agencies, and twenty-two Tribes, Nations and Pueblos on Native American programs and issues. He has served eight terms in Santa Clara's tribal government, including two terms as Lieutenant Governor. Secretary Warren played a key role in Santa Clara's reacquisition of the *P'opii Khanu* Headwaters Area, the first International Forum on Indigenous Mapping, and the enactment of the State-Tribal Collaboration Act (SB 196) and permanent funding for the Tribal Infrastructure Fund (HB 162). Secretary Warren graduated from Dartmouth College with a Bachelor's Degree in History with High Honors and lives in Santa Clara with his wife and children.

STUDY GUIDE

This study guide is intended to assist the reader, teacher, and/or professor in leading discussion, exploration, and reflection on each writer's thoughts, words, and ideas.

It is intended to guide a deeper exploration of how both collective and personal history shape relationships to specific places over time. The articles link past and present in an effort to show how historical experience underlies contemporary life.

We offer this study guide to you in the hopes that it may be useful if you use this book for a high school or college course, readers' club, or to further your own understanding and exploration of Native American experience in the southwest, specifically in relationship to Santa Fe, New Mexico.

Overview Questions

1. Why is Native American history central to American history?
2. Why do you think this book opens with a Blessing? What does the Blessing mean to you?
3. Why is academic self determination critical to Native America?

Chapter 1 – Greg Cajete

1. Dr. Cajete describes the downtown Santa Fe of his youth as a vibrant commercial center consisting of small and large stores established to serve the local community. Describe the transition and the subsequent transformation of downtown Santa Fe.
2. What criteria is required to write and submit a New Mexico history book for use in public schools?
3. What characterizes the "Coalition Period"?

4. What types of virus or diseases were a part of the Pueblo and Spanish life in the 1600s?
5. Describe the treatment for these diseases.
6. What was the average distance covered in a day if traveling by ox and wagon?
7. What is the difference between the *encomienda* system and the *repartimiento* system?
8. Describe how Pueblo and Hispanic communities prepared to defend their communities against raiding tribes.
9. Why was the practice of the Pueblo religion described as "witchcraft" by the Spanish?
10. Describe the characteristic of Spanish monarchy in the 1600s.
11. Define the term "ethnocentrism" and describe a situation in which this term can be applied.

Chapter 2 – Ramón Gutiérrez

1. Who is a Genízaro? What does this term mean?
2. How did African slavery as it was practiced in the American southeast prior to the Civil War differ from the slavery practiced by the Spanish in New Mexico?
3. What was most surprising to you about this article? Why?
4. What questions would you like to ask if you could go back in time to the early days of Santa Fe and interview a master/owner and an enslaved woman or child?
5. What does the term "detribalized" mean?
6. Why were Native American women and children preferred to Native American men as slaves in Spanish New Mexico?
7. Do Genízaros have a valid voice in Native American academia?
8. Can one compare the plight of the Cherokee Freedman to that of the Genízaro?

Chapter 3 – Herman Agoyo

1. Describe the ethnic backgrounds of European explorers in the late 1500s and early 1600s.
2. Describe the types of skills colonist explorers needed to support travel and settlement in New Mexico.
3. What did expedition leaders need to consider when establishing a new colony? What is the "Indian Removal Act"?
4. Describe church and state alliances that were established to further colonization around the world in the 1600s.
5. Describe how correspondence between the new world and Spain was conducted.
6. Describe the contributions of Dr. Florence Ellis to New Mexico history and to the Pueblos of New Mexico.
7. Why does Agoyo refer to the Pueblo Revolt as a 'Holy War'?
8. Describe how ancient road systems were constructed and maintained.

9. Describe archeological policies and procedures related to excavating an ancient site.
10. Describe examples of cross cultural integration ritual and agriculture between the Spanish and Native tribal communities that are evidenced in the Southwest today.
11. Describe the weather or meteorological patterns found in the Southwest in the 1600s.
12. Describe why Pueblo spiritual practices conflicted with Spanish Catholicism.
13. Describe the possible roles of people who were descendants of both Pueblo and Spanish relationships.
14. Describe the most important legal relationship established between the Pueblo and the government of Spain and its impact on Pueblo people today.
15. Describe the role of the Spanish Inquisition on the colonization of the Southwest.
16. Explore the basis for the American concept of "Manifest Destiny."
17. Herman Agoyo believes that research by non-Pueblo people is beneficial to Pueblo communities because it provides vital information to support Pueblo land claims. What other ways can archeological and historical research assist tribal communities?

Chapter 4 – Evelina Zuni Lucero

1. What is the literary genre called, "magical realism'? How is this story an example of magical realism?
2. Why do you think the author leaps back and forth over a period of 450 years in this chapter? What is the connection between these two time periods?
3. What was the yellow stone the Turk showed the *capitan*? Who was the Turk and who was the *capitan*? What is the significance of the yellow stone?
4. Who is Elsie? Why is she important to the story?
5. Where does this story take place? What is the name of the modern city described in it?
6. What are the common names today of the two rivers mentioned in this story?
7. At the end of the chapter another character is mentioned named Angel. Who is Angel? Why is he important?
8. What are some of the mysterious things that happen in this chapter?
9. What might be the relationship between history and mystery?

Chapter 5 – James Riding In

1. What Indian tribes were directly impacted by the Santa Fe Trail?
2. Describe what Riding In means when he writes of the "master narrative."
3. Why did Riding In characterize the founding of the Santa Fe Trail as illegal? (Answer requires additional research on the Trade and Intercourse Acts.)

4. Describe the conditions that led to differing experiences of the Indian tribes impacted by the Santa Fe Trail.
5. What are the names of the Native American tribes located along the Santa Fe Trail? Which tribes did the U.S. fail to make treaties with in order to pass through their lands? What were some of the consequences of this failure?
6. What were some of the Spanish laws imposed upon the Spanish people under Spanish colonization?
7. What were some of the impacts of the Mexican Revolution on Pueblo people?
8. A Pueblo Perspective of the History of Santa Fe/Greg Cajete
9. What were some of the main events that led up to the Pueblo Revolt?
10. What were some of the consequences of the Pueblo Revolt?
11. Did Pueblo people leave Santa Fe after the Spanish Reconquest? Why or why not?
12. What dialect of Spanish was spoken in the 1600s? Can you compare it to the dialect of Spanish spoken today in northern New Mexico?
13. Determine the worth in trade and/or currency for the following items for the following periods: 1600s, 1700s and 1800s.

Buffalo hide	Comanche woman captive
Rifle	Wagon
Horse	An ounce of gold

Chapters 6 & 7 – Kim Suina and Matthew Martinez

1. Two chapters discuss the economic impact of "the porch" or the selling of Native American arts and crafts beneath the portico at the Palace of the Governors in Santa Fe. What are some of the opportunities this presents to Native American artisans and what are some of the limitations it imposes?
2. Describe the participation and influence of women and Pueblo culture as it pertains to economy and gender politics.

Chapter 8 – Diane Reyna

1. Diane Reyna describes a moment of humiliation with her third grade teacher at St. Joseph's which "re-enacted centuries old dynamics of contrasting histories, ethnicities, and cultures of Northern New Mexico." Can you think of an experience you have had or observed that represented a clash in culture, experience or belief systems? Explain this experience and what it represented.
2. Reyna describes several public commemorations of ethnic pride and identity that she experienced in New Mexico. Think of a public commemoration or celebration that you know about, and compare different interpretations of this commemoration based on different understandings, experiences, or perspectives of history.
3. Reyna describes her participation in a public mediation process initiated by the Albuquerque Public Arts Program. What came out of this mediation process?

What do you think was helpful about this process? What is an example of another time such a process has been used successfully?
4. How is an understanding of history important for dispelling stereotypes and building community? Can you give an example of something you have learned about history that changed your perspective or belief about another group of people?
5. Who is a Nuevomexicana/o? What does this term mean?
6. What is the name of the indigenous people that the Spanish brought north with them when they settled New Mexico? What is the history of this group in New Mexico?
7. What is the problem with public celebrations that assume "pure" racial or ethnic heritage? What might be some approaches or solutions to this problem?

Chapter 9 – Carol Harvey

1. What is the impact of personal memory on place?
2. How do someone's personal recollections shape your understanding of a specific place?
3. What is significant to you about her memories of growing up in Santa Fe?

Chapter 10 – Alvin H. Warren

1. Name the three successive national governments that sought control in New Mexico since the 1600s? What are some unique characteristics of each period?
2. What are some of the core values that enabled tribes in New Mexico to adapt, to persist, and to survive over the 468 years of colonial powers?
3. Why is it important for the Tribes, Nations, and Pueblos to maintain control over their ancestral lands?
4. What year were Native Americans made U.S. citizens by an act of Congress?
5. What does it mean to be a citizen of both a tribal nation and the U.S.A.?
6. In what year did all Native Americans in New Mexico gain suffrage (the right to vote)?
7. What have been some of the major 21st Century changes to law or public policy in New Mexico that affect state-tribal relations today?
8. How was a compromise achieved between Tesuque Pueblo and the City of Santa Fe when burials were discovered at the site of the new convention center in 2005? How did that mark a turning point in Santa Fe/Pueblo relations?
9. In your own words describe why the future of the state of New Mexico is tied to the future of the 22 Tribes, Nations, and Pueblos located within current boundaries of the state?

NOTE: These questions were developed Diane Reyna, Ann Filemyr, Annie McDonnell, F. Richard Sanchez and Stephen Wall of the Institute of American Indian Arts.

Index

A

Abiquiu, 47, 54
Abo, 26
Acoma Pueblo, 23, 44, 58–60, 129, 137
Agoyo, Herman, 57–70, 173
Agualagu, Battle of, 59
Alameda Pueblo, 30
Albuquerque Public Arts Program, 130–131
Alcanfor, 24, 73–74
American Indian art, 108–123
   signatures and identification, 111, 114, 115
American Indian identity, 40, 113–114, 123, 126–132, 170
American Indian Policy Review Commission, 160
Analco, 54
Anaya, Toney, 161
Apaches, 25–26, 32, 40, 110. *see also* Jicarilla Apaches, Plains Apaches
   as captives or slaves, 45, 46–47, 52, 54–55
   image of, 109
   wars against, 34, 45, 54–55
Arapahos, 83, 88
   and conflict with Santa Fe Trail travelers, 89, 90–94
   reservation in Indian Territory, 94

Archaic Pueblo peoples, 22
art, American Indian, 108–123
   signatures and identification, 111, 114, 115
Atchison, Topeka and Santa Fe, 110
Atole, Leonard, 160
Awatowi, 32

B

Babcock, Barbara, 110
Barrio de Analco, 54
Battle of Agualagu, 59
Becknell, William, 86, 95
Belén, 53, 54
Bent, Charles, 97
Bent, George, 93
Bent's Fort, 99
Bernal, Juan, 28
Big Soldier, 90
Big Timber, 91, 92
Bolsas, Antonio, 64
Bonal, Maurice, 11, 15, 70
Brintnall, Sandra, 11, 70
Burawoy, Michael, 109
Burnside, Ambrose E., 92
Bursum, Holm O., 159

181

C

Cabeza de Vaca, Alvar Nuñez, 23
Cachupín, Tomás Velez, 46, 50, 51, 156–157
Cajete, Gregory A., 19–38, 173
Calhoun, John C., 157
Camino Real National Historic Trail Legislation, 61
captivity narratives, 42, 167
Casas, Bartolomé de las, 44
Castillo, Francisco Gomez de, 156
Cata, Jose de La Luz, 62
Catholic Church, 26–27, 33, 43–46, 51, 58–60, 63–65, 84
Catiti, Alonzo, 27, 29, 64
Catua, Nicolas, 28
Chabot, Maria, 106
Cheyennes, 83, 88
    and conflict with Santa Fe Trail travelers, 90–91, 93–94, 99
    reservation in Indian Territory, 94
Chilili, 26
Chino, Wendell, 160, 165
cholera, 82, 91, 99
Christianity, 26–27, 33, 43–46, 51, 58–60, 63–65, 84
Cimarron, New Mexico, 89
Cochiti Pueblo, 30, 101–103
colonialism, 84–87, 95, 99
Comanches, 34, 83, 87, 88
    as captives or slaves, 47
    and conflict with Santa Fe Trail travelers, 88, 89, 89–90, 91, 93–94, 99
    reservation in Indian Territory, 94
Conixu, Luis, 27, 64
Cooke, Philip St. George, 97
Coronado, Francisco Vaszuez de, 23–25, 63, 71–78
Coss, David, 164–165
Cow Creek, Kansas, 96
criados, 47–48, 52, 168
Crows, 88
Cruzat y Gongora, Gervasio, 156
Cruzate, Domingo Jironza Petriz de, 30, 68
Cultural Properties Review Committee, 164
Cuyumangue, 34

D

Dasheno, Walter, 160, 165
Davis, W.W.H., 98
Delawares, 84, 98–99
Delgado, Carlos, 48, 54, 55
Dietrich, Margretta, 112
Dilworth, Leah, 109–110
Domínguez, Atanasio, 52–53
Dosedo, Margaret, 161

E

economic impact of art and tourism, 108–123
El Ollito, Francisco, 27, 64
El Saca of Taos, 27, 64
El Tano, Juan, 64
Ellis, Florence Hawley, 53, 61
encomienda system, 25, 44, 47–48
epidemics, 25–26, 90, 91, 99
Espejo, Antonio de, 24
Estevanico (Esteban), 23

F

fake and imitation art, 113, 119
Fort Atkinson, 92, 96–97
Fort Dodge, 92
Fort Harker, 92
Fort Hayes, 92
Fort Larned, 92
Fort Leavenworth, 89
Fort Mann, 91, 92
Fort Riley, 92
Fort Union, 93
Fort Wallace, 92

Fort Wise, 92
Fort Zarah, 92
Franciscans, 26–28, 32–33, 59
Fred Harvey Company, 110

G
Galisteo Pueblo, 28, 34
Garley, Eloy, 159
Genízaros, 16, 36, 45–56, 167–169
    attitude towards, 52–54
    population, 48
    recognized as indigenous people, 67
    treatment, 48–52
Gomez, Cora, 161
Gran Quivira, 26
Grand Island, 91
Gregg, Josiah, 95–96
Gutiérrez, Ramón A., 39–56, 173–174

H
Harvey, Carol, 133–154, 174
Hawikuh, 23
Hendricks, Rick, 31
Hidalgo, Pedro, 28
Hoerig, Karl A., 170
Homestead Act, 68
Hopi Pueblo, 27, 32, 34, 44
horses, 25–26

I
Indian Arts and Crafts Act, 104, 122
Indian Arts and Crafts Fair, 106
Indian arts and crafts industry, 112–113
Indian gaming, 70, 71–72, 161
Indian Gaming Regulatory Act, 161
Indian Removal, 58–59, 93, 98–99
Indian Territory, 94
Isleta Pueblo, 30, 32

J
Jacona, 34
James, Thomas, 95, 96
Jemez Pueblo, 26, 27, 28, 34, 95
Jicarilla Apaches, 83, 84, 86–87
    and conflict with Santa Fe Trail travelers, 92–93, 99
    land and water rights, 157, 162
Johnson, Gary, 161
Jongopavi, 32
Jonva, Nicolas de la Cruz, 27, 64
Jumano Pueblos, 59–60

K
Kaafedeh, 57–70
Kanitobe, Randy, 129
Kansas-Nebraska Act of 1854, 93
Ka-'p-geh, 27
Kaws (Kansas), 83
    reservation in Indian Territory, 94
    and treaties, 87–88
Kearny, Stephen Watts, 157
Kessell, John, 25, 31
Kewa [Khe-wa], 27, 29, 30, 33, 59
Kiowas, 83, 88
    and conflict with Santa Fe Trail travelers, 89, 90–94, 91, 93–94
    reservation in Indian Territory, 94

L
La Cieneguilla, 28, 34
Laguna Pueblo, 110
land ownership, 40, 82
Las Vegas, New Mexico, 92
Laughlin, Ruth, 16–17
Levine, Frances, 22
Lewis, Robert, 160
Livingston v. Ewing, 115
Lobo, 92–93
Lucero, Evelina Zuni, 71–80, 174

Lujan, Ben, 160, 161
Lujan, Mabel Dodge, 112

M
Madrid, Roque, 32–33
Malacate, Antonio, 64
Manifest Destiny, 67, 82
Manzano, 26
Martinez, Maria, 111
Martinez, Martina, 127
Martinez, Matthew J., 108–123, 174
Matasina dance, 58, 62
McFie, John R., 158
Mendoza, Antonio de, 23
Mexican control of New Mexico, 67–68, 84, 157
Mexican War, 84, 85
Mishongnovi, 32
Missouria, 88
Mitchell, Mark, 163–164
Momaday, N. Scott, 9–10, 174–175
Montaño, Mary, 128
Montoya, Juan Martinez de, 22–23
Mora, New Mexico, 90
Morfi, Juan Agustín, 52–53, 55
Museum of New Mexico, 61, 115. *see also* Palace of the Governors; Portal Program
    children's annual fair, 118

N
Nambe Pueblo, 26, 27
    water rights, 162–163
Naranjo, Domingo, 27, 64
Naranjo, Tessie, 111
Native American Graves Protection and Repatriation Act, 164
Native American Vendors Program, 102–107, 114–122, 170–171
Navajos, 21, 25–26, 40, 63, 66, 84, 110
    as captives or slaves, 46–47, 54–55
    image of, 109
    vending on plaza, 110, 115–116
    wars against, 34, 54–55, 96
    water rights, 162
New Laws, 44
New Mexico Association of Indian Affairs, 106
New Mexico Board of Tourism, 109
New Mexico Commission on Indian Affairs, 160, 161
New Mexico Indian Affairs Department, 162
New Mexico Office of Indian Affairs, 161, 162
New Mexico State University, 127–128
Niza, Marcos de, 23

O
Oglalas, 88
O'gha Po'oge, 11, 15, 19
Ohkay Owingeh, 24, 27, 32, 57–70
    Heritage Center, 61
    tribal lands, 67–69
Ojo Caliente, 54
O'Keeffe, Georgia, 112
Old Tobacco, 91
Omahas, 88
Omtua, Pedro, 28
Oñate, Juan de, 23, 24, 44, 57–60, 129–130
    statue, 129–131
Oñate Cuarto Centenario Project, 130
Oraibi, 32
Ortiz, Alfonso, 23–24, 29
Osages, 83
    reservation in Indian Territory, 94
    and treaties, 87–88
Otermín, Antonio de, 28
Otoes, 88
Overland Trail, 98

P

Palace of the Governors, 103–104
    portal program, 102–107, 114–122
PaleoIndians in Santa Fe area, 21–22
Pawnees, 82, 83, 87
    and conflict with Santa Fe Trail travelers, 89–90, 91, 96, 99
    and epidemics, 90
    population, 91
    reservation in Indian Territory, 94
    and treaties, 88
Pecos, Regis, 161
Pecos Pueblo, 28, 46
    and Santa Fe Trail, 94–96
Peña, Tonita, 102, 169
Peralta, Pedro de, 23, 60
photography, 114, 120
Picuris Pueblo, 27, 29, 34, 46
Pike, Albert, 95
Pinto, John, 160
Pio, Juan Baptista, 28
Plains Apaches, 34, 83, 88
    and conflict with Santa Fe Trail travelers, 90–91, 93–94
    reservation in Indian Territory, 94
Point of Rocks, 92
Po'Pay, 27, 63–65
population of Pueblo people, 25–26, 35
    Genízaros, 48
Portal Program, 102–107, 114–122, 170–171
Po-sogeh, 27
Puaray, 24
Pueblo ceremonial and religious practices, 63–65, 66
Pueblo Indians, 83–84, 170
    image of, 109
    land rights, 156–159
    maps, 12–13
    population, 22, 25–26
    pottery, 111
    religious practices, 26, 29–30, 63–66, 158
    and Santa Fe Trail, 94–96, 99
    silverwork, 110–111
Pueblo Lands Act, 159
Pueblo Lands Board, 68–69
Pueblo Revolt of 1680, 27–30, 63–65, 84
Pueblo Revolt of 1696, 66
Purary, 30

R

raids by non-Pueblo Indian peoples, 25–26
railroads, 105, 110–111
Rayaldo, New Mexico, 92
Recompilation of the Laws of the Indies, 44, 46, 156
Reconquest of Santa Fe, 31–34, 65–66
Religious Crimes Code, 158
religious practices, 26, 29–30, 63–66, 158
repartimiento system, 25, 48
Reyna, Crusita Mondragon, 127
Reyna, Diane, 126–132, 175
Richardson, Bill, 162, 163, 165
Riding In, James, 81–99, 175
Roberts, David, 33
Rodriguez, Richard, 128, 131
Romero, Domingo, 64
Romero, Tomás, 97–98

S

Salazar, Nick, 160
Salinas Pueblos, 59
San Cristobal Pueblo, 28, 34
San Felipe, 26
San Felipe Pueblo, 30, 31, 32
San Gabriel de Yungeh, 24, 57–63, 69
    archaeological excavation, 61
San Ildefonso Pueblo, 27
    water rights, 162–163

San Juan Pueblo, 24, 27, 32, 57–70
   Heritage Center, 61
   tribal lands, 67–69
San Lazaro Pueblo, 28
San Marcos Pueblo, 28, 34
San Miguel del Vado, 54
Sanchez, F. Richard, 15–17
Sand Creek Massacre, 93
Sandia Pueblo, 30
Sando, Joe, 157
Santa Ana Pueblo, 32
Santa Clara Pueblo, 27
   land rights, 156–157
Santa Fe
   economic impact for Native peoples, 101–107, 108–123
   plaza, 20, 34, 104, 108, 112, 115–118
   and Pueblo people, 19–21, 101–107
   and Pueblo Revolt, 29, 31, 33
   and Santa Fe Trail, 84–85, 92
   Tewa name for, 21
   tourism, 104–106, 108–114, 120–123
Santa Fe 400th Anniversary, Inc., 15
Santa Fe Convention Center, 163–164
Santa Fe Fiesta, 20–21, 106, 128–129, 131
Santa Fe Indian Market, 106
Santa Fe Indian School, 127
Santa Fe Ring, 157–158
Santa Fe Trail, 81–99
   and impact on Indian peoples, 82–84
   and United States expansion, 82
Santo Domingo Pueblo, 27, 29, 30, 33, 59
Saritaris, 81–82, 96, 99
Shawnee, 84, 98–99
Simmons, Marc, 60
slavery, 26, 34, 36, 40–56, 63, 66–67, 167–169
smallpox, 25–26, 90, 91
Smith, Jedidiah, 90
State-Tribal Collaboration Act, 163

stereotypes of Indians, 85–86
Stratton, Hal, 161
Suina, Kim, 101–107, 175

T
Tagu of Ohkay Owingeh, 64
Tajique, 26
Taos Pueblo, 27, 28, 29, 126–128
   and Santa Fe Trail, 89, 96, 97
   water rights, 162–163
Taos Rebellion of 1847, 97–98
Tapatu, Luis, 27, 64
Tapia, Pedro de, 32
Taylor Grazing Act, 68
Tenorio, Frank, 160
Teotho, 27
Tesugeh, 28, 145
Tesuque Pueblo, 28, 128–129, 145
   and Convention Center, 163–164
   and Oga Pogeh, 156, 165
   water rights, 162–163
Texas invasion of New Mexico, 97
Torre, Mariano Rodriguez de la, 156
tourism, 104–106, 108–114, 120–123
Treaty of Guadalupe Hidalgo, 67–69, 157
Treviño, Juan de, 26–27, 63–65
Trujillo, Miguel, 159
Tucumcari, New Mexico, 93
Turk, The, 72–79

U
US vs. Joseph, 158–159
US vs. Lucero, 158
US vs. Sandoval, 159
Utes, 34, 83, 84
   as captives or slaves, 47
   and conflict with Santa Fe Trail travelers, 92

V

Vaca, Alvar Nuñez Cabeza de, 23
Vargas, Diego de, 31–35, 65–66, 128–129
Velasco, Captain, 59
Velasco, Fray, 28
Vizcarra, José Antonio, 96
voting rights, 158, 159

W

Walatowa, 27, 28
Ward, John, 158
Warren, Alvin H., 155–166, 175
Warren, Alvin K., 159
Watchman, Leo, Sr., 160
water rights, 162
Weigle, Marta, 110
Welai, 27
White, Elizabeth, 112
White, James, 92–93
world's fairs and expositions, 105–106, 114

X

Xenome, Diego, 27, 64

Y

Ye, Juan de, 28
Yope, Cristóbal, 64
Yungeh, 24, 57–63, 68, 69
    archaeological excavation, 61

Z

Zah, Peterson, 161
Zaldivar, Juan de, 44, 59
Zaldivar, Vicente, 59
Zia Pueblo, 30, 32
Zuni Pueblo, 23, 32

www.ingramcontent.com/pod-product-compliance
Lightning Source LLC
Chambersburg PA
CBHW080544170426
43195CB00016B/2673